Awakening to the Presence of God

An Intimate Story of a Pastor and His Companion

Karl Robert Viernstein, M. Div. and
Dale Suzanne Ditmars Viernstein, B.A.,R.N.

ISBN: 978-0-578-02723-4

Self-Published
Printed in the U.S.A.

Contents

*Dedicated
To Our
Living God*

Introduction

Whether you are a seasoned pastor, a seminary student, a regular churchgoer, or an agnostic who is not sure that God exists, this book will appeal to you. You will be charmed by Karl's and Dale's stories and fascinated by the way God's grace seems truly present in the difficult situations they have to face. You will shake your head over the answers to prayer that come to this pastor and his wife in situations where there seems to be no way to move ahead. You will laugh out loud as you read about Karl's dream of falling through the church roof and how it actually happens to him as he is repairing the floodlights in the attic above the sanctuary. You will chuckle at the embarrassing moments in a church service or wedding where Karl turns it into something humorous.

If you are a pastor or a trustee, or someone on a committee to make recommendations for changes in the church, you will get some helpful ideas about how to do this even when most of the members are in doubt. If you are a seminary student, you will get a rich sense of all that is involved in pastoring and guiding the people in a parish toward the opportunities that lie before them. Anyone questioning the reality of God, will begin to seek their answers to the deepest meanings of life even more intensely than before. As a church member dedicated to making the church work, you will be surprised by the insights that show what a church can be at its best.

If your prayer life seems to be on hold, there are suggestions for building up your confidence. This pastor and wife team has developed a way to enter into prayer together using Jesus' suggestion—an easier way to pray and more power—when two or more join together. Jesus promised that not only will the power of two be stronger than the power of one, but that he, himself, will be there.

Karl and Dale have found their own way of developing this promise of Jesus, and it works not only for them and their family, but also when they direct prayers for others. They call it "Companion Prayer," and it has worked for my family.

I have a son (47 now), who was going through a stressful time when he was in his late teens. One day, he disappeared and we were unable to find him even with the help of the police. For twelve years, he was gone from our lives and we had no idea how or where he was. We asked our friends and colleagues, Karl and Dale, to pray for him.

My husband and I invited them into our home and were soon caught up in the process of Companion Prayer. After some Bible reading and short prayers, Karl lay on the floor and became quiet and receptive to God's guidance. Dale gave him some suggestions to center and focus him, then read off the questions we had worked on together. After a time, Karl sat up and shared with us an experience he had had during the prayer time. He said that a beautiful woman had appeared before him (probably an angel), and assured him that our son was well, but not yet ready to come home. As soon as he told us what the angel had said, my husband and I shed some happy tears. It was the first time in twelve years we had been given even a glimmer of hope. Yes, he did come home to us.

Reading Karl and Dale's stories, brought up my own experiences as a minister and a minister's wife. Memories flooded back. I kept thinking if I had had access to a book like this, I would have been better prepared for my work in the ministry. Most young ministers don't have a clue as to what they are getting into.

Karl and Dale have been incredibly creative in meeting the crises that arose in their various churches and family life from time to time. Minister friends of mine with gifts like Karl's and Dale's have been reluctant to share these gifts publicly. I hope this book will encourage more to talk about them. I am glad the Holy Spirit has led Karl and Dale to reveal their intimate stories.

They have been bold in their sharing, and have found beautiful ways to introduce their congregations to the many ways God speaks to us in these times, offering hope and healing just as in biblical times. That is the promise of this book.

The Reverend Doctor June Avis Bro

Preface

For many years my wife, Dale, and I have dreamed of writing a book which tells the true stories of our years as minister and wife. As we've told people of these experiences, and I have even preached about them from the pulpit, many people have asked if any of these accounts were written down. Sadly, we had to say, "No."

Finally, a good friend and colleague, Dr. Harmon Bro, Theologian and Pastoral Counselor, said to us, "I've seen and heard the experiences of many people in my travels, and yours are some of the most valuable. They should be recorded so others may realize that God still moves upon the face of the earth. If I never receive another word of spiritual counsel from you, it would have been sufficient for me to have known you and to have seen the wonders God has worked through you both. Please, write these stories down!"

So, with the encouragement of Harmon Bro and the editing assistance we received from June Bro, my secretary, Meryl Osse, my sister Laura Anderson, my friend, Jerry Lazarus, parishioner, Ruth Van Why, journalist, Susan Jorstad, some friends both in this world and the next, we have written these accounts to the best of our ability.

Dale and I have written these stories so that others may find some helpful ideas for building a closer relationship with God, and with each other.

Forward

The following is a collection of stories about our spiritual journey as minister and wife and how God has interceded in our lives in astounding ways.

***Please Note: Dale's writing is in italics,* and Karl's writing is in regular print.** If it were not for the support of the faithful people in the churches we have served, we would not have been able to do half of what has been accomplished. Thus, I believe that the ability of a Pastor and spouse to succeed in a church is in direct proportion to the faith and support of the congregation and community of believers. Even Jesus could not perform any great miracles in his hometown because the people saw him as a child growing up in their midst. They did not see him as the Messiah. Ministry is at its best when shared. There must be a wholehearted and healthy sharing and trust between the minister and spouse, and between them and the church community. It is a two-way street.

Some of our stories are common, while others are quite miraculous. Yet, they are here to inspire you, to make you laugh, and at times, they may bring you to tears. I would like to thank all the people mentioned in this book who have been to us such inspiring examples of how to keep growing in the midst of joy and pain.

May this book be an inspiration to you, the reader. May it increase your faith as you come to know that God in Christ can do all things and will strengthen you. May it give you some concrete ways to enrich your life.

I would like to thank my wife, Dale, who has been such an inspiration to me. Without her help, these stories would not have been written. Except for our family and close friends, the names of people in these stories have been changed to preserve their anonymity.

As Karl and I looked back over the earlier years of our ministry, we saw how much thoughtful reflection was required of us in order to tell our story. Our research also brought with it the knowledge of how much more there is for us to learn.

I believe that living on the earth is like being in school. We have many lessons to learn. Some are easy, others are difficult. We hope that, as you read, you will realize that in your life's journey on this earth you are never alone. As in the poem, "Footprints in the Sand," God is there to carry us through our most difficult times.

Thank you, Karl, for being my life partner, the love of my life, and the inspiration to go through all the challenges that ministry presents to God's dedicated servants.

Chapter 1

"I will pour out my spirit on all flesh,
Your sons and daughters shall prophesy,
Your old men shall dream dreams, and
Your young men shall see visions."

Jonah 2:28

A Rude Awakening

I woke up suddenly from a deep sleep. I was yelling, my whole body was wracked with pain. It was a frightening experience, something that had happened to me only once before in my life. I grabbed my legs and screamed.

Dale, my wife, came running upstairs and asked, "What's wrong?"

"I don't know," I said. "My whole body is in pain. I heard the sound of a plane going over our house and I'm hurting."

I crawled out of bed with difficulty, and tried to walk around the room. It was as if my body was one big muscle cramp! There was something troubling me inside, an unsettled feeling that wouldn't go away.

"Dale," I said. "I have this ominous feeling."

My wife, a private nurse, said, "Why don't you take a hot bath?"

So, I went into the bathroom and got into the tub, and turned on the water as hot as I could stand it. Maybe the warmth of the water would help my body to relax.

Shortly after, I heard Dale scream, "Karl! Karl! A plane just hit the World Trade Center. They just announced it on the 'Today Show.'"

"Something is terribly wrong," I said.

As I lay in the warmth of the tub, I was still hurting from the shooting pain in my body, and not quite able to understand the events that were unfolding. Even though the water was soothing my pain, I knew I had to get out of the tub.

Just then, Dale started to scream again, running up the stairs of our house shrieking, "Karl! Karl! A second plane just hit the World Trade Center. I saw it on television with my own eyes!"

With that, I jumped out of the tub and ran, as best I could, down the stairs dripping wet, and with only a towel wrapped around me. I watched, horror struck, as events on the screen played out before my eyes – the towers were burning! We stood there aghast at the events that were taking place. What was happening?

This day had started out with me wailing with a strange incredible pain for which there was no explanation. I had awoken screaming and writhing, and I didn't know why. Now, we were witnessing on television these terrible events one right after another. Were the two connected?

There was a sinking feeling in my gut.

I had to go to work because I had responsibilities to fulfill. I got dressed as fast as I could, and hobbled over to my office next door, slowed down by the extraordinary events of the day and the pain I could still feel. I told my secretary of waking up in pain and added that both the World Trade Center Towers were hit by planes. She was in shock!

"I want to see a television!" she said bluntly.

At that moment, Dale ran frantically into my office and exclaimed, "One of the buildings has just collapsed!"

My secretary said, "I have to see this!"

So, while I sat at my desk grappling with the pain and vigorously rubbing my legs and arms, my secretary ran next door to watch the breaking news with Dale.

What was happening? Had I picked up on the pain of the events of this day as had happened to me many times before? Was the plane I'd heard earlier Flight 93 or Flight 175 as it passed overhead? Is it possible that I intuitively picked up on the pain and fear of those people soon to die in such a tragic way? Or was it just a strange coincidence and my pain entirely unrelated? I made my way back over to the house to watch the news that continued to get worse on that September 11th day of 2001.

I knew in my heart that I was connecting to the pain of the people and events that were taking place. But who would believe me if I told them? There was no scientific proof. If I were feeling the pain of the people involved in these events, why me? Why would I feel pain for people suffering so far away and before the events had even occurred?

Few people have heard our stories. There have been other similar moments when right in the midst of confusion and suffering, a loving God stepped into our lives to guide, bless and heal us. Yes, warn us, too! We want to share these experiences with you now, in this book.

Chapter 2

"Before I formed you in the womb I knew you,
And before you were born I consecrated you."

Jeremiah 1:5

Karl's List of Begets

My mother's story and her mother's story show where some of my sensitivities to the Spirit come from.

My mother, Frances Haywood MacRae, had a difficult time in her early years. She was a "doorstep" baby in Red Springs, North Carolina, and was placed on the step of Archibald and Kate Terry Bunting MacRae's home with a locket and note around her neck saying, "Please take care of me." There is a possibility that Archibald and Kate were in fact her real grandparents.

It was not socially acceptable to have children out of wedlock in the early 1900's. There was a tale that my grandparents' son, Marion, had gotten the green-eyed school music teacher pregnant. The teacher went away for a time and when she returned the "doorstep" baby appeared. The new "parents" promised they would always take care of this doorstep baby. The sad truth of the matter was, the baby's adoptive parents were advanced in years, her new father died when she was about 12 years old and her mother died while Frances was still a young woman. My mother had green eyes and excelled in music.

The MacRae's adopted Frances, but in order to do this they were required to adopt her as an "indentured servant." Frances was never treated poorly. If anything, she was treated like a queen. She never learned of her adoption until later on in her life. She grew up as a proud MacRae. When Frances found out the truth, the knowledge devastated her emotionally. She once told me, "Nobody wanted me!" and said it was difficult not to feel rejected. She explained that an indentured servant was another name for being a "slave." However, she said that she never felt that way growing up because her parents always treated her as if she were their child.

Frances was fascinated by her family history. She learned how the MacRae's had fought with Stonewall Jackson, and she was proud of her Scottish Presbyterian heritage. She had two brothers who were very much older. Colin, the younger son, served in the Navy during World War I, but unfortunately he was swept overboard in a bad storm and lost at sea. His sacrifice resulted in a financial remuneration from the government which helped the family during difficult times to survive. Marion, the older son, was called "Brother," and took care of Frances like a father (as we suspect he was). She always felt loved by her parents and Brother.

An interesting story told to me, took place when Frances was nine years old. A maid was doing the laundry in a big black iron kettle over the fire. Frances wanted to have her dress ironed, and told her to do it, but the maid refused. Frances took Brother's shotgun, pointed it at the maid and told her, "You will iron my dress!" The maid was forced to iron her dress at gunpoint! When Brother found out, he just laughed and laughed. Archibald and Kate were not happy with Frances at all. Needless to say, the maid quit and never returned to the house. I am sure that some of my "daring to rush in where angels fear to tread," comes down to me from my mother.

My grandfather and grandmother were very religious, and strict Presbyterians. There was no work to be done on Sunday at all! Food had to be prepared the day before. There was no dancing, no card playing, and no movies! In fact, you did not smile when you were in church. Worshipping God was serious business!

Frances learned to play both the piano and the organ and played for church at an early age. She became very faithful to the Presbyterian Church which her "parents" attended, and this love of music and faithfulness to the church was passed on to me.

There is another story about Kate that reveals how spirited a woman she was. She believed in natural medicine, and would brew sassafras tea in the Spring and "cleansing" herbs and teas at other times. The doctors felt this "cleansing" had been too hard on her system and eventually contributed to her death.

Kate also believed in drinking "pot liquor" (the juices from cooked vegetables), and swore that this caused her to have her own "pearly white" teeth until the day she died.

A Warning Comes to Kate as to Karl on 9/11

When my mother was a child, the MacRaes took a long trip together. It was pouring rain and the driving conditions were poor. The family stayed at a motel along the way because they were not making good time. They settled in and went to sleep. Very early the next day, Kate was the first to wake up. She had had a dream and in that dream she was told that they needed "to leave now." So, she woke everyone up, although it was still dark outside. They packed their bags and got ready to resume their journey. Someone looked at the clock and saw that it was only 3:00 a.m. They had slept only a few hours, but decided to check out anyway since they were all ready to go.

The rain was pouring down heavily. It must have been a tremendous tropical storm because the downpour continued for a long time. They left the motel and continued on their way. After a time they crossed a large bridge that was quickly beginning to flood. The water was just starting to cover the bridge at this point, but their vehicle made it safely across. Suddenly, just after they made it to the other side, the water rushed over it like a mighty flood, and the whole bridge collapsed. They could see it as it was being swept away. What frightened them was, had they been on that bridge just a few seconds later, they would surely have been swept away. Besides, this was the only bridge for many miles around that could have transported them to their destination on the other side of the river.

Why did this dream come to Kate? Why did she have such a sense of urgency to get on the road?

Frances accepted this story of her family's near brush with death as a sign that God was helping them through the trials of life. It was another indication that the intuitive ability that Kate had was also present in Frances and her children.

Mom's Intellect

Mom was 16 when she went off to college. She entered Flora MacDonald, now known as Queens University of Charlotte, North Carolina, and finished school in an incredible three years. She was extremely intelligent and graduated at the top of her class. Later, she regretted going through school so quickly, even though she did very well. She was the youngest student, several years younger than the other students in her class and because of this, her social life suffered. She had difficulty making friends and meeting boyfriends.

After Frances graduated, she taught school in Broadway, North Carolina for a time. She then got a job in Washington, D.C., working for a governmental intelligence agency, where she decoded cryptographs during the Second World War. I remember her telling me that she was one of the few people that knew exactly what was going to happen on D-Day before it even happened! It was top secret, but it was part of her job to be aware of these things. She provided some keen insight for the Intelligence Department during World War II, and was a valuable asset.

Sudden Footsteps

The following story lends credence to the intuitive ability that runs in our family.

Before Kate and Archibald passed away, they promised that they would always protect Frances and take care of her. There is one story that my mother told me a number of times for which there is only a spiritual explanation.

Frances was in her early twenties and living in North Carolina. At this time, she was a junior high school teacher and played the piano in a Presbyterian church. As she regularly attended worship, she developed a love of God.

One day she went to see a doctor for a problem, and was given the last appointment of the day. When she arrived there was no one but the doctor in the office. In fact, no one else was in the whole building. I don't believe this is common today, but this was in the late 1930's.

Believing they were alone, the doctor started to assault my mother, and she was terrified. All of a sudden, footsteps could be heard outside the door of the doctor's office. The doctor yelled out, "Who's there?" But when he opened the door, there was no one there. So he continued his assault on Frances who kept pushing him away as he attempted to rape her. Once again, footsteps were heard outside the door. The doctor repeated, "Who's there?" He went to open the door and still no one was there. But now, these phantom footsteps were enough of a distraction that Frances managed to slip away and escape.

Frances considered telling someone, but who would believe her? The most important thing was that she was able to get away unharmed.

Who was outside the door making footstep sounds? Not only were the sounds heard once, but twice! There was no evidence that anybody had been there at all.

Frances had become a very religious person. She had a strong faith in God, and He answered her prayers. She told me, "It was my father who had passed away some years earlier who came to my aid as a guardian angel, because before he died, he promised he would always protect me."

Love of Music that drew Frances and Larry Together

Some of my love of music comes from my father. He loved to sing! My father, Larry, went to work at a local Chock Full of Nuts restaurant so he could save money for singing lessons. When he joined the U.S. Navy, his aptitude scores were so high, that he was asked what he would like to do. He said, "I like to sing." The recruitment officer said, "Okay. We don't have anything in singing, but singing is about music; music is on the radio; radio is about electronics; so I think you'd be good in electronics." And, that's how Larry got into the electronics field.

He received a lot of training in electronics while in the Navy, and because of his high aptitude, he served as an electronics teacher during his time. After the military, he continued his schooling on the GI bill and received his College Degree at Oklahoma A & M, and later went on to California Institute of Technology to receive his Masters in Electrical Engineering. Finally, he received his Ph.D. in Electrical Engineering and Neuro-Physiology at Johns Hopkins, where he went on to teach as a visiting professor, and worked at the Johns Hopkins Applied Physics Laboratory.

My mother and father met at a USO gathering in Washington, D.C. during the Second World War. Larry was looking for someone to accompany him on the piano while he practiced his singing. Frances was playing the piano for the USO social gatherings, so Larry asked her if she would play while he sang. This was the beginning of their love affair. They were married in the National Presbyterian Church by Rev. Peter Marshall April 16, 1945.

I recall how my mother spoke fondly of Rev. Peter Marshall and his wife. He was a dynamic pastor and my mother enjoyed listening to his sermons. Frances was impressed with the inspiring words that were spoken by Rev. Marshall when she and Larry went to pre-marital sessions. They had a simple but beautiful service and, judging from their wedding photograph, Larry wore his Navy uniform.

During the postwar baby boom era, Larry and Frances had two children, Laura on March 7, 1946, and Karl on February 4, 1950.

Chapter 3

"Where you go I will go,
And where you lodge I will lodge,
Your people will be my people,
Your God will be my God."

Ruth 1:16

The Roots of Dale's Passion for the Church

My grandfather was an intelligent and resourceful man. As a boy, he worked in a drug store with an old-fashioned soda fountain. He told me about the big tank in the basement, and how it was his job to move it back and forth to create the "bubbles" for the soda. He also helped the pharmacist prepare prescriptions and often talked about his opportunity to become a pharmacist and go into the business. His boss offered him the chance, but his mother was not keen on the idea, and so Grandpop ended up moving to the Philadelphia area to work for his Uncle John Seyfert, his mother's sister's husband. Grandpop later became a salesman with Porter and Cable, a company that sold belt sanders. Included here, in his own words, is one of his many stories about his faith in God and how he felt a miracle had occurred in his life while working for Porter and Cable:

"I have had many Miracles during my lifetime. I started selling machinery at the age of 23 on commission and I worked that way until I retired. It was very rough during the Depression. People only purchased what they needed to operate their limited businesses. I always prayed before going out in the morning that the Lord would help me find a buyer. It didn't always happen but it happened often enough so that we could pay for our home and take care of the needs of our four children.

I remember one miracle that really 'paid off.' I sold some floor equipment to a woman who had a paint store in Pennsylvania. She signed a conditional sales contract – payments

10

to be made monthly. In about 30 days, she packed up most of the equipment and disappeared. Being responsible for such sales, the machines were charged to my commission account. This was quite a shock. I prayed that the Lord would help me to find the address of the place she had moved.

A few months later, the machine manufacturer received a letter asking for a price on these same models. The letter came from Ocean Grove, New Jersey, which is an old Methodist Camp Meeting Town. I stopped to see another customer near Ocean Grove and he mentioned that there was an advertisement in the local paper offering machines for sale. The ad gave a P. O. Box number, which was the same as the one on the letter I received. Unfortunately, the Post Office Department was not allowed to give the address of a box holder. I asked the lady clerk and she refused. I explained that they wanted to see me and failed to give me their address. The Lord was with me, she gave me the address.

I went around to a boarding house and rang the bell. An elderly lady asked if I came to see the machines which one of her boarders advertised. I said "Yes," and she escorted me to the kitchen. I got down on my knees to check the serial numbers. They matched. She said the woman who owned them would return shortly. I said I would return. I rushed to the Police Station and told my story. The Chief told me to go back and tell the Boarding House Mistress that he said to let me take the machines. When I told her the story she said, "We don't want any trouble in our town." I loaded them in my car and drove away thanking the Lord for his help. When the woman heard about my visit, she 'skipped.'

The next day was Thanksgiving Day. A very happy one for our family! Anyone who has been through a depression can understand how much the recovery of the machines meant to us, a wonderful miracle.

I can tell many more stories where Miracles were involved. I have had surgery six times, plus a Pacemaker a year ago. If it wasn't for Miracles I wouldn't be here today, at the age of 81."

My grandfather lived another 15 years. Grandpop gave me these words of wisdom. He said, "You should always save a little money each month. It doesn't have to be much. We lived through tough times in the depression, but we always had enough, even to go to Florida on vacation."

I believe my grandfather must have received his faith in God not only by going to church when he was a boy, but also through his mother. He talked about going to church twice every Sunday, once in the morning and then again later in the day.

I want to share with you a letter from my great-grandmother to my great Aunt Ruth, my grandfather's youngest sibling, in reference to her bequests. This letter shows me that my great-grandmother loved all her 10 children equally, as all parents try to do.

August 14th, 1961

Dearest Ruth,

You have always done what I have asked you when I lived and know you will carry out my wishes now.

Give Anna the green lamp and something she may want. Give to all my children something they may want for I know you will not want all the junk I leave which I loved. I do trust there will be no hard feelings the way things are left, for I loved one as much as the other. Please love one another- as I have loved you.

Lovingly, Mother

The Roots of Dale's Passion for Healing

My mother's mother, Julia Inge Emilie Petersen, went by the name of Emilie, although it was pronounced Amelia. She came to the United States from Denmark with my "Aunt Hulda" and to pay for their passage, they worked out West in Nebraska for the family who had paid their way. She later attended Nursing School at Providence Hospital in Washington, D.C. She excelled in her studies and graduated at the top of her class. At the same time, she took classes to learn English. She was in Washington during the great flu epidemic of 1918, where many who died were loaded onto wagons and buried in a mass grave. My grandmother also contracted this flu virus, but recovered. She was a friend of the Busch family and stayed with them at this time. After graduating from school, she became a private nurse in a well-to-do family for a Mrs. Webb, and went to live with them in New York City.

My mother is extremely intelligent, like her mother. She never missed a day of school throughout her childhood years. She even skipped a grade in high school and graduated early. My mother wanted to be a nurse like her mother, so she attended the Brooklyn Hospital Nursing School. She also took piano lessons and could play quite well enough to substitute for the organist at church occasionally. I recall that she was fond of African violets and loved to propagate them. Later on, she became interested in making quilts and has made a number of them for her children and grandchildren.

The Roots of Dale's Passion for the Ministry

I have always felt close to the church and the teachings of Jesus Christ. When I was given a copy of the Borglum family tree, I began to see the connection between my heritage and my religion.

I have the Borglum family tree copied from the records at Borglum Cloister, about their pastors from the earliest times after the Protestant Reformation. These records date back to 1439 when the Moth family came to Denmark with Kristoffer of Bavaria.

My father updated this tree and made a family tree of the Ditmars. He did this because I asked him to. This was another of my "projects" for him. The other major project I assigned him was to write his memoirs of World War II, which he called "Recollections of a Foot Soldier."

Upon examination, the Borglum family tree lists a number of "prasts" or priests in it. The language is Danish. There is a village in Denmark with a church called Borglum Cloister which is where my *family tree originates. I find it interesting that years earlier when I was in my Sunday school class at church, I told my minister that I wanted to be a minister's wife when I grew up. How prophetic this was for me, as I had not even seen the family tree yet!*

My grandfather on my mother's side was Axel Peter Borglum who was a sailor and later a painter. His father had a brother who emigrated to the United States. He made a life in Idaho where a son was born to him. He named his boy Gutzon Borglum. Gutzon went on to become a sculptor who worked on such impressive projects as Stone Mountain in Georgia and later went on to carve Mt. Rushmore in South Dakota. His son Lincoln later finished this project. Gutzon Borglum was my grandfather's first cousin.

I sometimes think I might have inherited some of my artistic ability such as my love of painting, from not only the Borglum side of the family, but the Ditmars' as well.

My Ditmars background is also impressive. My great-grandfather, Wallace, was a painter and, as my grandfather put it, "Painters in those days had to know how to mix paints and design and cut stencils. It was an art form." The painting tradition still holds with my Uncle Robert and his sons who each started painting businesses.

I also developed a love for oil painting and watercolors. This was due in part to my association with a girlfriend named Marie - her mother was a wonderful artist and Marie inherited these qualities as well. My parents encouraged my artistic endeavors and purchased my art supplies, which encouraged me to draw and paint.

I started to sing at a very young age, and believe I must have been born singing, since that is what I most like to do. If I am not singing, I'm humming. I've sung in many choirs and choruses throughout the years, and as a young girl, I sang solos in church and then in later years, at weddings. I still hum frequently, and if I'm not humming, it means I'm generally sad or struggling with emotional issues. Mostly though, music has gotten me through many a bad day.

I took piano lessons for six years, like my mother. This was great because I became my own accompanist! Before I could do this on my own, my mother would play for me. In later years, I learned to play the organ out of sheer necessity and I continue to serve as organist and choir director of our church today.

I am very artsy/crafty and love doing all kinds of projects. I've learned to knit and crochet, as my mother did, and I sew as well. I've learned needlepoint and other needlecrafts, and have even learned how to make jewelry, and to arrange flowers too! Gardening is also a big interest.

I must say I learned a great deal from my mother.

Three Generations of Healers

My mother grew up in Brooklyn, New York with her younger sister, Doris. Both she and Doris became nurses like their mother. I followed this same path and am the third generation in a family of nurses.

My father, Kenneth, and my mother, Ruth, met at a resort in the Pocono Mountains, Pennsylvania in 1948. It was at a vacation spot where you could get a room and enjoy meals in the dining hall for a week at a time.

My mother liked to vacation there with friends from Brooklyn who had a summer home there as well. When she met my father in the summer of 1948, she was on vacation with her sister Doris.

My Dad happened to vacation at the same resort with a friend who was there to practice his soccer. Dad's friend was an excellent athlete and played for a semi-professional soccer league.

Early in their vacation, my father and his friend went down to the lake, where they spotted my mother and her sister sitting on the dock. The two men approached the women and struck up a conversation. Before long, my parents were dating. They were married 10 months later on June 18, 1949.

I arrived on the scene on June 3, 1950. They named me Dale Suzanne Ditmars.

Chapter 4

"He leads me beside still waters, he restores my soul.
He leads me in paths of righteousness for his name's sake.
Even though I walk through the valley of the shadow of death,
I fear no evil; for thou art with me."

Psalm 23:2-4

By the Still Waters

Larry and Frances Viernstein moved to Stillwater, Oklahoma and there, Larry attended Oklahoma A&M University. They lived in a small trailer with a little garden in the back yard. It was located right next to an Indian Reservation. It was there Frances gave birth to their second child. She had had difficulties giving birth to their first child, Laura Kate, earlier in Washington, D.C., and after a previous miscarriage, was told by the doctors that she would not be able to have any more children.

Frances' blood factor was RH Negative, which is a component in the blood that made it difficult to have children and bring them to full term. However, she did become pregnant again, and she was determined that things would be different. So, Frances prayed to God, and prayed often! The doctors placed her in the hospital with her feet elevated for the last several months of her pregnancy. Karl, a healthy baby boy, was born on February 4, 1950 at 11:05 a.m.

While living in Stillwater, Frances and Larry got to know some of the local Native American Indians who were their neighbors. Some helped to care for young Karl. It was so hot in the trailer that Larry put a fan in a window. One of their Indian friends was curious about the fan and unfortunately, cut his hand severely when he touched it. Frances and Larry were there and wanted to help the man, but he refused any help. What amazed them too, was that he didn't seem to feel the pain!

After Larry graduated from school, he earned a scholarship to Cal Tech, and the family moved to Baldwin Park, California. There they purchased their first house using a VA loan Larry qualified for after his time in the service. One of my earliest childhood memories was of playing with a large multi-colored plastic ball in a yard with a huge fence, and there were gigantic electric power line towers behind the house. Everything was huge! From my perspective, everything looked big because I was only 3 years old. Then, very early one morning, I woke up screaming. Both my parents woke at my cries, and realized that everything in the house was shaking! It was an earthquake! It wasn't a big one, but strong enough to knock stuff over. I got the blame for alerting everyone when the earthquake occurred.

After graduating from the California Institute of Technology, my father got a job working for Johns Hopkins Applied Physics Laboratory (APL), in Silver Spring, Maryland. That meant we had to move again.

Traveling across the country was quite an experience for us. My parents, sister and I made frequent stops along the way, and one of our layovers was at the Grand Canyon in Arizona. That night it snowed. I was the first person up in the morning, and when I saw all this white stuff outside on the ground, I was frightened. "Wake up, everyone, wake up!" I yelled. "Something is wrong! There is all this white stuff outside!" I was amazed to see this "white stuff" all over the place. Recovering from my outburst, my parents were amused by my reaction to the first snowfall I had ever seen.

Kensington, Maryland

Shortly after arriving in the Washington, D.C. area, my parents rented a house in Kensington, Maryland, and quickly settled in. One day, while at home with my family, I began to draw. I started making lots of circles on paper, over and over again. Larry and Frances, uncertain what this meant, consulted a psychologist. He supposed that I was probably suffering from the trauma of the move and demonstrated this with my drawings. He also suggested that the circles I drew represented the breasts of my mother. Maybe, he thought, I was yearning for my mother's breasts. I, however, remember exactly what I was drawing. On our trip cross country, I was impressed with the maps my parents had used to navigate. They were the AAA Trip Tics, a kind of driver's guide we would follow that had lines drawn on the roads marked in yellow magic marker, and with circles around the cities where we were going. My childish drawings were my attempt to recreate that which impressed me!

I also kept asking to play with Stanley, my friend. I couldn't understand why I couldn't play with him, not realizing that Stanley was a neighbor, way back in California.

I didn't talk very much as a child, which had my parents concerned. Consequently, making new friends was not exactly the easiest thing for me to do in a new community. I remember standing in the middle of the sidewalk in front of the house, when a couple of kids came down the sidewalk riding their tricycles. I stood there in the middle of the side walk and spoke up, "This is my sidewalk, and you are not allowed to go on my sidewalk!"

At that, the other children were taken aback and argued with me and said, "We have always ridden our bikes on this side walk."

Insistent, I said, "No, you are not allowed to ride on my sidewalk!"

At that point, my mother heard the commotion and came out to see what was going on, only to find out that I had refused to allow the other children to pass. I didn't want them riding on our sidewalk!

It took awhile to convince me that the sidewalk was not really part of our property, but by that afternoon, I had made some new friends, Robbie and Suzie. Later, I was invited to their house and had milk and cookies with them.

Racial Discrimination

While in Kensington Elementary School, I made a new friend named Harriet, and we enjoyed playing together during recess. She was black and I was white. We climbed through the jungle gym, which was a complex structure of iron bars. The other children were teasers, as kids are and started chanting, "Karl and Harriet, sitting in the tree, K-I-S-S-I-N-G, first comes love, then comes marriage, then comes baby in the baby carriage."

Shortly after, my mother received a phone call from the principal of the school who said, "Mrs. Viernstein, your son has been playing with another child in school at recess. We think it is inappropriate for them to be playing together and we want you to tell your child that he can't play with her any more."

Frances asked, "Why, did he do anything wrong?"

"No, we just don't think they should be together because she is colored and he is white."

Later that day, when my mother spoke to me, I got very upset and said, "Why? Why can't I play with Harriet?"

I just didn't understand why the grownups were telling me that. "What is wrong with playing with her?" It just did not seem right to me, and I was only 6 years old!

My mother also seemed to be unhappy with what she'd heard from the principal, and admitted that I was right. "It shouldn't matter," she said. "But, it's the times we live in."

Jesus loved everyone: color was not an issue, love was.

Warner Memorial Presbyterian Church

Faithfully, I attended Sunday school at the Warner Memorial Presbyterian Church, and sang in the children's choir. My mother was the substitute organist at the Church, and played for the children's choir led by Mrs. Bailey. My mother also played the organ at NIH, National Institutes of Health for the Catholic, Protestant and Jewish services. Since my mother usually took me with her, it was then that I was exposed to many different religions and gained an appreciation for them all. Just living in the area north of Washington, D.C. was an experience in ecumenical training because of the diverse religions and cultures of those people who had migrated there from different countries around the world.

Trying To Be Helpful

There were many escapades that happened while I was a child that often revolved around my mother, who was very hospitable to all the kids in the neighborhood. I remember whenever I got a cut, which was often, my mother would put some iodine on it to kill the germs, and then put a band-aid on it to keep it clean.

One day, my friend Robbie and I were playing at my house and we decided to drop a rope out the second story window to climb down it. I said, "Robbie, you go first." Robbie climbed out the sill and immediately slid down the rope. And because he was unable to hold on tightly, he burned his hand. I told him I knew exactly what to do! I brought him into the house and got out the iodine and band-aids, but when I put iodine on his rope burn, he let out a blood-curdling scream, and ran out of the house! I didn't realize that it would hurt so badly. I thought it would help.

Signs of Being Empathic: Sensitivity to the Pain of Others

In some ways, I was just like every other kid on the block, but in other ways, I was very different. One evening, my parents were in the kitchen talking while I was in the other room. All of a sudden, they heard me crying, and came rushing into the living room. "What's wrong?" they asked. I was holding on to my leg as I sat on the floor crying, "My leg. My leg!" They examined my leg thinking I had cut myself or perhaps twisted it somehow, but they could find nothing wrong with me. Then, my mother noticed the TV show that was on. It was "Lassie" (a popular television show about the adventures of a boy and his collie dog). Timmy, the main character, and a boy not much older than I was, had got his leg caught in a fence and could not get it free. He was crying and needed help, so Lassie raced to get help to rescue him. I remember how that caused quite a stir in the family. My parents were disturbed by how strongly I was affected by what I saw on TV, and wondered if I should be allowed to watch it. If "Lassie" upset me, how would I deal with the pain of others in real life? As a

result of this episode, my parents thought I should have a dog and they got me a Collie whom I named "Bonnie."

Bonnie's Bomb Shelter

During the 60's the cold war was brewing between Russia and the United States and our president sent out detailed plans to all residents in the Washington, D.C. area to build bomb shelters as a precaution. We had the Cuban missile crisis to contend with as well! My beloved Collie, Bonnie, was my friend and protector, so I decided to build a bomb shelter for her in the back yard of our house. I gathered all the kids in the neighborhood, and with shovels we began to dig a hole in the hill that would become "Bonnie's Bomb Shelter." The neighbors were quite amused but perplexed as to how all the kids in the area came together on their own to help protect the dog they loved.

Fearless

One summer, our family went on a trip to North Carolina. As my father was driving through a small town, we suddenly heard police sirens behind us and the police officer motioned for us to stop. The car was a station wagon, packed with luggage, and I was sitting in the very back section. The police officer informed my father that he had gone through a stop sign without stopping. My father apologized and tried to explain that we were from out of town, hoping that the officer would not give him a ticket. For some reason, I was disturbed by all the commotion and not happy with the police officer stopping our car, so I said in a loud voice, "Aw...Shut up!" My parents were dumfounded, but ignoring me, they again tried to explain how they were looking for direction signs and did not see the stop sign. Their apologies fell on deaf ears. The policeman said, "You should have been looking at the traffic signs." Still perturbed, I said in a loud voice, "Aw...Shut up!" At this point, my father and mother were trying to stop me from talking, but I was too far back in the car for anyone to get to me. For the third time I said, "Aw…Shut up!" With that, the policeman said, "Wait here while I write up the ticket!"

My mother was upset, of course, and said, "What is wrong with you?"

I replied, "That man shouldn't be talking to you that way!"

"But he's a policeman!" She said.

After we received the ticket, we left the town in a hurry. My sister laughed and laughed at what I did. Who would have thought quiet little Karl would say such a thing!

This story was repeated many times because it was so out of character for me. It wasn't until much later that I told them that when I said, "Aw…Shut up!" I was only mimicking what Ralph Cramden, played by Jackie Gleason, said on the Honeymooners on TV when he was fed up with what was going on. At the time, I don't think anyone believed me. However, I was a very impressionable child, and sensitive to things around me.

Unusual Sleep Happenings

As a child, I remember sleepwalking through the house. I would sometimes wake up during one of my "walks" around the house, and wonder, "What am I doing here?" I was sleepwalking! I was awake walking, but I was also asleep!

I remember one time I had the most unusual out-of-body experience, of seeing my body from the top of the room. It seemed like I was floating on top of the room looking down, and when I tried to move my body, I couldn't. Then in a flash, I zoomed down to where I was sleeping and woke up. I remembered what had happened very clearly. Did I actually leave my body? Was that possible?

There were different times, other people would tell me, that I fell asleep with my eyes open. My friends thought it was funny that I slept this way.

I've always felt different from my friends and others since the beginning of my life. I never felt handicapped, just that I was different from others in several ways.

Slow Going

From as far back as I can remember, I felt God had something special in store for me, a direction for my life that was different from many others. I felt I was to accomplish a task that would help others. But, life was not easy for me. In fact, the beginning of my life was unusual and different from the start.

As a child, I didn't speak very much. I could talk all right, but I was usually quiet. It was a concern for my parents, so they took me for psychological testing. I'll never forget it. After all the tests were given and we were on our way out the door, this lady said, "Mrs. Viernstein, I'm sorry, but your child is so unusual, we can't use his scores to compare with other students. We have to throw them out."

For a while, I was withdrawn and shy. However, as time went on, I began to realize on my own that I was unique. The results of the tests showed that on simple tests such as assembling blocks and puzzles, I performed poorly. However, on the advanced and more complex tests that most people find difficult, I performed exceptionally well. As for talking, it took time for me to develop my verbal skills. Speech was difficult and I stuttered.

Reading was another problem. Doctors had determined that I wasn't stupid, but they couldn't figure out why I couldn't read. To me words often came out reversed and slow. This is well before Dyslexia, the learning disability, had been diagnosed and recognized.

I remember my mother would ask me, "Why don't you talk?"

I would respond, "I don't have anything to say."

There were times in my life when I really did have something to say, and I would raise my voice to be heard over the voices of others and say, "I want to shay something," slurring the word "say." I was kidded for years afterward, "Karl wanted to 'shay something.'"

Evidently, because I did not talk very much in my early development as a child, I had some difficulty speaking later on, and even slurred different words. Yet, I had the gift of being ambidextrous. I am able to use both my hands while doing different tasks. My right hand became the dominant hand, but there are times when I can do equally well with my left.

I remember how very difficult it was to learn how to read. In fact, I couldn't read at all! I could learn certain words, but stringing them together in a coherent order was next to impossible. My words usually became reversed. I would read the second word first and then read backwards to catch the word I should have read. Again, my parents took me to the best ophthalmologist in Washington, D.C. to have my eyes examined, but there was nothing wrong with them, according to the doctor.

So, why couldn't I read? The teachers said I was one of those slow children. "Not all children are smart enough to read, and Karl is one of them." But, I could read, word by word, very slowly. I had one special reading class after another, but it didn't seem to help. Since I was a good boy in other areas, they pushed me through school.

The guidance counselor in Junior High said, "Karl, you will probably never graduate from high school." I went home, very discouraged that the school guidance counselor was telling me that I was doomed to fail! I was a dummy! How could you explain then, that whenever I played with my friends at board games or chess, I usually won! It was a mystery.

Was I that stupid? How could I get A's in Math and barely pass English? It didn't make any sense.

My mother had some good friends at our church. Some were teachers, others were musicians. Mrs. Stickley was a 7th grade English teacher, but she was different from the other teachers. I knew she recognized that I had a problem, and took a personal interest in tutoring me - not as punishment, but out of genuine concern. She praised me often, and was the first teacher that believed in me.

I struggled with tests in class, but she knew I wasn't stupid! I just had a reading problem and that was my Goliath, something I had to overcome. Moreover, I could do it! She believed that God had something special in mind for me, though I didn't know yet what it was. Someday I would find out.

I started reading comics. I began to get the story line and enjoyed the short phrases. Soon, I was reading Tom Sawyer, and enjoying the story. I had a lot of catching up to do! Nevertheless, it seemed like I was always behind the others in class. I had to study twice as hard as the other students just to do the work. By the time I was in high school, I had developed study habits that required time and discipline, while other students, not used to studying hard, were now having difficulty. Thus, the teaching and support of my 7th grade English teacher has been a lifetime of benefit.

I do believe that I am the result of the many people who took the time and effort to help me on my journey through life. It does 'take a community' to raise a child and to provide the support that will help them develop confidence.

Science Experiments in High School

It was 1964, and I recall an experiment I did in high school with two magnets. I observed that if only one magnet was standing, nothing happened outside of an energy field that ran from north to south. However, if you placed two magnets together in close proximity and passed a group of wires between them, it would generate a kind of energy that could pass between the two almost indefinitely. I entered this device into the science fair at school and called it "Perpetual Energy!" No one understood it. It just received a lot of curious questions, such as "What does it do?"

One interesting thing about the device was that once you started the motion by moving the coil of wire through one magnet, that in turn would move the coil of wire through the other magnet. In other words, one affected the other in an equal and opposite manner.

This is another principle I learned in Sunday school. Jesus taught us the laws of reciprocity. Do unto others as you would have them do unto you. Forgive, and you will be forgiven. Love and others will love you. Give and it will be given to you, all edicts that paid tribute to my scientific theories.

I found an old tube electrocardiograph (EKG) machine at a local junk yard and, with my father's help, fixed it up and got it working. I began taking EKG readings of everybody in the community including my dog, Bonnie. I put her front paws into two small butter tubs filled with salt water. Then, I put a flat piece of lead that had wires connected to the EKG in the bottom of the tub that she stood in. After the test, I took the various EKG strips to a local doctor for evaluation, and discovered a friend of mine had a heart murmur. I entered my old tube EKG machine with the heart beat results of my friends and dog into the High School Science Fair in 1965.

I built a 3-bit computer using relays the following year. I had a tremendous vision of the future with computers, and I learned about computer programming early.

Music Uplifts and Tunes me In

In my youth, I was particularly sensitive to certain types of music. I recall listening to music and, when it was exceptionally beautiful, it would send "chills" running throughout my whole body. I asked other people if they felt this way too, but I would get a strange look from them. After a while, I stopped asking, because I realized that other people didn't always feel the same sensations that I felt. And, I didn't feel this way all the time, just when the music was superbly lovely. I've since met others who also sometimes got chills, but they were usually very good musicians or sensitive people who appreciated very good music.

For me, there are two elements that can cause music to be uplifting. First, good vocal or instrumental music is the result of the emotional and spiritual character of the artists themselves that produce the music. The notes and sound waves are only vehicles for the uplifting music to energize me.

The second element is a live performance of the music and you are in the same room with the performer. There is a remarkable difference when you are actually in the presence of the one who creates the music. The overtones of the music and the 'presence' of the performer are much more dynamic. However, if the performer is "angry" or "off key" emotionally, it makes for lousy music.

I loved music and asked my mother if I could learn to play the violin. My mother was delighted, but thought I should learn to play the piano first. Then, if I wanted to play the violin, I would be ready because I would already be able to read music. I agreed. I took two years of piano lessons, even though there were times when I was not happy with the piano. I still wanted to play the violin. So, my mother took me to a music store to buy a violin. I was so excited! I remember going into the store and seeing all kinds of instruments, and many violins. She started me out on a small violin and I soon advanced to a larger one. I took violin lessons for six years, and played in the school orchestra, and for a brief time, I played in the youth symphony in Washington, D.C.

I also learned to play the guitar and performed in a number of professional bands throughout high school. I sang in choirs throughout high school, college and church. Music became a bridge that drew me closer to God. It was important to me to hear good music, but bad music would grate on my nerves. Music would comfort me in times of sorrow, whether playing or listening. Music would lift me up when I was bored, and energize me to study for long periods. Music penetrates you and touches you deep inside. I have found it to be a wonderful gift we can use to uplift others.

My First Spiritual Experience

I had my first spiritual experience when I was about 12 years old, while riding my bicycle about half a mile from my home. Several of my friends and I tied cans to a string and attached them to our bicycles with the cans dragging behind us down the street, making a loud clashing noise. All of a sudden, the cans fell off my bike and this strange feeling overcame me, as I had never experienced before. My whole body tingled from head to toe, and I heard a voice telling me to go HOME. Something was wrong! It was urgent that I go home immediately! As I started peddling frantically for home, my friends yelled at me, "Where are you going?" and, "You've left the cans behind, come back!" But there wasn't any time to explain my actions, I didn't know why. All I knew was that I had to get home, and as fast as possible! "I have to go home!" I yelled to my friends. It was not like me, to abandon my friends and the cans I'd worked so hard to put together. Home! Home! Home! Home was the urgent message!

I ran into the house and as I entered, I noticed that there was blood all over the front steps and through the door onto the floor inside. I found my mother lying on the floor. She had cut a major artery in her leg, and was bleeding profusely. She had been trying to call for help, but the doctor's phone number was busy. She even went to the front door to call for help, but the people across the street couldn't hear her although she was crying desperately for help! I was the first one to enter the house. She had a towel wrapped around her leg and I knew enough to apply direct pressure to stop the bleeding. Finally, we were able to get someone on the phone and soon after, an emergency vehicle pulled up to the door.

When I had time to think, I realized that the tingling I had telling me to go home was right. Somehow, I knew that something special had happened to me that day, even though I didn't understand it. It was a blessing for my mother, whom I loved. Somehow, the love we shared for each other transcended the barriers of time and space, and there was a communication between us that defied the laws of the science that we know today.

The Physicist

There was a physicist who taught his son in a different manner than most fathers. When his son returned home from school each day, he would ask him, "Did you ask any good questions in school today?" Although most other parents would ask, "How did you do in school today?" or "How was school?" The Physicist knew if his son asked the right questions, he would learn. By getting his son to reason out the why, how, when, and where of a situation, the knowledge would come as he would seek the truth.

That physicist was my father. The ability to ask questions was especially important to my father because he was never allowed to ask questions in his youth at the Catholic orphanage where he grew up.

Defending the Weak

When I was in Junior High School (grades 7-9), I had a friend named Peter, and I became Peter's defender. He was a fellow student that the other kids would always pick on. They would play cruel jokes on him, especially during gym. The trouble was Peter was very immature, and he would suck his thumb occasionally and the other kids would make fun of him, which compounded the problem and made him even more insecure. Instead of standing his ground, he always ran from his opponents. I remember on several occasions I got fed up with the other kids giving Peter such a hard time. After all, Peter didn't do anything to them to deserve it!

I would yell at the other kids, "Leave him alone. He hasn't done anything to you!" I screamed at them, raised my fist, and I banged the lockers making lots of noise. I never had to hit anybody, because they always ran. I believed the scare tactics I used, yelling and banging, and making as much noise as I could was frightening to them. I acted like a crazy person, but it was just an act.

I went to Peter and asked, "Are you all right?"

"I'm okay," he said.

After that event, Peter would run from the other kids and hide behind me. I was shocked. The kids did not want to mess with me, but wanted Peter. Again, I told them, "Leave him alone!"

The Puzzles of Life

Chess was a favorite game I played when I was young and I was almost undefeated. I also loved to play "Risk" with my friends, and the only way they could win was for everyone to gang up against me. I also loved to play "Hex" (a game based upon a board made of hexagons – similar to the game "Go") and it was also hard to beat me in that game. A boyfriend of my sister, Laura Kate, was doing a research paper on the game "Hex" and thought he had figured out a foolproof method to win. He played me several times and lost every time. He was so devastated, he quit writing the paper and stopped seeing my sister!

A Happy Family Life with Exotic Pets

My father worked in a laboratory with rats and monkeys, so you can guess the kind of animals we had as pets growing up. It was unusual, but my sister and I had white rats for pets, and a ring-tailed monkey as well. We also had turtles, hamsters, rabbits, fish, birds, and of course cats and dogs. My sister had several science fair projects that involved our pets. The monkey had four levers built into his cage. One lever turned a light on, one rang a bell, one shook the cage and the last one was a dummy. We tracked his habits with a pen recorder my father built, and we discovered he turned all the levers on and off before eating time, to get our attention. He liked to keep the light on at night. In addition, he soon learned not to shake the cage except before dinnertime.

The monkey came to be known as "Monkey Doodle." It was interesting to take the monkey for a walk around the block. The neighbors would look twice. Once the monkey got loose and my friend next door saw him in the tree right outside his window. He called out to his mother, "Hey Mom, there's a monkey outside my window!" She didn't believe him. So he yelled out again, "Mom, there's a monkey outside my window!" So, just to amuse him, she went upstairs and asked, "What are you talking about?" Then low and behold, there was a monkey right outside the window hanging on the tree. They opened the window and let the monkey in the house. She continued, "Whose monkey could this be? I bet it belongs to the Viernstein family! They always have strange animals, like white rats." Soon, all the neighbors came to know us as the exotic animal house people.

The Cedar Brook Swim Club asked me to be the Organ Grinder with the monkey in their South Pacific "Water Show." I remember a well known TV celebrity who was the commentator for the show, got angry with me. As he was reading the story, I was walking around the

pool with the monkey, and all eyes and ears were on me and the monkey. The TV commentator was jealous of the attention the monkey got and said, "Get that damn monkey out of here!" It seemed like I always managed to get in the middle of things. The monkey was stealing the show.

One day, my friend, who often played at our house, was teasing the monkey, and the monkey got upset. My friend ran and the monkey jumped on him and bit him in the behind. That became the talk of the neighbors and all my friends. I felt sorry for my friend because when word got around school that he had been bitten by a monkey, the other kids teased him that he had rabies! Watch out for the Viernstein monkey! That was the only time I knew the monkey ever bit anyone, but after that we had to be careful with him.

It was wintertime when the monkey died and the ground was totally frozen. So we could not bury the monkey in the ground. My father put the monkey in a bag and placed him in the freezer. I was aware of this, and when my friends wanted to know where the monkey was I told them, "He's in the freezer.' They did not believe me. So, I started showing all the kids in the neighborhood our frozen monkey. In fact, I started charging them 5 cents to see the "Monkey in the Freezer." Then my mother got a call from one of the neighborhood mothers, "Mrs. Viernstein, is it true you have a monkey in the freezer?" My mother was mortified! I was in the doghouse when she found out I was bringing all the kids in the neighborhood into the house to see the monkey and charging them a fee.

It got even funnier, when a few weeks later, my father finally buried the monkey in the back yard. The following day, there was a knock on the door. I opened the door and a policeman was standing there. He asked, "Is this the Viernsteins' residence?" I said, "Sure, come on in." I welcomed the policeman into our home and he asked to speak to my parents about a report made by one of our neighbors who said they saw my father bury a fetus in the backyard! My father and mother were horrified. My father explained that it was a pet monkey that had died and was buried. The officer insisted that my father go outside and dig up the monkey to prove to the police officer it was not a baby, but a monkey. The monkey got the last laugh in the end!

Our family just laughed and laughed at how bizarre things could get. The good thing about all of this was that we were enjoying life and laughing together. We had lots of good friends and we opened our house to all. We did show love to one another through the events and experiences of life.

What a preparation for ministry! Every congregation has its exotic, its clever, its faithful, its bizarre, and its wonderful collection of people.

Training for the Ministry: Boy Scouts of America

As I grew older, I became active in the Boy Scouts of America, going on camping and canoeing trips, and each summer I learned skills at the Chesapeake, Maryland Boy Scout Camp. I was the senior patrol leader of Troop 1072 with over 100 scouts in the troop. I found myself teaching basic skills such as first aid, swimming, cooking, camping and even Morse code to other scouts. The most valuable lessons I learned in Scouting were leadership skills, and the confidence that I could succeed if I applied myself.

It is interesting that my most difficult merit badge was for "public speaking." I recall my father taking me to a women's organization where I was assigned to give a speech. In the middle of my speech, my mind went blank, and I forgot what to say. So, I improvised and I raised my hand forming the scout sign and said to them, "And now I will tell you everything that a scout must do." I then recited the Scout Law that I knew by heart, and the Scout Oath. I regained my composure and finished the speech. It was a big hit with the women and I got the public speaking merit badge.

Part of my training in scouting was a religious award, "God and Country." I was on my way, developing knowledge and skills that I would use later on in ministry.

And They Will Soar Like Eagles

Becoming an Eagle Scout was a long road of hard work and much discipline. To attain this I needed to get 21 merit badges (I got 26), develop a project (mine was working with the mentally ill), demonstrate leadership abilities (I was senior patrol leader), and submit to an interview with a council of men involved in scouting.

The interview was the most difficult for me. I was nervous to the point of shaking and displayed a nervous tick. As I waited for the results of my interview, I overheard the discussion of those who interviewed me. One man said I was too nervous to be an Eagle Scout. Throughout my whole life, people have tended to judge me without understanding me. Other people have seen that I possess some unusual abilities. I believe everyone has the same capabilities, but they haven't developed them yet.

Another man spoke up and said, "Of all the boys I know, Karl deserves this the most. He best displays the qualities of an Eagle Scout because he goes out of his way to help others and his resourcefulness is amazing."

The vote was positive. I was to become an Eagle Scout!

My ability to be resourceful has continued to be part of me throughout my whole life. I have had to be resourceful at most everything in the home and in the church because money was often scarce. I can't tell you how many jobs I have completed using only a few tools. Either I could not afford the right tools or I didn't have them available, but I still managed to complete the task at hand. Every church congregation needs a minister with the ability to figure out a way to get a task done in an emergency.

Light in My Hands

My hands have been God's greatest gift to me. I feel blessed to be able to do many things with my hands. As a child, my father would joke that I was able to use a screwdriver before I was able to use a fork at the dining room table. My father taught me many things, but other things I was able to figure out myself, as I observed others. I could build with wood, deal with plumbing problems, handle electrical malfunctions, repair broken appliances, lay tile, and even add a room to a house. By the time I was 14 years old, I was able to use many tools.

I remember trying to drill a hole through a shark's tooth so that I could thread a cord through the hole and wear it around my neck. I did not realize that the shark's tooth was fossilized and was harder than the drill bit I was using. The drill slipped off the shark's tooth and drilled a hole through my finger. So, I went to the hospital and got some stitches and an x-ray of my hand. The doctor showed me the x-rays and pointed out the "white spots" in my hand. The doctor said these were God's gift to some people who were provided with extra lubricating points. He explained that not all people had been blessed with these extra oil spots, but it would help me with my dexterity.

All my life I have tried to use my hands to help others. The Bible says that those who shall ascend to the hill of the Lord will have clean hands and a pure heart. I feel that when I use my hands to be helpful and uplifting to others, I am serving the Lord. When I play the violin or the guitar, my hands are being used to inspire the listeners.

I also discovered that I could use my hands to bless others. When I hold a baby in my arms at the Baptismal font, my hands are blessing that baby. When I pass out the bread and the wine during communion, I am blessing the congregation. When I hold up my arms for the benediction, and my hands reach out to one and all, I am blessing them. When I touch an elderly person in a loving way, I am blessing that person with my hands. When I visit an ill person in the hospital, I lay my hands on them and bless them.

So, my hands have been an important part of my ministry. You could say I'm a "hands on pastor."

Learning Grace and Speed

I attended a dance and decorum school for two years on my mothers' advice, so I could learn to get along with others socially and be more confident. It did give me the knowledge to approach others with grace and style, and I ended up winning my first trophy. I took first place in couples dancing.

I also took tennis lessons at Georgetown University for high school students, and won my second trophy, also first place. I enjoyed the sport, but I believe I won because the other players couldn't keep the ball in play as well as I could. I was not an outstanding tennis player, but my best abilities in the sport were my speed in running and the ability to figure out a good strategy.

The Queen Bee

During High School, a group of my friends and I went by the nickname, "The Crew." We met in the basement of my house. We had black lights, psychedelic posters, pictures, drawings, and a strange assortment of items we collected. We camped out together, made snow forts together, ate together and had a great time. It was all good clean fun. We never did anything bad and were basically a good support group for one another.

However, it was my mother, Frances, who really was the gracious host of the "Crew"! She invited my friends into our house, and we had a grand and glorious time. We even formed a rock-'n'-roll band and practiced right in the middle of the living room. We built a clubhouse on a hill in the backyard, and developed a close relationship with one another, but it was because my mother was the one who encouraged us to work together and then guided us in a better direction, especially, when we came up with ideas that were not realistic.

Here is a true story about a "queen bee" that best describes the relationship between my mother and the Crew. There was a bee keeper who had years of experience taking care of bee hives. He started a new hive and had to get a new queen bee. As usual, the workers would follow the guidance of the queen, but he noticed that the bees were very agitated and were stinging people all the time. So, he took the queen bee back and got another one. However, this time he noticed that most of the bees were lazy. They didn't make honey, they didn't move very fast, and the bees just laid around. These were the same bees, but now with different work habits. Again, the bee keeper exchanged the queen bee for a new one. Now, this time, the bee keeper noticed that the bees were doing just fine. They didn't sting people because they were busy working to produce honey. They were not lazy, but very productive. That turned out to be the best queen bee that the bee keeper ever had. This story illustrates how very important leadership is in any organization, be it a home, church or a nation.

Our real leader was mom. She wasn't agitated or lazy, but she was a compassionate leader, who taught us how to be peaceful and be productive in what we did as a group and as individuals. She was a wonderful "queen bee."

Thus, I developed a leadership style of peace and reconciliation. Jesus did not come to divide the world, but came that the world would be reconciled together in peace and love.

Summer Jobs: A Preparation for my Future Work

During the summer months while in high school I worked at several jobs. "DISCOM" or Display Communications was a shop where I worked putting together advertising displays for military recruitment offices and other companies. The production of plastic parts from an injection mold machine was also used to fill other display orders. I learned a great deal about shop tools, electronics, and a variety of other general skills by working there.

Another summer I worked for Ostronics, an electronics company that built deep-sea microphones for the military.

Finally, I worked for a private contracting company during the summer of my senior year and also several summers while attending college. I helped to build additions to homes. I learned framing, wiring, plumbing and concrete work.

These jobs helped to fashion in me what I am today, a "Jack of All Trades." My abilities have aided me every step of my way in life, especially in the home and in the church.

Life Guard – Swim Team
Learning about God's Saving Grace

It was not unusual for me to work two full time jobs at the same time each summer. After working during the day, I would come home, grab something to eat, and leave again for the Cedar Brook Swim Club. I was a lifeguard and swim instructor. On two occasions, I pulled children out of the water. First, there was a child who jumped into the deep end and did not know how to swim. He saw other kids jumping in, so he thought he could jump in. I remember seeing his frightened eyes as he struggled in the water going down. I pulled him out and, fortunately, he was able to cough the water out of his system. I saved the life of someone I may never see again, but it gave me courage to face the future, and to understand that God could use me to help others in ways I did not know.

The second time I was called upon to save a life was when there was a child in danger of being exposed to a deadly chlorine gas. While I was on life guard duty, a chlorine gas tank exploded. Almost instantly, dangerous chlorine fumes were spreading throughout the area. I immediately blew the whistle and cleared the pool of all the people to prevent exposure to this toxic gas. One child however was swimming straight toward the lethal gas, so I jumped into the water and swam like there was no tomorrow to get him out as fast as possible. Fortunately, I was able to reach the child before he sustained any injury, and I guided him to safety.

I was on the swim team and we practiced about 4 hours a day. A short-lived claim to fame was when I competed in the Junior Olympics swim event in Chevy Chase, Maryland. They were looking for the best swimmers who would go on to compete in the Olympics. My best stroke was the breast stroke, and I entered the competition, but alas did not have a qualifying time. I did get a medal for competing in the Junior Olympics.

Preparation for Serving the Living God

My high school experiences were also quite remarkable. I usually received A's in math, but English was always a struggle for me. I loved sports, especially varsity team basketball and track. Early in the football season, I sprained my ankle three times in a row. That kept me from being involved in sports. Even though I was discouraged, I believed God had another plan for me.

In my junior year at Albert Einstein High School, I became involved with the Key Club, a service organization sponsored by the Kiwanis Club. By my senior year, I became the president, and had a large following of dedicated people, both young men and women. We had the biggest dances and the biggest raffles, with prizes such as TV's and radios. I organized a program for mentally handicapped children, in the school gymnasium. Individuals from the Key Club, other students and faculty would volunteer to work with these children once a week. The program was so successful it continued after I left high school.

A Remarkable Premonition

I was driving down Ambler Drive in Kensington one day, when suddenly I heard, "Step on the brake." I thought to myself, "Okay, I'll do it." So I did. And, just at that moment, five or six children came darting out of a side street on bicycles into the middle of the road! Had I not heeded the warning to brake, I would have run into those children, and they could have been killed or injured. I thanked God for sparing their lives and preventing me from hitting them. I was in awe! I vowed that if my intuition ever told me to do something, I would do it! To this day, I try to follow the prompting of the Holy Spirit. This was another spiritual experience I will never forget.

Dating

I was a bit shy when it came to dating girls, although I was always attracted to girls who were genuine and honest. There was one girl I dated, who stuttered. She was not the most beautiful girl in the school, but that was not what love was all about. I was not ashamed or afraid to face any of our human faults and frailties. I tried to look beyond physical appearance and upon the inside, the heart of a person. When I did go out on a date, we usually ended up talking about philosophy or religion.

Bandstand

There was a show on TV in the Washington, D.C. area called "Wing Ding" and it was like American Bandstand.

Several girls in school came up to me and asked, "Karl, do you want to be on TV with us and dance?"

I said, "How is that possible?"

They said, "We have two passes for this Friday's afternoon show, but we have a plan to get all three of us on the TV show."

They explained the plan and I agreed I would go along with it. The worst that could happen would be for one of us not to get in, or so I thought. The plan was this: I would escort one of the girls into the studio, using the two passes. Then once in, the girl I escorted in would go to the bathroom. I would then go back outside and escort the other girl in, still using the same two passes. The deal was one girl would always remain in the bathroom, and from time to time switch with the other one. They would dress exactly alike and wear the same hairstyle so no one could tell the difference. It was a very clever plan, and to be on the hottest TV show in the Washington, D.C. area seemed like a great idea. So, we followed our plan exactly and it worked! There I was on TV, dancing with one girl while great songs were being played, and then when we took breaks, the other girl would take her place. Toward the end of the program, one of the girls decided she didn't want to wait in the bathroom anymore, and I ended up dancing with them both on the dance floor! It was a bit chaotic with people dancing everywhere to the fast music and not as partners arm in arm, but we got away with it. Even if the camera people noticed it, they didn't care. We had a lot of fun.

There was one glitch. I didn't get a chance to tell the girl I was dating at the time, of the plan. As soon as I got home, I got a telephone call from her.

"What in the world were you doing dancing on TV with two girls? I was shocked to come home, and turn on the TV, and see you, my boyfriend, dancing with not one, but two other girls!" she said.

Boy was I in the doghouse! I tried to explain that it had all happened so fast that I did not have a chance to tell her, but she was angry about it. Well, that was the end of our relationship.

Learning to Take a Stand

When I was in high school, there was a small group of us, which included a girl who wanted to play a joke on her girlfriend. At the time, there was a silly practice of "rolling" your friend's house with toilet paper. Remember, it was 1968! Some of the girls cajoled me into going with them to "roll" their friend's house. I was sort of dating a girl who also agreed to go along. So, we all went, in different cars, rolled the house, and took off.

The angry father, who did not take rolling his house lightly, grabbed a girl in the front yard of his house. He had a tight hold on the girl and she was crying. The rest of us were running away, and everyone headed for home. I stopped and told the girl I was with, that I could not let the girl who was caught, take the whole rap and I could not leave her.

So, I walked right back to the house to rescue the girl, even though it put me at risk. I could see that the father was holding the girl as she was desperately trying to get away. He had her in a headlock. So I shouted, "Let her go, she didn't mean any harm! It was supposed to be a harmless joke."

At that, the man released her, but then went after me! I stood my ground only to be "captured" by the angry parent. He hit me and I fell to the ground. His wife, who was standing at the door, started screaming to her husband to leave me alone. We didn't know where his daughter was, but she wasn't at home. She was probably out on a date! I found myself trying to explain to an angry stranger, that it was just a friendly joke, not meant to be of harm to anyone, and I promised to clean everything up by myself. I told him not to take his anger out on the girl. I said, "I did not have to come back here! I did come back, so you would not harm an innocent person!" Finally, the frustrated father let me go, and he apologized for hitting me. It was obvious that the mother was furious that he had hit me, all over a stupid joke on their daughter.

I went back to my car, and my date was still there, as well as the girl I had helped rescue. They could not believe that I had taken such a risk confronting an angry father!

The next day, the story spread throughout school, as well as the neighborhood! It was not long before my mother heard the story from her friends, and she praised me! She had heard through the grapevine that I was the only one who stood up, and was willing to take the heat! Well, that was who I was. I wasn't afraid of anyone if I believed in the cause. My mother often said to me, "Fools will go where angels fear to tread." Of course, she was saying that I would go places where even the angels would not go. This was my first "peace settlement."

A Nudge by the Holy Spirit

I was in my senior year in high school, and I was standing in the living room in front of the piano, thinking reflectively as I often did. All of a sudden, I heard a very faint voice speaking to me from the piano, "Karl, I have bad news for you. Your parents will be getting a divorce." That was it. That was all I heard. I said no, that can't be! I tried to put it out of my mind, but I had received impressions before, although none like that, and never before the piano. Why the piano?

41

For years, the piano was a place where we would gather as a family to sing Christmas carols and other favorites. Why not the piano?

Then about two months later, I got the bombshell. My father told me, "We're getting a divorce." I was in shock, yet I couldn't help remembering what I had already heard before the piano. I was warned by that still small voice. It was hard to believe, and it affected me greatly. I did not want to take sides, and that is exactly what I told both my parents. However, I lost something. I'm not sure what, but I think somehow I lost confidence in myself, I began to doubt myself and my abilities. My will to excel and do well went out the window. My grades suffered, and by the end of my senior year, I was so depressed that I handed in my final exam in advanced algebra and trigonometry by answering only one question. I decided it did not matter to me if I failed. The teacher never asked me if I had a problem.

I guess the hardest thing for me was listening to my mother cry every night. One evening she was so distressed, she told me she wanted to commit suicide. She said, "Tell me one reason why I should live?" I answered, "Me!" It was enough to change her mind. From then on, she never mentioned suicide.

My sister was already away at college. She didn't have to deal with the trail of tears, except when she spoke to my mom by phone. I felt like the whole world was caving in on me and I just wanted to get away. I couldn't wait to go to college and begin my own life.

There were times I felt like the mediator between my father and mother, both strong-willed souls. I couldn't help but feel like a failure or that I was part of the reason why they were getting a divorce. Surely, it was my fault, but it wasn't.

I had just started seeing a girl who was the lead singer in our band. When I started telling her of my woes about the divorce, she quickly withdrew from me. I didn't blame her because I was no longer any fun to be around. My friends, "the Crew," didn't know what to say to me. When I told them, they responded in silence, and were just as shocked as I was. I would hear neighbors saying they couldn't believe it. As I look back, however, I realized that my parents never showed their love outwardly toward one another in front of their children. Any problems were hidden or never explained to my sister or me.

High Idealism and Destiny

Somehow, both my sister Laura and I shared a common goal growing up in the 50's and 60's. We wanted to help save the world!

Those were the turbulent years, during the Vietnam War. I remember registering for the draft at age 16. In fact, I even considered joining the service. I asked the man who was in charge of registration about one of the exemptions on the application: "Only surname." He said that it was an exemption only for men who had no other last name like that in the country, but that couldn't possibly apply to me unless I was the only Viernstein besides my father in the United States of America! That was the first time in my life when I ever wondered if there were any other Viernsteins in the U.S. How could I find out? I didn't think about it again until many years later through the internet, I discovered that I was indeed, the only male in the U.S.A. with the last name Viernstein, besides my father, at that time. However, I decided that if I were drafted, I would go serve in the military. I put it in God's hands.

SAT Story
Learning the Value of Intuition

An important test required for all people interested in college was the Scholastic Aptitude Test (SAT). I was concerned about taking it because I knew I didn't usually do well in English, even though I was confident in my Math skills. The first time I took the test, I did poorly on the English "Reading Comprehension" part.

I wanted to improve my scores, so I took a short course on "Improving your SAT Score," in Silver Spring, Maryland. It was intense, and the instructor shared some tricks for improving your test scores. They gave us a list of the words most frequently used on the test in the vocabulary section, and taught us how to increase our speed by reading the first, middle and last paragraph of each section. Then if all else failed, guess! The next time I took the test, I tried to follow some of the suggestions, but I found it just as hard as the first time, except the only thing I did that was significantly different was that I guessed! I never left a blank, and guessed at every answer, even if I did not read the question. At the one-minute warning bell, I went through the answer card and just guessed at all the rest of the answers.

When I got the test results back, my teacher said, "Karl, your test scores showed the most remarkable increase of all. You improved your scores over 150 points in the English section alone." I was pleased but knew the reason I had done better was because I had guessed!

I was amazed the very next week, when I heard a radio announcement advertising that this company could help you improve your scores by 150 points!

I remember a friend of mine who said to me, "Hey Karl, why don't you take that course and improve your SAT scores 150 points?" He didn't realize I had already taken the course, and it bothered me greatly that they were using my scores to promote their business. I told my friend, "You know, that was me. I was the one who improved their score by 150 points."

"No way," he said. He didn't believe me. I told him it didn't matter anyway, all I did was rely on my intuition.

Someone's Pulling My Arm
My Sister Has the Gift of Intuition, too

Here is an unusual story about my sister, Laura, that occurred while she attended Queens College in North Carolina.

Laura had a roommate and her dormitory room was on the ground floor on campus. While she was sleeping, she had a terrible dream. She dreamt someone was pulling her arm and shaking her and saying, "Wake up, Laura! Wake up!" She woke up screaming, shaking, and feeling as if someone had been pulling her arm. Immediately, her roommate woke up and turned on the light.

Laura was still screaming, "Someone is pulling my arm!"

Her roommate said, "No one is pulling your arm."

Laura said, "I felt someone pulling my arm."

At this time, other girls in the dorm were coming into her room, wondering what was going on. Again, Laura explained that she felt someone was pulling her arm, and her arm was sore! Meanwhile, someone ran down the hall and immediately called the security guards.

The next morning, they discovered that someone had attempted to remove the screen from their dorm window. The screen was hanging off the hinge. Security also reported seeing someone running from the dorm that evening. They attempted to catch him, but he escaped.

Neither Laura nor her roommate saw anyone entering their room.

The question remained, who was "pulling her arm" and telling her to "wake up"?

The best explanation that seemed to make sense was that while Laura was in a dream state, someone from the other side (an angel?) came to warn her about the impending danger and pulled on her arm telling her to "wake up."

It still remains a mystery to this day, but what does remain constant is the intuitive help from the other side that comes to help our family through difficult times. God has been present with us to save us time and time again.

Chapter 5

So faith, hope and love abide, these three;
But the greatest of these is love."

I Corinthians 13: 13

By the City of Brotherly Love

I was born in 1950 at Pennsylvania Hospital in Philadelphia, Pennsylvania. My parents were living in an apartment in Germantown, at the time. I have been told that as a child, I was quite a handful. I was on a schedule where I would arise early and go to bed early. I slept in the same bedroom as my parents and would greet them in the morning with a bubbly "Hi!"

I kept my parents on their toes, as I walked and talked early. While my mother was on the phone one day, I climbed up on to the counter in the kitchen and got into the spice cupboard. I opened up all the jars and dumped them on the counter. My mother had quite a mess to clean up!

I remember some experiences from early on in my life. One was going with my parents to a lake where there were big white ducks waddling around. I recall the softness of the feathers as I put my arms around a duck. I have seen pictures of this, and I wasn't very old.

As our family grew and my brother Kenny came along, we moved into a row house on Homer Street. I remember different things about this time of my life. I had a friend next door and we would play together. Mary Ellen had a toy metal stove which fascinated me. It had pushbuttons on the top to turn it on. I remember how much fun I had pretending I was cooking and pushing those buttons.

When my mother was expecting my brother Paul, we moved to Barlow Avenue in Merchantville, New Jersey. It was a small house with two bedrooms, and I was almost 4 years old at the time. My brothers and I shared the same bedroom for a while. They had bunk beds and I had a single bed. When I grew older, I was moved to the enclosed back porch to sleep. That wasn't so bad in warm weather months, but winters were cold, so they moved me into the dining room.

Coming to Terms with Death

I had always wanted a dog and begged my parents for one. Finally, we went to a farm where I chose a Boston terrier I named Pixie. She was a tiny little thing and I loved her very much. Unfortunately, we didn't have her very long because she developed distemper and my parents had to have her put to sleep. I was very upset about this and it took me a long time to get over it. We did eventually have several other dogs, one named Patches, and another named Fluffy. I was never really as close to them, nor did they mean as much to me as Pixie did. It wasn't until after Karl and I were married and we were given a tiny little toy fox terrier- rat terrier mix that I finally got my Pixie back. We called her Midget and she was my faithful dog and helped me through many a difficult time throughout the years. She was over 15 years old and had lived a long, happy life before she died. Thank you, God, for Midget!

Pets can be fantastic healers and faithful, loving companions. They teach us about kindness, loyalty and forgiveness, and they never hold a grudge!

Another Lesson

I remember an incident that occurred when I was 8 years old, and living on Barlow Avenue. It upset me a lot and made me very aware of people who were a little different from me. I was playing with a group of children who lived two doors down the street and their cousins were visiting for the day. We were all laughing and having a good time. One of the cousins was wearing braces on his legs and was having difficulty running as we played ball. The neighbor boy thought I was laughing and making fun of his cousin who was trying to play. He came up to me and very angrily started to shove me and shouted at me not to make fun of his cousin. I didn't know what he was talking about. I wasn't laughing at his cousin, I was laughing because I was having fun! No matter what I said, he wouldn't listen. It really upset me, and put a damper on the rest of my day. In my heart, I knew I would not have consciously hurt him. However, this situation made me more aware of those who were struggling to overcome problems in their lives.

Growing Up and Learning that Life is an Art

We lived on Barlow Avenue for six years until we eventually outgrew the house. We moved to Cinnaminson, New Jersey, and our new home had four bedrooms, a recreation room and two and a half bathrooms. What a step up, I even had my own bedroom!

While living on Cornell Avenue, I met a girl named Marie who lived around the corner. She and I were quite friendly for four or five years. Marie's mother was an artist and she was a major influence in my life. Marie also could draw and got me interested in art. Before long, I was trying my hand at drawing, too. I even went with her to the Moore College of Art where we took classes on Saturday mornings. I learned a lot from Marie and her Mom, and especially learned to love the smell of linseed oil, turpentine and paint as I watched her mother paint whenever I would visit. I have also done some paintings myself over the years, and my favorite subject to paint is birds.

I have discovered that ministry is an art, as well! There is an art in listening to other church members, and in sharing your skills wherever your church needs them. There is an art to beautifying the sanctuary with banners and flowers for Sunday service and special occasions. And, there is also an art to providing the music that fills the sanctuary with joyous sounds. All of these require an artistic effort. The ambience of every church service is a blending of God's creation on a canvas that is called His Church.

President Kennedy Assassinated

It was while we lived in Cinnaminson, New Jersey that I met my closest and dearest friend, Jane. I had always wanted a sister when I was growing up, and she fit the bill nicely! Two brothers were a bit much, and she and I hit it off quite well. The day we truly became friends was actually a very sad day for our country. We were in history class when we heard an announcement over the loudspeaker. We were told that our president John F. Kennedy, had been shot and we were to report back to our homerooms. Jane sat behind me and we hadn't really spoken to each other before, but when the principal got on the loudspeaker again to tell us President Kennedy had died, we cried in each other's arms. From then on, our relationship grew. We confided in each other and our combined love of the musical group, The Beatles, gave us a common bond, (she loved John and I, George). We just loved to make up stories about them!

Our ultimate experience occurred on August 30, 1964 when we got tickets to a Beatles concert in Atlantic City, New Jersey. We went to the concert as planned and stayed with Jane's Aunt Myrtle, from where we were to leave to go home the next afternoon, when my mother picked us up. Unfortunately, we were two 14-year-old girls who had such a fixation on the Beatles that we spent our last fifty cents to see the film, "A Hard Day's Night," thereby loosing track of time and missing our ride home! Fortunately, Jane's older brother had been working at a political convention at the Atlantic City Convention Hall earlier and he was going home that same afternoon. We were able to hitch a ride home with him.

Of course, Jane and I shared the same experiences as most teenagers, talking about boys, and being involved in talent shows. Jane tried out for the school's Color Guard and later became their Captain. Her team went on to do well in competitions. Together, we supported our school sports teams and sang in the school chorus. We even took an art major class together our senior year.

I would visit Jane at her parent's vacation home in Townbank, New Jersey, where I learned to water ski on the Delaware Bay, and she would come with me on vacation to Paradise Falls in the Pocono Mountains.

The thing that drew Jane and me together was our deep love for God. We went to each other's churches for different events. Jane went to Luther League with me, which was my church youth group, and I went with her when her church had youth retreats. I especially liked going to the Sunday evening worship services at her small church in Northeast Philadelphia. Since this was a small congregation, she and I would often sing a duet in church. We'd sing old hymns, and did this for years. We also sang in my church as well. On one memorable occasion we sang "O Holy Night" on Christmas Eve.

We have been through much together over the years, and our religious bond has held us together. Through good times and bad, we have remained close friends.

Dale's Summer Sleeping Experiment

The summer of my 15th year was 1965. My family took our annual vacation for three weeks to one of our favorite destinations—the Pocono Mountains of Northeast Pennsylvania. One of these weeks, my friend Jane was able to come along. I was delighted since I did not have to hang out with my brothers the whole time.

At this time in my life, I experimented with different ideas. The most recent one that grabbed my attention was hypnotism. Actually, it was called, "mesmerization," after a man whose name was Mesmer. He had developed a technique of "mesmerizing" or hypnotizing other individuals, and this was a popular parlor game during his time. I was so interested in this technique, that I wrote a term paper on it in school.

I had also heard from some other source that while a person was asleep, you could ask them questions and they would respond truthfully to you with the answers. So, my curiosity got the better of me, and while my friend and I shared the same room, I tried a little experiment with Jane while she was sleeping.

When I woke up one morning and my friend was still asleep, I decided "now" was the perfect time to try my experiment. I proceeded to ask her innocuous questions such as, "What guy do you have a crush on? What's your favorite class in school?" and the like. I was anxious to see if she would answer me. To my surprise she did! When she woke up, she did not recall answering any question I asked her. Thank goodness, Jane didn't get mad at me either!

This experience opened my mind to other ways of thinking and doing things. Much to my surprise, I employed some of these techniques with Karl, years later.

Family

The family certainly can be a training ground for being the wife of a pastor. I was part of a large, loving family on both sides. From them I learned how to care for those near and dear to me, and how to care for others, too. The church is just like a family, only larger.

My parents were both firstborn children and so am I. I am the second oldest of thirteen grandchildren on my father's side and the oldest on my mother's side. I was fortunate to grow up with both sets of my grandparents and got to know them fairly well. I spent more time with the Ditmars than the Borglums because I lived closer to them. I was twenty minutes away from the Ditmars and several hours away from the Borglums, my mother's parents, who lived in Brooklyn. The Verrazano Narrows Bridge had not been built yet, so we took the Staten Island ferry to see them. It was fun to be on a boat.

I grew up with my father's siblings and their children nearby until they began to move away. I feel especially blessed to feel the closeness and sense of belonging that a large family offers. My grandparents' siblings were also nearby along with their families as well. My mother's sister lived two hours away so we would see them on holidays and other special occasions. This is my family background and an important part of who I am.

The Church is Center Stage in my Life

My parents always went to church and took us with them. This is how I learned about God and our Lord Jesus Christ. He has been my mainstay through the major traumas of my life.

The first church I remember attending was Temple Lutheran Church in Pennsauken, New Jersey. This is where I sang in my first church choir.

My mother recognized that I loved to sing and had me join the children's choir. I was blessed to have been trained under the direction of Dr. Carlton Lake. He was a fabulous musician and later became the director of music for the Philadelphia Public Schools. I remember he lived in a small row home in the old colonial part of Philadelphia near the historic home of Betsy Ross. He was from Wales and freely imparted his love of music to me. He taught me to sing and before long, I was singing solos in church at a very young age. Church, quickly, took center stage in my life and my whole life revolved around it.

Not only did I learn to love music, but I learned about God. I began to think about where I came from and where I was going. I felt as if I had been here on earth before and I could almost visualize it.

I also began to wonder about life and death. I knew I came from somewhere. I couldn't have been born out of thin air, could I? And what was my purpose in life? I remember looking out the window of my bedroom and asking God about my future, "Where am I going?" This later became the title of a song I wrote.

I wondered about who I was going to marry. Sometimes I felt so lost and alone. I also felt as if a major part of me was missing and I would cry myself to sleep at night.

I went to Sunday school and church every week, and can honestly say I loved it. There may have been times when I was tired and didn't want to go, but it was still an important part of my life.

My First Experience with Death

My first personal experience with death was frightening, and I wasn't quite sure how to react. I was 15 years old when my mother received a telephone call from a policeman in Brooklyn, New York. He said my grandfather had become ill and was taken to the hospital. My mother told us what happened and my brother Paul said, "What if Grandpop is dead?" Of course, we didn't want to even think such a thing. Unfortunately, fifteen minutes later the policeman called back and told us he had died.

We were shocked and saddened and also very concerned because my grandmother was not with him at the time. We knew she was becoming senile and we didn't know where she was. My mother called a family friend, Luther Dittmer, to help find her until we could get there. Thankfully, my grandmother was found and Luther stayed with her until my parents could be with her.

My father's parents came and stayed with us and then took us to Brooklyn for the funeral. Unfortunately, we did not arrive in time to go to the viewing of my grandfather's body, and anyway he had requested a closed casket at the funeral. Still, I was devastated. It took me years to recover from his death, and partly because I hadn't seen him dead and couldn't believe he was gone.

I learned a valuable lesson. I feel it is important, in most cases, for a child to see someone in death in order to grieve and accept their passing. This is why, from a very early age, my husband and I took our own children to the funerals at which my husband officiated in order to help them understand the process of death.

I was 15, and I knew in my heart of hearts that I would live on even in death and that there was much more waiting for me "in heaven" beside what was here on earth. I came to understand that my grandfather was all right even though he had physically died, because I felt God's love reassuring me that this was so. My grandfather was not gone but had moved on to another plane.

As I worked through the grief process, I would talk to my grandfather and often felt his presence. I remember telling my mother that Grandpop came to me and she asked, "Why can't I talk to him?" I couldn't answer that. I didn't know. I knew that I was able to sense the presence of people who had passed over.

When I saw a change in the light of a room, I knew there were other souls in the room with me and could often tell who they were. If I told anyone about this, my observations were met with skepticism. I quickly learned to keep my 'talent' to myself.

Learning to take Care of the Elderly
More Training for Ministry and the Nursing Profession

Learning to live with my elderly, senile grandmother was good for my church career. It taught me patience, understanding and compassion, especially dealing with those who were struggling with chronic illness and conditions.

Living at home became increasingly difficult. After my grandfather died, we quickly realized my grandmother could not live alone and would need constant supervision and care. She came to live with us for two months at a time, and then would go to live with my Aunt Doris and her family for a turn, but since Aunt Doris' children were younger than we were, we sometimes had Grandmother longer.

My grandmother was given the room next to mine. I was a light sleeper and would hear my grandmother get up in the middle of the night. In her confusion, she thought it was daylight and time to get up, and would try to dress herself. I would have to get up and help her get back into her nightclothes and back into bed. My sleep was constantly disturbed and my grades began to fall. As a result, I had to go to summer school for English and French in order to pass. I did well and did pass, but for the next several years, while my grandmother lived with us off and on, I learned firsthand what Alzheimer's disease could do to a person and those who care for them.

Preparation for a Career in the Church

I took a College Preparatory curriculum while still in high school. I wasn't sure, but I was leaning toward becoming an elementary school teacher where, I felt, all my talents would be put to good use.

I had always loved music and participated in music programs at school. I sang in the chorus in elementary school and danced whenever they had school programs. I went to the Children's Concerts in Philadelphia when conductor Eugene Ormandy and the Philadelphia Symphony Orchestra played. This helped me to appreciate classical music.

I tried out for a Madrigal Choir called the Cinnamin Singers and was invited to become a member. We were a group of select singers who sang for special occasions, such as business luncheons, and even went Christmas Caroling. I also took individual voice lessons to improve my singing voice, not knowing that, in the future, I would be directing and singing in church choirs. Choral Concerts were also a highlight for me. We even performed Vivaldi's "Gloria," and it was no wonder that when I began to look at colleges, I chose one with a college choir, so that I could sing.

California or Bust

Being the eldest child, and a girl, I took a lot of ribbing from my brothers. Perhaps they thought of it as good-natured teasing, but being the sensitive person I was, it hurt. Not only physically, when they hit me, but mentally, too. I was teased unmercifully. I was told it was normal for brothers to act this way, but I didn't like it. It all came to a head for me when my parents decided to take a camping trip out west to California, in the summer of 1967.

It was a wonderful trip, most of the time. I was amazed and moved by the beautiful and interesting scenery we saw along the way. But, I was teased continually for my comments about the scenery, as I would gaze in awe at its beauty and size. Unfortunately, every time I would exclaim, "How beautiful!" the countryside was, my brothers would tease me. My parents told me to ignore it because by my reaction to them, they got a rise out of me and they enjoyed it. It was hard for me to ignore them.

Finally, when we visited Yosemite National Park in California one day, my parents left to go shopping and left us alone at our campsite. My brothers began picking on me again almost as soon as they left. They teased me so much that I couldn't take it anymore and I had a major crying episode, which lasted for some time. My brothers had hurt my feelings so much and I couldn't understand how they, themselves, did not see the awesomeness of our country. I couldn't stop crying. They began to get upset when they realized that I was inconsolable and tried to cheer me up. Finally, I was able to calm down before my parents got back and my brothers were nicer to me for the remainder of the trip.

A Magnificent Promise Comes in a Dream

During my senior year in high school, several interesting experiences occurred. I was dating Chuck at the time, but somehow felt he wasn't the man I would spend my life with.

That same year, my parents took my brothers and me on a trip to Washington, D.C. It was Christmas 1967, when we arrived. I felt drawn to the area. I looked around me and somehow felt that my future husband was nearby. I felt a yearning for a man I hadn't even met, and my loneliness intensified.

A few weeks later, I received word that I had been accepted at Davis and Elkins College. Later that night I had a dream, and that dream turned out to be prophetic. In my dream, I was singing in the College Choir, and the man I was to marry was sitting in the bass section - second seat from the end, third row back.

"D & E" College

*After my high school graduation, I prepared to go to Davis &
Elkins College. It was scary as D & E was located in Elkins, West
Virginia, ten-plus hours away, and I wouldn't be able to go home until
Thanksgiving. When Labor Day weekend finally arrived, my parents
drove me to college. What made this trip exceedingly difficult for me
was the fact that I had some plantar warts on my left foot frozen before
I went to school and the blisters were large and painful. During my
orientation I hobbled around the campus, which was built on a hill.
All of the buildings had many stairs, and wouldn't you know it, my
classes always seemed to be on the third floor. My English class was
also on the third floor and there were no elevators to help me out.*

*At my first class, I noticed a young man sitting in the front row on
the other side of the aisle. He was rather good looking and was
sharply dressed in matching shirts and socks. He wore a dickey under
his shirt. His favorite combinations were baby blue shirts and socks
or yellow shirts and socks. He seemed interested in the lessons and
was always willing to offer his opinions on various subjects. A week
into the class, I ran into him in the bookstore and we talked a little.
Several weeks later, I was at a student get-together at the Student
Union, when he came over and asked me to dance. It wasn't long
before we were moving to the music and talking the whole time. I was
really attracted to him. Later, when I watched him leave the room
with another girl, I was upset. In just the few minutes we'd talked
together, I knew that this man was very special, and I wanted to get to
know him better. I was falling in love. How could this happen so
quickly? I felt that I had known him forever and that we belonged
together. Since he had already left the dance, I left too. There was no
reason to stay.*

*When I got back to my room, I told my roommate that I had just
met the man I was going to marry. Ironically, my roommate lived in
the same area that he did and attended the same church. His name
was Karl Robert Viernstein, and I married him two years and nine
months later. He told me he was from the Washington, D.C. area and
he sang in the college choir, in the bass section, in the second seat*

from the end, third row back, exactly as I dreamed it. This couldn't have been coincidence, the dream was too specific. Surely, this is one way God speaks to us! I truly believe so.

Karl and I began to date and would see each other during the day. It wasn't long before we were eating together every day in the cafeteria and we would talk for hours on end in the lounge in our dorm. We discussed everything from spiritual/philosophical issues to the everyday problems in life. Karl was upset because his parents had recently gotten a divorce and this had devastated him. We talked about that a lot.

One night we went to the "Ice House," which was an old icehouse which had been renovated for students to use as a club/coffee house. While we were sitting at the table in the dimly lit room, I suddenly felt the presence of my grandfather, Axel Peter Borglum. I wasn't certain whether I should say anything to Karl about this, because I didn't know how he would receive the information. However, since we were discussing metaphysical things I jumped at the opportunity to tell him about it. Karl was totally receptive to the idea that my grandfather was there. In fact, he too felt my grandfather's presence. I felt as if I was no longer alone. I had finally found someone with whom I could share all of my unusual experiences.

Chapter 6

"Now the Lord had said to Abram,
'Go from your country
And your kindred and your father's house
To the land I will show you.'"

Genesis 12: 1

Breaking Away - The College Years

I wanted to further my education, but struggled with which school would be best for me. I believed if I went to Maryland University, I would be just a number and get lost in a crowded school. The scuttlebutt was that Maryland University had to accept all students who applied as long as they were residents of Maryland. However, they were very strict and hard on the freshman class in order to weed out those they felt were not "college material". This was how they controlled the size of the classes. That certainly was not the school for me, and was too intimidating.

I looked at one school my mother thought might be a good fit for me. It was in the South, St. Andrew's College. However, after visiting the school, I saw how high the standards were for the students, what was expected of them, how formal and organized they were, and felt that was not for me either. Again, I felt I would get lost in the process because I could not excel and be myself. I would be just another student.

Davis & Elkins College was a small liberal arts school in the mountains of West Virginia. It seemed to be in the middle of nowhere, away from all civilization. That seemed to be perfect for me. I wanted to get away from family, friends, and the commotion of a busy metropolitan area. Maybe I could find myself, focus on my studies, and because it was a small school, be more than just another number, a person in search of my purpose in life.

Therefore, I applied to D&E with average grades of B's & C's, a slightly-below-average SAT score, and good recommendations. Because my overall Math scores were very high, although my English scores were low, I was accepted on a conditional basis. I was expected to overcome any deficits that I needed in English.

My first day at College, I was filled with great apprehension and excitement. The fall leaves were beautiful in West Virginia, and it seemed like the perfect place for me to center myself and make new friends. I lived in Darby Hall, a co-ed dorm with men housed on the one side, women on the other, and locked doors between the two sides. It was quite advanced for the day. Most colleges segregated the men and women in totally separate buildings.

My roommate was black, and we were one of the few integrated rooms in the college, also quite advanced for the day. I was excited because ever since I was a little boy, I had believed that all races are equal in all ways.

I started to meet new people and to make new friends. There was a student activities committee on campus, and I was invited to join, so I attended one of the meetings where I learned that they needed someone to run the movie projector. Did anyone know how to do it or know of anyone who did? I sat there thinking to myself, how hard could it be? I was fairly good at operating machinery and I could figure things out if I didn't know how already. So, I volunteered to operate the projectors, even though I had never done it before, but was willing to learn. Thus, I became the school projectionist for new release, TOP named movies! I had to set up two projectors at once in order to run the reels back to back, and I always had to have a spare bulb if there was a problem with either projector.

I wasn't sure what I wanted to major in, but I was leaning toward Business Management, because whatever field I eventually entered, I could always use the management skills. My problem was that I could do so many different things that it was difficult for me to choose only one specialized field. A liberal arts education would give me a broad background in many areas, so that later on I could select whatever specialty suited me.

Love at First Sight

It was like a storybook romance. People won't believe this, but it's true. It was a few weeks after college began and the school was having its first big dance. I was fairly shy after having dated a few girls in high school who had hurt me. I didn't want to get involved in another relationship, plus, I was still reeling from my parents divorce. I resolved within myself that there would be no serious relationship with any girl. I was there to study!

Suddenly, I caught a glimpse of a girl across the dance floor. She was a gem. She was petite - just my size - and she had a glow about her that seemed to shine out above all the others. I said to the person standing next to me, "I have to meet that girl." So, when the next song began, I sauntered over to the other side of the room and there she was, standing there with a pure, innocent aura and a sparkling smile.

"Would you like to dance?" I said.

Without hesitation, she replied, "Yes."

We introduced ourselves, and she said her name was, "Dale Suzanne Ditmars."

We walked out onto the floor and began to dance. It seemed so natural, though I was a bit nervous. I could tell she was a good dancer because she followed every move I made. What do I say? I told this perfect stranger that, "I can't get involved because I have plans to go into the military service after college." Why did I say that?

We danced for a while, and then I left to take another girl back to her dorm. She was just a friend I had come to the dance with. When I returned, I was disappointed to find that Dale had already left. I would just have to wait to talk to her again.

The next time I got a chance to talk with Dale was on our first date. There was not much to do on campus, but there was a recreation room where you could play pool or ping-pong. So, we played a little pool. But, I really just wanted to talk with Dale. That was what I enjoyed doing with the dates I had been with, and Dale was no exception.

So, we went to the "Ice House" because it was a good place to talk. As we were sitting there, Dale grabbed my arm and said, "Karl, wait a minute, my grandfather is here!" I didn't say a word, but I immediately knew that this girl was different from the rest. She went on to explain how close she had been to her grandfather and how she thought about him often. She was still grieving his death of a few years before.

"How," I asked, "do you know that your grandfather is here?"

She told me that her grandfather spoke to her from the other side, consoling her that everything was all right. With all of my own unusual experiences, I could understand this was possible.

Dale was one of the first and few persons I felt comfortable with, talking about deep spiritual matters and the 'other' side.

She and I had reached a point in our relationship where I wanted to get closer to her, but she was apprehensive, although we knew we loved one another. Dale wanted to be free to date other people, and I agreed with her. I remember saying to Dale, "If you truly love me and it was meant for us to be together, other people wouldn't matter." I felt confident that my love was pure and my intentions were honorable, to do the best for her. I did not want to manipulate her into making a decision she would regret. Being pre-engaged or "pinned" had to be a decision Dale acted upon from within.

The analogy I thought of was being like an animal on a chain. Over-simplistic perhaps, but there is a tendency for a chained animal to want its freedom. I don't believe God ever intended animals to be chained or caged. The same is true with people. God never intended us to be in chains or in slavery to one another, and I learned early on that a good, strong relationship between people is never based upon manipulation or control of the other. So it is with our relationship with God.

I believe that God never intended to be our master or for us to be slaves, or for us to be the master and manipulate God. For two people to share a right relationship, both must be free to be co-creators, loving one another because they choose to love, being faithful because they choose to be faithful. Two wills that agree because they choose to agree.

Now God, who first loved us, and who chose to love us, can only be in a relationship with those who choose to love Him. It is often repeated in the Bible, "If ye will be my people, I will be your God." That's the 'If' clause in the Bible. Always, "If" we choose to love

God with all our minds, and hearts, and souls, then He will send the Holy Spirit, the counselor, and will teach us all things. I learned these beliefs early.

Now to continue our story, Dale and I agreed to date others, but she really loved me, she said. She tried for a few months to see others, but alas, she always found herself drawn back to me.

I had other girls interested in me as well, and some were even friends of Dale's, but I wasn't interested in them. There were opportunities for other serious relationships, but there was no spark, no real common destiny with any of them. It was providence, after awhile, that Dale and I began to see one another again.

We were the typical young minds exploring all the universal questions about God and the future of the world, the problems of human suffering, and how one defined love. As we shared our ideas, and expressed our similar beliefs, we came to realize how much we loved one another.

Our Love of Music

Music was an important part of our college experience. As members of the choir, we went on tours to New York City and other interesting places. In the city, the choir performed early and was given the afternoon off to go wherever we wanted, so Dale and I decided to live it up and eat out at the Cattleman's Restaurant. There we had a grand dinner with wine, and we felt like a couple that belonged together.

The choir also toured in New Jersey, and throughout West Virginia, in towns such as Wheeling and Charleston. It was in Charleston while Dale and I were in the chapel praying and listening to the organist practicing for a wedding, that a fellow choir member appeared, and hearing the "Wedding March," jokingly pronounced us husband and wife! He eventually went on to become a minister. That was on December 18, 1968, and we felt God's Spirit had blessed us on that day.

The choir was rehearsing for the Messiah and both Dale and I tried out for solos. As it turned out, we were both fortunate to get parts. Dale sang the aria, "He Shall Lead His Flock," and I sang the recitative, "Thus saith the Lord." I began to get the feeling that maybe God wanted us to speak on his behalf. Maybe He wanted us to warn people of future events that they needed to be preparing for. Music was a path that provided the way for us to speak these words of wisdom.

Other Interests

While in college Dale and I had some unusual dates. We would often go to the music room in Halliehurst Hall, and play piano and violin duets on Friday night.

At times we enjoyed talking about different religions, and discussed people's beliefs. We spent every moment together we could, and as a couple we decided to explore different churches such as Presbyterian, Episcopal, Baptist, Pentecostal, Methodist, and the Church of God. We also studied the teachings of The Church of Jesus Christ of the Latter Day Saints, Jehovah's Witness, and other faiths.

While in college I joined the Alpha Phi Omega fraternity, a service organization that helped disabled children and other people in need. During my junior year, I was elected the president of the fraternity and started a "Phyettes" chapter well before it became nationally recognized. Dale joined the Chi Omega Sorority.

YMCA Swim Coach

While at D & E, I took a part time job as a swim instructor at the YMCA, and I agreed to be the swim team coach. For two years, I coached and we competed with other teams throughout West Virginia.

One of the younger girls on the team was only 14 years, and she was attracted to me. She seemed to have a crush on me. She made several advances towards me, but I had my ground rules. I had my moral beliefs and I was a bit old fashioned. I believed in honor and trust, and would not take advantage of someone, especially a vulnerable 14-year-old girl, whose parents trusted me to teach her how to swim.

I'll admit that when I wore my brief "Speedo" swimsuit there was not much left to the imagination, and physical attraction can be an enticing antagonist in such situations, but I took it to be a test of one's character and strength as well as to be a good role model, and truly to help others by using the skills and talents that we are given.

The Vietnam War

School was going well, and I learned a great deal about many subjects, but the U.S.A. was in war with Vietnam and it loomed over everyone like a dark cloud. It was constantly in the news, and everyone was sick and tired of it. Some students on campus demonstrated against the war, and I was sympathetic with them.

I remember when the lottery draft was instituted. It was based upon the date of your birthday, and regardless of who you were, and how well-educated you were, you would be drafted in the order of your number from 1-365, plus leap year. My number was 210.

The day after the lottery draft numbers were drawn, a young man who was a fellow student went yelling across campus, "I'm number one, I'm number one!" We all knew he was a staunch anti-war demonstrator on campus. How ironic it was that of all people his birthday was selected to be number one. The next day, we were terror-stricken to learn that that same young man had committed suicide.

There was a time during my second year, when the draft number had reached as high as 200, that I was feeling compelled to quit school and join the service, forgoing my education. Dale could sense that I was not happy with the mess the world was in and knew that I would be willing to sacrifice myself even in a senseless war. I was fearless, and I would have volunteered to go to the front line. I was not afraid to fight and bear arms, although I probably would have been killed.

However, Dale and my mother convinced me not to quit school and join the military. They helped me to understand that war was a terrible thing, and that I could still be patriotic without having to serve in the military. Sometimes the United States gets involved in conflicts such as the Vietnam War and it's wrong. We never participated in anti-war demonstrations, but we respected the right of others to protest. In some ways, we admired the courage of others to speak up during those peaceful demonstrations. We had good friends who were serving as soldiers in Vietnam. Some came back missing limbs, while some never returned at all.

The lottery draft never did reach 210, but it was close. Fortunately, the war finally came to an end.

Mom's Counsel

It was October of 1969. I was in love with Dale and decided to ask her to marry me. But she said she was uncertain and needed more time. "Okay," I said.

It was Parents Weekend that fall and my mother had come to visit. Dale and I were struggling to get a bearing on our relationship and needed some advice to determine the best direction for our future. I suggested that we consult my mother.

Mom was very perceptive and had a keen awareness of people and how they thought. She would have made a good counselor had she chosen that field. She was very popular with the young people in my neighborhood, and they would come to our house to talk to her about their problems. She understood. People enjoyed her presence and she had many good friends.

Dale and I agreed to ask her for advice. I knew my mother was good at reading tarot cards, and because I was curious, I asked her to give Dale and me a tarot reading with an interpretation. I was keenly aware of her intuitive perception and her gift for seeing things others couldn't see. After all, she was the one who taught me how to use my gifts and talents and encouraged me to use them to help others. Who could know whether the cards worked or not? That wasn't the point.

What was important was the fact that the cards were simply a tool by which my mother could impart her intuitive guidance and wisdom to those who needed it.

She was glad to read the cards for Dale and me. She knew what we were going through, the struggles and uncertainty about our future. What concerned me most were the choices Dale and I had to make for ourselves. No one else could make these choices for us. There was no manipulation on Mom's part. It was as if we were standing before a mirror. Mom's counsel was reassuring. She told us not to rush into marriage, but first be sure of our choices and decisions.

We were certain that our souls must have a unique purpose. I always felt that Dale and I were meant to be a team, and that we were strongest when we were together. All we needed was to be patient and together we would grow in wisdom.

My mother had a dream about me. I was alone in the midst of a conflict. People were fighting with each other and there I was in the thick of it, trying to bring peace out of chaos. She said it was an important task.

There were many times in my life where I was called upon to be a peacemaker. During those difficult days after my parents' divorce, they expected me to help resolve certain issues. When my sister was dating different men and there were conflicts, I was able to restore peace. There have always been times when someone got upset in church, or there was some confusion, and I stepped in and helped to solve it. I believe that there is never a problem so huge that in time, it can't be resolved in some way. It may take years to resolve, but all things come to those who wait, and for those who have a genuine desire to arrive at a righteous and just decision.

College Experiments

I always believed there was a spiritual purpose to my life, and during those college years, Dale and I began to experiment and experience things that would deepen our understanding of life and death, dreams and reality, the earthly and the spirit worlds.

Some of us began experimenting with "hypnosis." I was usually the person that gave the suggestions, and directed the session. We were amazed to find that some of the students were susceptible to hypnosis, while others were not. The positive subjects could be hypnotized to not feel pain for a brief moment, but with others there was no effect at all.

We were searching for the answers to many questions. We even looked at reincarnation as a theory. Dale confided in me that she sometimes felt that she had lived before, and that we had known each other in a previous lifetime. This was all very interesting and I thought it would be worth exploring. We practiced regressions through hypnosis, and although we received a little bit of information, we were uncertain about the reliability of the information which came through. It was fascinating to imagine Dale having lived in ancient Egypt long ago. She felt it was there she had known me, and fallen in love with me, but we were separated because it was against the law for people to marry someone of a different class.

I had always been drawn to Egypt and was fascinated by that culture. I was particularly drawn to the period when Nefertiti reigned. I felt a strong connection with her. Karl and I decided to try a hypnosis session where we could do a past life regression. It was during this session that I saw myself as one of Nefertiti's attendants or slave girls. Could this be true? It was no wonder I had been drawn to that particular period in time. I also discovered that it was here that I had known Karl in one of his past lives. We apparently knew each other and would have pursued a relationship. Unfortunately, his position in society was different from mine and we were forbidden to be together, and we were punished for trying.

Dale was exactly what I was looking for in a woman. She was very sensitive, and it was easy to converse with her. We shared the same high ideals and were both interested in discussing the same philosophical and religious issues, and she was open to exploring new ideas. Perhaps she would be accepting of the strange impressions I received about future events, as I was accepting of her feelings of previous lives and of her ability to communicate with the dead.

More Strange Processes

It was fascinating for Dale and me to discover things for which there was no explanation. Unfortunately, we did not always feel we could share with too many people the spiritual events that were taking place in our lives. For example, we tried using the Ouija Board to see if there was any validity to it. We were curious and felt like experimenting. Dale and Sara, two people who were receptive to impressions, were selected to operate the board, while I asked the questions from quite a distance away. There were seven other people who sat around the board.

We chose to experiment in Halliehurst Hall, an old building on campus in the upper "ballroom" as we called it. As I asked the questions, the house seemed to respond in time with the Ouija Board. At times the marker would spin in circles, as if reluctant to answer the questions, and the house would rock and creak back and forth. Then, there were times the marker on the board would remain perfectly still, unwilling to respond. You could hear a pin drop as the house became perfectly still, as if in sympathy with the board. I would repeat questions several times in different ways knowing full well that whoever or whatever we were talking to was reluctant to give any information.

Then, all of a sudden, the Ouija Board went flying up into the air and then fell to the floor. Everyone sitting around the Board started screaming and running out of the room, except for me. Everyone experienced a burning sensation, and felt as if they were on fire! Dale said the sensation shot right up her legs and into her hands and throughout her body. I stood there astonished, as they all ran out of the room. They were calling for me to get out of the room. As I watched all this with amazement, I felt nothing, until 10 seconds later. All of a sudden, I felt this wave of hot air envelope me as if there was an invisible wave of electric energy penetrating my body. I felt like I was on fire! With that, I decided maybe I should leave too! I usually try to analyze things and figure them out before taking any action, but this time, I was afraid that maybe I was in over my head. Here was something I could not understand, and I high-tailed it out of there!

We never tried that again! It did leave us curious and bewildered. Perhaps we may never know exactly what happened, but something physiological DID happen, and at different times and places.

We also experimented with the tarot cards with some unusual results. I had actually learned about tarot from my mother, and I considered her a master. She taught me that it was not the cards that revealed information so much as it was the talent of the reader to interpret them. The cards themselves are just paper, and do nothing by themselves.

I began reading cards for people with mixed results. In most cases, everyone can relate to travel, to issues of success or failure, and even life or death. I realized that all the cards accomplished was to affirm certain basic fundamentals of life, and that it was left up to me to interpret them.

The Accident That Never Happened

It was wintertime and very cold outside. The fog was terrible as we drove back from my mother's home. It was late in the evening, and as I was driving, both Dale and I began to get tears in our eyes. We both sensed something was terribly wrong or that something very bad was about to happen. I heard a still small voice say, "Karl, stop the car in time. It's important to stop the car." Then almost like magic, a gas station appeared out of the fog, one that I had never noticed before, so I stopped. For some reason it kind of shook us up, and we didn't know why.

I decided to buy a pack of cigarettes since I was smoking at that time. I walked into the gas station and saw a cigarette machine. As I approached, I heard that still small voice say, "Karl, this machine will need the exact change." As I reached into my pocket to get money out, a man behind the counter yelled out, "Hey mister, you will need exact change for that machine."

I started to shake even more, and was glad to have a cigarette. Why was I told to stop the car at that exact time? I may never know why, but to confirm that what I did was the right thing to do, a follow-up piece of guidance came true within seconds! After we got back on the road again, Dale said, as we approached a specific point in the road, "On this curve we would have been hit by the big truck that passed us earlier!" It is never imagination or coincidence if you listen to that inner voice. And having two people hear a warning is even better confirmation.

Religious Debates

There were a few students who were considering ministry as a profession in college, and we had many theological discussions with a friend in our school dorm. I would usually take the side of the questioner and challenge the others with their belief. I would often say, "Prove it to me!" or "What is the basis of your belief?" or "Do you have any evidence to back you up?" One of the religious professors at the college had taught me how to question ideas that people had, and use reason to make sense of what was said.

Dr. Phipps

Dr. Phipps was my philosophy professor. I had many discussions of the religious and philosophical thinking processes of people living in different cultures, times and places with him. He wrote the book, Was Jesus Married? which led to several discussions about the pros and cons of such an argument. I was very curious and skeptical about such arguments. I learned a great deal from him and will always appreciate it. At that time, I began to develop a greater understanding of the possibilities of Mary Magdalene's role in the early church. According to Dr. Phipps, it was probably richer than we ever dreamed. Until recently, it has not been understood how important women have been in the life of the early church.

In a similar way, Dale has been an important influence upon my early life as we prepared for ministry, using our gifts together and working as a team.

71

Premonition of Death

It was April 1971, and Dale and I were having unsettling feelings about my roommate, Matt. He was having some difficulties sleeping at night and I was becoming concerned. One night, he just talked, and talked, and continued to talk all night long. At first, I was tired and responded, "Yeah," or "sounds interesting," but as he rambled on, what Matt said made less sense. This worried me, so I sat up with him for the rest of the night.

I came to visit Karl in his dorm room the next afternoon and noticed that Karl's roommate, Matt, was taking a nap. I looked at him and saw him dead. I had the strangest premonition that he was going to die, but he was only 23 years old!

When Dale came into the dorm room, she told me privately that Matt looked like he was dead. Later, when he woke and left the room, I decided to do a tarot card reading right there on the floor. I couldn't believe it, the final card was Death! I became worried for him even more. I called Matt's parents to let them know he was not well. He was not sleeping and seemed agitated. They took him home for a few days and later, when he returned, explained that he was on medication for his nerves.

He told me a story about being in church and, for some unknown reason, he suddenly jumped out of the window. Fortunately, the church was on the ground floor so he wasn't hurt, but the church elders were so concerned by his behavior, that they performed an exorcism on him and encouraged everyone to pray for him. Matt was the fourth generation of a line of preachers in his family, an only son that did not want to go into the ministry, but was expected to do so. Matt wanted to study biology. Several weeks later, after he had returned to school, he disappeared. I got word from his family that he was in the hospital and would not be returning to school any time soon.

Later, I wrote a letter to his parents asking how he was doing. I received a letter shortly after informing me that he had died of a massive heart attack. The next day, Dale saw Matt in a vision. My roommate was walking up into the clouds and as he turned, he waved, and she knew he was all right.

Could Karl's Career turn out to be Ministry?

I wanted to marry Dale, and do things in a way that would be right with God. After receiving the "Yes" decision from Dale that she would marry me, I went to her father and asked to speak with him privately. Ken Ditmars worked for an accounting firm in the Personnel Department, and was responsible for hiring and firing employees who worked for the firm. Even though I found him to be a bit intimidating, I needed to speak with him. Though it may have been simply a formality, I asked his permission for his daughter's hand in marriage.

I could tell he was pleased, yet concerned for his daughter's welfare. His first question was, "What's your profession going to be?" At the time, I was only a sophomore in college. My major was Business Management and I was planning to go into Hospital Administration when I graduated. I had told Dale this many times. Yet when Mr. Ditmars asked me, "What's your profession going to be?" I paused and told him, "I want to be a Minister." I know he was surprised, because I had never said anything to him about this before, and even Dale was surprised when I told her what I had said. She asked me, "Is that what you plan on doing?" And I replied, "I don't know why I said that."

I told Karl the story about when I was a young girl in my Sunday school class. The Pastor asked the students in my class what they wanted to be when they "grew up." I piped up and said, "I want to be a minister's wife!" I felt very close to God and wanted to be deeply involved in the work of the Church.

All my life, since I was a young child, I have felt drawn to the church. I envisioned myself becoming a nun one day and I wasn't even Catholic! But when my pastor asked our class that day, I knew that I wanted to be a pastor's wife — not a minister, but someone who would assist her husband in a ministry that they could build together.

73

Wedding Plans

It was in March of 1970 that Dale and I went on Spring break and traveled to Washington, D.C. to pick out an engagement ring. I sold some shares of Sperry Rand stock that I had received back in high school, and bought Dale a ring. We planned the wedding for June, 1971, and would live in Elkins, West Virginia our last year of college.

Some of our family members were concerned that, if we were married, we wouldn't finish college. But this was never an issue because we were both determined to finish what we had started, and to maintain a good grade point average as well. It would not affect the "guaranteed cost plan" that we had both enrolled in from the beginning. We were the last graduating class that had the opportunity to enroll in the plan that "guaranteed" no inflationary expenses if we attended school there for all four years. It was a financial plan designed to attract students to attend their school, and it was beneficial for us as inflation really took off at that time. The total cost for Davis and Elkins College at that time was $2,400 a year for tuition, room and board. We had to pay for our own books, but we could buy used books from other students if we could find what we needed.

Our Wedding on the 19th of June 1971

What impressed me about Dale was how well organized the wedding plans were, and how well executed everything was, from beginning to end. I thought, wow, Dale must be a really organized person. She made all the arrangements for the wedding and they were carried out in a beautiful way.

The wedding itself was a little different from a traditional service, because Dale and I decided to have a religious processional song instead of the typical "Bridal Chorus from Lohengrin." We selected, "Jesu', Joy of Man's Desiring" by Bach for the entrance of the bridal party. There were Scripture readings, from both the Old and New Testaments. Dale's father read one of the readings, and three different ministers offered special blessings and prayers. One minister offered what he claimed was the true "Apostolic" blessing granted to him by another apostolic minister. I was not certain what he meant by that, at the time, but he assured me that we were receiving a true apostolic blessing which had been passed down from generation to generation with the laying on of hands from the time of Christ!

The wedding reception was at the "Hawaiian Cottage" in Cherry Hill, New Jersey (which has since burned down). It was exciting to have the hula girls dance the ceremonial "wedding dance" before us.

When it came time for the DJ to play the couples favorite wedding song, Dale told him to play "The Hawaiian Wedding Song." So, there we were, on the dance floor and the DJ announced, "And now, ladies and gentlemen, we will play for you the couples favorite song, the Hawaiian Wedding Song!"

I was shocked that Dale selected that as our favorite song! It wasn't a bad song. I just had never heard it before, and what made it really funny was that I did not even know how to dance to the music. I had several years of training in dancing school just to shine at moments like this while everyone was watching. So, I grinned and acted as if I knew what I was doing! The other couples were later asked to join the Bride and Groom on the dance floor, and it was obvious that no one else knew how to dance to this song either. We all muddled through somehow with lots of smiles, and commented on what a wonderful song it was.

When the band leader came to me and asked me what song we would like to dance to as our favorite song, I didn't know what to say. Karl wasn't nearby and we hadn't discussed this earlier. So, since we were at the Hawaiian Cottage, the band leader suggested "The Hawaiian Wedding Song." And I agreed. Later, as I began to dance with my father and we struggled to find the rhythm to the song, my father said to me, "Who the hell chose this song?" I didn't have the heart to tell him it was me.

The Southwestern Company

After our wedding, Dale and I traveled to Alabama where I had a summer job working for the Southwestern Company selling books door to door. My roommate had gotten me the job and I thought I would give it a try. Perhaps I might learn something about people and it could help me to overcome feelings of rejection, and that is exactly what happened. I learned not to be offended when a door was slammed in my face or when I received rude remarks. One man threatened, "If you don't leave now I'm going to get my gun." So, I left and said, "Have a nice day!"

During this time, I met some extremely poor people on my sales route. Some were so poor they even had dirt floors in their homes. I didn't sell many books there, but I got to know many of them and witnessed first hand, standards of living in our own country, that I had never seen before. There were times when I was so moved by the poverty of a large family, that I gave them a children's book of Bible stories at no charge. I did this numerous times. It wasn't easy to confess to Dale that not only did I not sell any books, I gave some away for free!

What an eye opener it was to live in the rural South. I was from suburban Philadelphia and had never seen poverty like this. What a learning experience! I truly learned to appreciate what I had, compared to the poverty I was seeing. But, I also came to appreciate that it did not matter what socio-economic background you came from, people were people, with the same feelings, wants and needs as those with greater economic means.

One family had so many cats that they were anxious to get rid of them, so we were given one that we called, "Tiggy Tiger," who was orange with white stripes. He was the only cat we ever have had that learned how to retrieve.

One of my fondest memories was of a family we met that had saved their pennies in a large pickle jar in order to buy a Bible with children's stories. When I collected the payment for the book at the end of the summer, they paid me in pennies. I told them I trusted them and did not have to count their change, but they were so proud of saving their money each day, they insisted that I count every penny!

Another fond memory is of a woman who wanted me to autograph the Bible she had received because she said, "You're going to be a good minister someday." I told her that I was not planning on going into ministry, but she said, "Someday, you will." This was before I had made a decision to go into the ministry!

After that summer was over, I sent some of the money I had earned to the parents of my old roommate, Matt at D&E, the friend who had recruited me for this job. They replied with a lovely thank you letter. There was just enough money left to buy a new mattress set for our bed.

Senior Year

When we returned from Alabama, we moved to a duplex in Elkins, West Virginia to complete our education.

Our senior year in college was a great challenge. I worked two jobs, and took my responsibilities as a husband quite seriously. I worked on the work-study program, mopping floors, cleaning school buildings, and worked a second job at a local supermarket, "Garden Fresh," where I stocked shelves. During this school year, I received all A's and B's in my classes. This was in stark contrast to my freshman year in college when I had no responsibilities and was merely a C student.

My senior year in college turned out to be a time when I became more focused upon my spiritual life, and what God wanted me to do.

Tarot Cards for Me or Not?

I did a tarot card reading for a woman I had never met before, and knew nothing about. I surprised myself with my observation. Dale was present for the reading and witnessed what happened. After looking at the cards, I looked up at this perfect stranger and said, "You're pregnant!"

She turned bright red, and said, "You're right, but there is no one who knows that except me and my mother. How do you know?"

I confessed to her, that was what I saw.

Then I told her that the baby's father was in the military, and was running away from it.

Again, she said to me, "How do you know these things?" She confirmed that the baby's father was indeed AWOL from the military, and then she asked me, "What do I do with my life?"

I got scared when she asked that particular question. The other information was easy. But "What do I do with my life?" was frightening to me, because I knew she would hang on to every word I said. I wasn't about to tell her what she should do with her life, that was up to her! There are people who would have no trouble telling others how to live, but I believe that it is our God-given right to choose our own paths. Yes, I saw possibilities, but what she did was up to her.

I soon learned that the tarot cards could be a way to manipulate people, and I knew that was wrong! Perhaps, it might be a way of gathering some information, depending upon the reader, but if used to manipulate people, that would not be God's work.

Where was this information coming from? Was it from somewhere in my own head, the Holy Spirit, or some other source? That was the question. I did not really know how to answer it. If it was from my own unconscious why do it at all? It would not change anything. But, if it was from the Holy Spirit, it could be very helpful in furthering God's work.

My options were clear to me. I didn't know a way of measuring the source of this information, and could not always depend on it to be helpful or reliable. Then I asked myself, "What kind of a person lives their life based upon a tarot reading?" A tarot card junkie? Is that how God would have us live? Would God want us to be slaves to a deck of cards in our hip pocket? "Oh, wait a minute. I have to consult my cards to tell you if it's okay to drive the car today." Some people can't function without consulting their daily horoscope. I decided this was not the route for me.

I tried another experiment that was interesting, and invented my own "Ouija Board," or "KV Board," which was made out of plain paper, and used only my hands. Why do you need two people to operate the board when one can do it? I tried it and it worked! I could get information from it, but where it came from, I don't know. But, it seemed to work for me. Then one day, I got into a kind-of-argument with the source of the information. It seemed unusual to me that when I questioned advice coming through this source, I was shocked and offended by the responses. They used foul language and that was the end of that! This approach to helping others was not for me!

As I matured, I realized that God had blessed me with the spiritual gift of vision, through clairvoyance, and at times in a dream state. I had been gifted with a spiritual sensitivity. I could empathize with others who were hurting, and I wanted very much to use this talent for good. But how was I to use these gifts, the dreams, the sensitivity, for others? It wasn't by way of the tarot cards or KV board!

I tried sharing my concerns with others, but whenever I talked to them about these things, I never received a clear answer that made sense to me. Sometimes, I was even scared of the feelings I had, and frightened of the premonitions that came to me. However, these experiences were an important part of my life. How could I deny it? I couldn't. It seemed that the only one that really understood what I was going through was Dale! Thank God for my wife, a true, wise, spirit-filled partner.

The First Divine Call

I was praying in the living room of our duplex, with all the lights out except for a faint light coming from the kitchen. Dale had gone to bed early. I was meditating upon my life and what God wanted me to do, and suddenly the most amazing thing happened to me. The room started to fill up with light, and then it became a brilliant glare! A figure stood in the middle of the room in the midst of the light. I was amazed and humbled when I heard the figure say, "Karl, follow me! You can't go in two directions at once." I sat as if frozen, astounded by the experience. The figure disappeared and the light slowly faded away, while I felt a wonderful sense of peace and love. I know that somehow I had been touched by the Light of our Lord, Jesus Christ.

I knew, then, exactly what He was telling me. I could not pursue "occult" ways at the same time that I followed Him. I had to go in one direction. At that moment, I gave up tarot cards and the ouija board, and decided to follow the path to which Christ was calling me. The tarot cards may work well with certain people, but that wasn't the direction He had in mind for me. I discovered that I didn't need the cards anymore. I had found a better way.

I began to focus my thoughts and prayers upon God in Christ, and to talk directly to Him. I have always felt the presence of God in my life, but now I was beginning to discover that there was a greater purpose for my life than I had ever realized. At this time, I was 22 years old and this was a profound, transforming experience for me.

Dale and I continued to pray together and we had dialogues with one another about how we could help the world. Could two people make that big a difference? Could we touch the lives of others and provide guidance and compassion? We had long talks trying to discern just what all these feelings meant. Was I going crazy? Dale assured me, *"You aren't crazy! You just have to learn how to use what God gave you."* We had to search for the right answers, and trust in God that they would come.

In our search for God's will, Dale and I began to pray more often and dialogue with one another on a regular basis. We tried various approaches. We found it helpful to first pray and then to meditate. We would write down a series of questions we would like to have answered. Then as we were praying, we got the idea to offer suggestions to each other as we asked the questions for which we were searching answers.

The outcome of our search was amazing. We discovered that we were both very susceptible to the suggestions we gave each other. We were astounded at some of the questions and answers given when in a subliminal, prayerful state, always keeping in mind that we wanted to learn more about what God wanted us to do with our gifts. The Bible says, "Ask, and it will be given you; seek, and you will find." (Luke 11:9)

On Christmas break, that same year, Dale and I went to visit my mother in Kensington, Maryland, and Frances recommended that I talk to Professor B about using special gifts for helping others. The professor was a friend of the family, so we made a special trip over to his home, and he seemed genuinely glad to see us. The professor was a doctor of Osteopathy and I remember swimming in his pool as a child. He was very interested in hearing some of our stories and recommended that we read several books, among them, There is a River: A story about Edgar Cayce by Thomas Sugrue, and The Search For The Girl With The Blue Eyes, a story about reincarnation by Jess Stearn. We thanked him and were glad that we had found someone sympathetic with our quest for understanding. These books answered many of our questions and demonstrated that Edgar Cayce, with a solid church background, had gifts similar to ours and used them to help thousands of people.

All of a sudden, I started having dreams about events to come, one after another. I woke up one morning and told Dale, "George Wallace will be shot, but he will not die." Why would I receive this information? I really was not following the politics of the world, but was concentrating on my studies and work. The following week, it was all over the news, television, and radio. "Wallace has been shot!" I dreamed it earlier in the week, and now I was hearing about it on the news. I was in shock! But Dale said, "I'm not surprised. It's what you do."

Shortly after, I had another amazing revelation that came to me in another dream. It was in the spring of 1972, I had a vision that I would meet President Nixon. The Vietnam War was raging and there were violent demonstrations in the streets with public pressure from U.S. citizens for the United States to get out of Southeast Asia. I confided to Dale that I was confused about my life. I had dreamed I would meet the President, but how was that possible, when I was in West Virginia, and only a college student? And besides, he wasn't even near by! Three weeks later, we were surprised by an announcement at school that the President of the United States would be visiting Elkins to speak to the students and community on the college campus. There had been no previous plans for the visit, but due to a schedule change, he had accepted the offer to make an appearance on campus.

Again, I was in shock. Was my dream going to come true? Dale took it all in stride.

After Karl told me about his dream, I knew it was possible for him to meet President Nixon. However, he doubted it. I pointed out to him that he had just predicted the attempted assassination of Gov. George Wallace. Wasn't it also possible for him to meet the President of the U.S.A., as his dream suggested?

As Karl dawdled and took his time to go to the college to see him, I encouraged him to follow through and see if his dream would come true. After all, the only thing he had to lose was his self-esteem. Maybe that was the crux of the matter.

This latest prediction concerned me. I began to struggle seriously with issues such as: Who is in control of my life? Me? Jesus? And what about the dream of meeting the President? It was a simple dream in which the President shook my hand and left. Should I trust it? Was it of the Spirit?

Was this dream showing me that I should trust my dreams as long as I was praying and living as faithfully as I could, and following the teachings of Jesus, the Christ? Is it what Jesus promised when he told his disciples he would be leaving them, but he would send his Holy Spirit who would "show them things to come?" (John 16:13)

When the time came for Nixon to speak on campus, I waited at home until Dale finally asked me, "Aren't you going to go and hear the President?" I was a bit afraid, but I thought if I waited long enough and let everyone else get a good seat, the chance of me meeting the President would be slim. After all, it was just a dream, not reality.

At this point, Dale and I went to the college, as we were living off campus, and sure enough, the whole place was packed. I stood off to the side and took some pictures with my camera. I was into photography at this time and had my own dark room.

After all the speeches, the President apologized and said he would only have time to greet a few people. At that, the crowd rushed forward to the rope in front of the stage. I just stood there and thought to myself, "This is ridiculous; I'll never get close enough, so why should I rush toward him? I turned and started walking to the right side of the lawn to leave. All of a sudden, I felt the press of the crowd pushing me from all directions and within a few seconds, I was up against the ropes on the far side. Then, who do I see standing almost in front of me but the President of the United States. He was greeting people who were up against the ropes on my left and he was approaching me! I was flabbergasted! So, I resigned myself, stuck out my hand for a shake and figured this must be my fate. The President shook the hand of the person on my left, turned around and started walking away.

My heart sank to my feet, what a let down! The President was right next to me then turned and walked away? Suddenly, I then called out to him in a stern voice, "President Nixon, you come back here and shake my hand!" To my amazement, he stopped dead in his tracks, turned around and looked right at me. After seeing my face, he walked all the way back and shook my hand. He spoke to me and said, "You know, I can't stay here forever." He moved on shaking a few more of the hands reaching out to him and then left.

I was quite ecstatic! And, I believe God was teaching me some of the greatest spiritual lessons in my life.

First, I learned that someone may have a clairvoyant dream about a certain event, but the individual's will is supreme! The dream may set the stage, but the dreamer has to make it happen. Had I not said anything, I wouldn't have been able to shake the President's hand.

Second, it was my choice to go see him or to stay home. I could have chosen to stay at home. Therefore, making the choice to participate in the event shown in the dream is an important factor.

And finally, by touching his hand, I could feel the weight of the world on his shoulders. I saw that the Presidency is a job with tremendous responsibility. This may have been my greatest insight. A President needs prayer support, and President Nixon needed my prayers.

I had followed through with what was set before me in the dream. Thus, I realized it is one thing to have a vision, another to make a decision in regard to it, and finally, it is important to follow through with what you have been shown and what you know to be the good and right thing to do in light of it.

Chapter 7

And I heard a loud voice from the throne saying,
'Behold the dwelling of God is with men.
He will dwell with them,
And they shall be his people,
and God himself will be with them
And be their God.'"

Revelation 21: 3

Self Discovery

After graduating from college, there was a period of searching and trying to discover what God wanted me to do. I considered getting a Masters in Business Administration, but I was tired of studying and needed to get out into the world and start working. Besides, I simply did not have the money to continue my education.

I had several job interviews with companies that came to recruit on campus. I was encouraged by the placement office to get used to interviewing. One organization that was interviewing students was the Government Accountability Office (GAO) in Washington, D.C. They were looking for a few honest people to come work for them. I was interviewed and was surprised to find out they wanted to hire me! I told them that I had a prior obligation with another company for the summer. They responded that this was a full-time job in Washington, D.C. with the opportunity to deal with many influential people. Few people ever turned them down.

I knew it was a great opportunity, but I wanted to be ethical and do the right thing. I had already promised I would work for the Southwestern Company one more summer, and I had a team of people I had already hired to work with me. I felt obligated to them, and did not want to let them down. I was torn. I struggled with my decision but finally decided I had to be true to my word even if it meant giving up a great opportunity.

We left Elkins and moved all our belongings to my mother's home in Kensington, Maryland. There, in a small chapel, we attended the wedding ceremony of my sister Laura Kate and her new husband Robert. My sister had a strong spiritual bent; however, she leaned toward Eastern spirituality, and became a teacher of Transcendental Meditation in Spain where she had met Robert at a conference. Laura went on to teach other styles of meditation, and became President of the American Meditation Society.

My own style of prayer and meditation was more traditional. I take time to pray to God in Christ, and then take some time for silent meditation while reflecting upon a Biblical passage. Afterward, I listen to hear what God would have me do. It seems that whenever I enter into a deep prayerful state, a bright light surrounds me and there is a wonderful feeling of God's love and peace. It is very common for me to spend 20 or 30 minutes in prayer.

Covington, Georgia

Dale and I left Kensington, Maryland on sheer faith, to go to Covington, Georgia. We had no money, no place to stay, and only the clothes on our backs. My job involved selling books door to door for a second summer. We were led to a small trailer park where there was one vacancy, a very small trailer. The lady we talked to gave us $50 to buy some food and gas so I could go to work! What a beautiful, trusting soul she was. Surely, God was with us. We were living by faith, praying morning, noon and night.

I was able to sell a few books a day to pay for our expenses, and I worked from morning to night. It was hard work, but I know I was making a difference in people's lives. I saw and learned a great deal about how people in this country lived. The most endearing people I met were the poorest of all. They had a wonderful spirituality that warmed my heart. I saw hundreds of people, each different, yet each with a purpose to fulfill.

Hurricane Agnes

One day, the rains came, and kept coming and coming. I did not have a radio with me, but I'd heard people talking about a hurricane called Agnes. I continued to travel on the road until my car got stuck somewhere in the red mud of Georgia. There were no houses close by so I got out and walked, and continued walking on those lonely country roads. I had lost track of where I was, but I kept walking in the rain, and asking myself why was I out here working in what appeared to be a major storm? I had faith that God would guide me through anything, but this was not exactly what I had in mind. I must have walked for hours, and still hadn't seen any houses.

I eventually made my way to an old abandoned, ramshackled house. I was standing in the rain, soaked, cold and freezing. Suddenly, I heard a voice saying, "Karl! You must go back the way you came!" I felt that I had walked so far, there must be a house soon, why go back? It didn't make any sense to me. I had always followed my intuitions before, and this one was very strong. It was as if even the trees and the house were telling me, "Go back!" I didn't want to, but I said, "Okay." I had come a long way and I was cold and tired, but I turned around and started back. I began to run, and then walk, run, and then walk, because I was feeling dizzy, and cold, and I was exhausted. I knew I had to get back as fast as I could and follow the voice I heard. "Go back!" That was all I could think about.

I got back to my car, got in, and turned on the engine to warm up. My clothes were soaked, but it felt good to be warm again. But I couldn't stay in the car, I knew I had to get back to the last house I had visited. It, too, was a long way from my car, so I got out and started back to the last house and asked for help! It wasn't easy to go back to that house, because the people there had treated me rudely earlier. But I swallowed my pride and knocked on the door. This time the people were very concerned and even drove me all the way back to the trailer.

I didn't sell any books that day, but that didn't matter to me. What was important was to know that God was with me all the way. I'd heard that people all over the countryside were suffering from the fury of hurricane Agnes. The damage was worse than anyone had expected. There wasn't anything I could do about my car until the weather calmed down, but my heart was filled with gratitude to God for his constant care and protection.

The next day, I hired a tow truck to pull my car out of the mud. The driver told me that the direction in which I had been walking, looking for help, led directly into a state park. There were no homes in that park. He said I was lucky that I had turned around when I did because, had I continued walking in that direction in the rain, with no shelter to be found, I could have died of hypothermia!

The Monastery

I had a dream of a Monastery in which I saw in great detail a beautiful garden. Dale and I were curious about what this dream meant. Was there a Monastery close by? After some exploring, we discovered that there was a Trappist Monastery not far away. So, we went there, and found that there was a hidden garden in the courtyard inside the Monastery walls, but it was off limits to everyone but the Trappist Monks. We did see a postcard that pictured the garden exactly as it was revealed in the dream. We went back home in awe that we had found the garden, although we weren't able to see it.

Then, that night, I had a second dream showing me that I would be struck by lightning at the Monastery near a pond, but I would not die. We didn't understand what the lightning dream was all about, so we decided to go back the next day, and try to figure out what it could possibly mean. It was a beautiful day when we left the house, and there wasn't a cloud in the sky. When we arrived on the Monastery grounds, we noticed, to our left, a pond next to a group of trees. We walked over to the pond, and that was when we began to hear the sound of thunder in the distance. When we arrived, it was a clear day, yet within a few minutes, dark clouds began to form. Dale and I looked at one another and wondered, "What does this mean?" In the dream I was struck by lightning, but the good news was that I would not die.

That fact was not very comforting to Dale. I told her that I felt I had to trust in God, because of my dream. I had to have complete faith in God.

I wasn't sure I wanted to go to the Monastery with Karl, but I couldn't stay away. I certainly didn't want Karl to be alone to possibly meet his dream of lightning striking him. Therefore, I straggled along. When I saw the grove of trees by the pond that was near the Monastery, I was afraid. But follow, I did.

Meanwhile, the sounds of thunder were getting closer, and closer. And, there we were, under the trees, standing near a pond of water! It started to rain hard. Dale felt she was in this with me, and grabbed my hands and held on tight. She also had a deep faith in God. All of a sudden, a CLAP of thunder and a Huge FLASH OF LIGHT came. Dale jumped off the ground, and we saw the streak of lightning go between us. Neither of us were hurt. There was no sign of injury or burns or anything, just our fast, pounding hearts. At that moment, the thunder and the rain stopped.

I was amazed! Not only did the lightning strike right between Karl and me, but we survived! I was certainly frightened, but wherever Karl was going I would go. We were uncertain as to the purpose of this event, but we were in an explorative mood and followed what we felt we needed to do.

I said, "This was a test of our faith." I knew it didn't make much sense. I would never stand out in a thunderstorm for fun or just take a chance at being struck by lightning, but this was different. I knew the dreams had to be teaching me something. I believed I wouldn't be hurt, and I wasn't. Thank God! It was amazing that the first and second dreams came true.

Dale and I got back in the car and drove home. We observed that as soon as we left the grounds of the Trappist Monastery, the ground was dry and the roads surrounding it were dry! I stopped the car and got out to feel the ground. It was perfectly dry, not a drop of rain had fallen here! I drove, as best I could, around the Monastery to discover it was all dry. In fact, as we headed home, there was no indication anywhere that it had rained at all, and the sky was perfectly clear.

Surely God was trying to tell us something! What were we supposed to learn from this experience? We prayed for an answer.

Shortly after getting back, our friend Tom showed up. I had recruited him as part of my sales team, but he was feeling discouraged. He needed to take a break from selling and needed some encouragement. So, we extended an invitation for him to stay for a while, and shared with him our experiences of the past two days.

That night, I had a third dream in a row about the Monastery. My dream said that I would be asked by a Monk who stuttered to enter the Monastery, but if I did, I would not be able to leave, as it was a trap. I was the only one who would be allowed to go in.

We explained to Tom that we were going back to the Monastery to see if the third dream would come true, but we were very apprehensive. The dream revealed that it would be up to me to say, "No," if I was asked to go inside. Tom was so curious about what happened, he asked if he could come along, and we agreed.

I was very uneasy about driving to the Monastery. This was the third time we planned to go, and each previous visit was an experience to remember. When we arrived on the Monastery grounds, we went directly to the spot under the trees next to the pond. Nothing looked disturbed. Everything looked fine as usual, and there were no signs of lightening damage to any of the trees in that place. We then went inside the gift shop to show Tom the picture of the garden. There was a Monk that we had not seen before behind the counter. I asked him if he had a cross with a hole in the middle for sale.

When the Monk spoke, we were amazed to discover that he stuttered! Tom and Dale's eyes got big when he started stuttering.

He asked me why I wanted that particular cross, and I told him that a dream had come to me suggesting I would find such a cross somewhere and it would have great significance for me. He told me he did not have such a cross. I asked him about the garden in the Monastery and how long it had been there. He explained that the Monks took care of the garden and it had been there a long time. He went on to say that he would be glad to take me inside and show me the garden. I thought, "Oh boy, here it comes!" I looked at Tom and his face was pale white. I looked at Dale, but she just smiled. I asked, "Can I take Dale and Tom inside, too?"

"Oh, no. I can't let you do that," he said. "If I take you inside, you have to wear a robe, and I can't take anyone else."

I responded to him, "If my friends can't go, I won't go either."

Dale said, "Let's get out of here."

I agreed and was satisfied. We had lived out the third dream. The dream symbols and the reality were one and the same.

I was truly amazed at these dreams and what they taught us about the dream process. I knew that Karl had dreamed other dreams that became a reality soon after, but this was a truly unique experience.

For years after, we tried to understand what lessons we were supposed to learn from those dreams. In each dream, it appeared God was trying to teach us something. I believe there are several possible interpretations, but I would not limit them to these few.

Some dreams can be interpreted as symbolic of what is going on in our external lives or in our inner minds and hearts. Some dreams are precognitive. That is what these dreams were. Dale and I concluded that the dreams were a test of our faith in God to follow through with what He would have us do.

Dreams also reveal something about our inner lives. Within each of us lie hidden gardens of truth and beauty for those who seek them out. Dreams are one way to uncover the beauty within us, and find where God is leading us. In the Bible, Abraham's faith was put to the test when God asked him to sacrifice his son, Isaac. This happened before Abraham was blessed by God. (Genesis 22) In any spiritual development, having faith in God is one of the most important lessons.

Dreams also bring to us the reality that we are given choices between good and evil, or between two directions lying before us as possibilities. I was given the choice of getting married or leading life as a single man. I chose marriage. No monastery for me in this lifetime! I was also given the choice of going to Washington D.C. to work in the Government Accountability Office, but I chose to satisfy a previous commitment I had made even though it paid far less.

After these events, Tom had never been baptized, and asked me to baptize him. I agreed, and baptized him with water in the Name of the Father, the Son, and the Holy Spirit. We were in the bathroom of our trailer. It was a wonderful spiritual experience for all of us and Tom was convinced this baptism marked him for a life of service to the

Lord. Maybe the reality of the dreams coming true opened the way for him to seek baptism and draw closer to God.

The Lady who saw Sparkles

I continued to sell Bibles, going from one house to another, introducing myself, and being welcomed in to chat for a while. In one home, there were several people there that were especially nice. They all seemed interested in what I was doing, and asked a lot of questions about my life as a student.

One of the women commented to me, "You have lovely sparkles around your head." I wasn't sure I had heard her correctly, so I asked her to repeat what she said. "Oh, around your head, you have such beautiful white sparkles, like the Fourth of July sparklers."

I asked her, "You can see these things?"

"Yes," she said. "I see different things with different people." I thanked her and said, "I hoped these were good sparkles."

"Oh yes!" she said. "But I don't think I have ever seen sparkles like yours before."

She also told me that she had never been more than six miles from home. She was born and raised in that house, and had never traveled very far from it. The other people in the room confirmed her story. I thanked them and left the house.

One of the women escorted me outside and once on the porch, said to me, "By the way, did you know that 'Mom' is blind?"

I said, "No."

"Yes, she is," she exclaimed, "but from time to time she can see the 'aura' around a person's head."

I left the house, glad that I had another interesting story for Dale. Where else would I ever find such non-judgmental, open-hearted and sympathetic ears?

I have always felt that there is an energy field around the body. I'm not sure why some people can see this energy field and others can not, but it's probably a gift some people have developed. However, the woman in this story was blind. How could she have seen an aura?

Maybe she was legally blind, but perhaps she could 'see' with more than her eyes.

Dale's Divine Revelation

One night shortly after I went to bed, after having said my evening prayers, I went into a meditative state and was told that I would give birth to a son on or around February 11th. No year was indicated as to when this would take place, but I knew it was going to happen. I was very excited and so sure this was to be, that I jumped out of bed and ran to tell Karl of my vision. We both were aware that only time would tell whether this would come to pass or not. So wait, we did.

Cayce the Cat

While we lived in Covington, Georgia, I got a job working at the Wishbone Fried Chicken fast food restaurant. I worked long hours and the pay was minimal, but it helped pay the bills. One day after I arrived at work, I noticed a small cat outside the restaurant that meowed loudly for such a tiny creature. Its leg was broken and all the hair had been burned off its ears, poor baby! I got a box from the storage room and put the cat in it. Later, I took the kitten home and Karl and I adopted him. We took him to the veterinarian, and he put a splint on his right leg. The kitten quickly learned to maneuver, and even climbed up onto the bed with the cast on. We enjoyed having him as a pet as he was very sweet and added a lot to our lives.

The cat had been abused and was severely burned on its head. The veterinarian said he didn't think the cat's hair would ever grow back, so I suggested to Dale that we put castor oil on his head every day to see if his hair would grow back. This was an old remedy that was recommended by the sleeping prophet, Edgar Cayce, for many people. So, we put castor oil on his head every day, and after several months, the cat not only healed from its broken leg, but it also grew back all the hair on the top of its head! You would never know the cat had been abused. So, we named the cat 'Cayce.'

Another reason for the name was because, not only are cats intuitive, but we started to learn more about another intuitive, Edgar Cayce. We had experienced many unusual events in our life together, and the man Edgar Cayce seemed to be one of the few people to whose own life and abilities Dale and I could relate. We were trying to understand how to use our intuition and subtle feelings in constructive ways following the Christ.

Angel for an Hour

Something happened to me that was right out of the "twilight zone." I had been praying to God, asking for his guidance on how I could use my intuitive feelings to help others. Then, the very next day, I had an experience in which I felt like I was an angel for an hour.

I was driving down the country roads, trying to sell my books and I got lost. All of a sudden, there was a clearing in the road, even the pavement changed, and there in front of me, was a row of three houses fairly close together. The construction of the homes looked different from the other houses in the area. These houses had driveways, unlike all the others, and it was as if they had appeared out of nowhere.

I stopped at the middle house because there were several cars in the driveway. I knocked on the door, and a woman answered. She was standing there with tears running down her cheeks. In sympathy, I changed my whole approach, and decided not to sell anything here. I would use my intuition to do what I could to help.

I said, "Hi! My name is Karl Viernstein. I just stopped by for a friendly conversation with you."

She said, "Please, come in."

At that moment, the bells of the grandfather clock began to chime. It was 2:00 p.m.

I said, "Tell me what happened."

She told me that a family member had just died. I began to comfort her with words of hope and quoted scripture. I said, "If you believe in Christ, He will be the resurrection and the life to you." She seemed surprised, and told me to wait a minute, while she rushed out to gather her family in the living room. She asked me to repeat what I said. So, I spoke to the whole family, reassuring them with words of hope for their loved one who had just passed on.

As I spoke to them it got so quiet you could hear a pin drop, and suddenly everyone began to cry. They said that what I told them was exactly what they needed to hear. They asked me several questions about God, and I did my best to answer. I'd been there almost an hour, when I finally said, "I'm sorry, but I have to go now." At that moment, the clock began to chime 3:00 p.m.

The people in the room started to cry again, but this time they were tears of joy. The woman who had first answered the door said, "I know who you are. You're an angel! Yes! You're an angel!"

I said, "No, I'm just a person like you and everyone else."

But she exclaimed, "You have to be an angel! You came into our house to tell us what we needed to hear, and you came exactly at the right hour. You did not ask for anything. And now you are leaving at 3:00 p.m. I know you're an angel!"

I just put up my hands and said a prayer and blessed them. They all thanked me, and I left. I got into my car and drove away. I didn't even bother with the other two houses. But as I drove away, I still wasn't sure where I was. Suddenly, the road ahead of me seemed to change again, and somehow I was back on a road I recognized from earlier.   Later, I tried to find those houses again, with the different pavement, but I couldn't. I even asked about those three houses and described them to locals, but nobody had ever seen houses like that in this area. All I knew was that somewhere, I was an angel for an hour!

I came to realize that when I talked with people about God, they would tear up as we talked. I was not trying to proselytize anyone; I was simply trying to help people to deal with their problems. They were not tears of sadness so much as tears of joy, and a feeling of being touched in a meaningful way. I enjoyed talking with people on all kinds of topics, and I always tried to uplift them with words of hope. Without knowing it, I was well on my way to becoming a minister.

The Second Divine Call

I was going from house to house throughout the Covington, Georgia area selling books, and I stopped at the house of a woman who was receiving chemotherapy to treat her cancer. She told me how difficult it was for her, and how she had lost her hair and had to wear a wig. Because her illness was so advanced, she was on the heaviest dose of medication that could be administered. Her immune system was so weak from the treatments that she had to be careful not to get a cold. She didn't understand why she had to suffer like this, and said that she might die soon, unless the cancer could be controlled.

She said she used to go to church, but lately, was having a hard time getting around because of her illness. I asked her which church she attended.

"The Presbyterian Church in Covington," she said. She explained that the church had a rich history and that it was Peter Marshall's first church. I was very interested in this bit of news because the same Peter Marshall married my parents.

I asked her if she had talked with her pastor about what was happening to her, and she said, "Yes." "Good," I said. She told me how wonderfully her church had treated her, and that she needed all the prayers she could get. We said a prayer, and I left.

The next house appeared to be far away. I saw a small church surrounded by a cemetery on top of the hill. It was almost 12:00 noon, and I thought I would stop and rest for a while.

I stopped at the cemetery and reflected upon the last house I had visited, and said another prayer for the woman. I prayed to God that someday there would be a cure for cancer, for all types of cancer. I had seen so much of it, that I prayed to God that maybe I could help people to be healthy and whole again. I prayed that He would use me as a channel of His blessings for others. I wanted to show the love of God and bring healing to others.

I was still uncertain about what God wanted me to do with my life, but I knew I wanted to help others. I sat there in contemplation, giving thanks for the beautiful day, the sunshine and the white clouds in the sky, and feeling a soft gentle breeze. Then, all of a sudden, I felt this tingling all over my body, from my head to my feet.

At first, I thought it was a moment of divine inspiration, since I had felt that before, but this was different. The feeling became quite intense. I can't recall ever having such a strong sensation throughout my whole body, and I began to shake.

Then, I heard a still small voice say, "Karl, follow me."

I was out in the middle of the country, and there was no one around. I was standing there shaking, my hands were trembling, and my whole body shook all over. I got in the car and drove to a phone booth to call Dale. I met her at a restaurant and told her the story. I was still shaking, and my hands trembled for hours afterward. Could this be Jesus calling me into the ministry as he called his disciples? If so, why me? I didn't think I was good enough. I was soft spoken, and I didn't have a rich sonorous voice. I didn't know why God would want me when I was afraid to get up in front of people to speak.

It didn't make sense! My scientific mind was trying to explain that there had to be a logical explanation for why I was shaking all over. It wouldn't stop. This had never happened to me before! Did something like this happen to everyone called by God?

I knew God worked in mysterious ways. Maybe this was the way God was speaking to me to come follow my Lord Jesus. This was the second time I had received the message, "Follow me!" This time I was physically shaking in the middle of the day. I couldn't do anything but pray.

Dale said, "If this is what you feel God wants you to do, I will support you."

Karl was deeply shaken by this experience. However, I had tried to encourage him whenever he was called to serve, and this time was no different. I encouraged him again, but he still doubted himself.

I think I shook for about two hours. I decided to take the rest of the day off and reflect upon this new experience.

Chapter 8

"Who shall ascend to the hill of the Lord?
And who shall stand in his holy place?
He who has clean hands and a pure heart."
Psalm 24: 3-4

Fall 1972

Getting Started after Fulfilling Obligations

My summer job came to an end. Dale and I returned to Kensington to live with my mother until we could get new jobs and set up in an apartment. The money I earned selling door to door barely covered our basic living expenses.

We were grateful to my mother for letting us stay with her until we were settled. She always opened her door to us and I always did whatever I could to take care of her. I would fix the house, which always needed repairs, and do any other errands or chores. Dale and I lived there for four months.

We got along all right, but after four months it was starting to wear upon Dale, because I was doing so much for my mother. My mother could be very demanding and I was trying to make everyone happy. I knew the scripture, "A man should leave his mother and father and cleave unto his wife," so it was just a matter of time before we would be getting set up in another house.

I got a job working for a large company that specialized in building homes and Dale got a job working for Elizabeth Arden.

The construction company I worked for built homes in the Washington, D.C. area. They were prefabricated houses that were partly assembled in the plant and then completed on the site. I started out becoming familiar with the on-site construction, and was part of the construction crew that actually put the buildings together.

I was interested in home construction, and worked for a business that was building $250,000 homes in a few short months. That seemed very lucrative to me, as people always needed housing. I stayed with the company for about six months, but I was not on a management track, and found myself restricted to physical labor.

Without an opportunity for advancement, I could not visualize myself doing this job. I questioned, too, some of the unethical practices I saw, and decided I could not be a part of it. The company was using sub-standard material to build the homes. There were flaws in the construction, and workers didn't care whether the floors were level or the walls were plumbed straight. I was beginning to see that my honesty made it hard for me to overlook certain things.

The foreman and I did not see eye to eye on the project we were working on, and since I was the new kid on the block, I decided to quit instead of compromising my ethics.

Dale understood my decision. However, who is to say I would not have experienced the same thing in any business. I was beginning to feel I was too ethical to be in the "business field." The schoolroom study of business was one thing, but practicing in the "real" world was something completely different. It just seemed to me that everyone was trying to take advantage of everyone else, and if that was true, I was in trouble. I didn't realize it then, but I was getting closer to choosing ministry as a profession.

Working at Elizabeth Arden

When we moved to the Washington, D.C. area I needed to find a job. I had a degree in Elementary Education, but at this time, there was an influx of teachers in the field. Not only would it have been difficult to find a job in that area, but also I had low self-esteem and I doubted my ability to be a teacher. I had a severe case of stage fright.

So I decided to look for a job in another area. I went to a job placement center and interviewed in different venues in Washington, D.C. I had interviews with congressmen at the Capitol, banks and other businesses.

I finally accepted a position at Elizabeth Arden in their business office. It was a wonderful place to work. Elizabeth Arden was a high-class beauty salon and famous people were there all the time. I spoke with Rosalind Russell, and Roberta Flack came in. Once I saw the signatures of many notables including Bob Hope's wife on the register. As a perk, I got 50% off all services, and also received a discount on makeup and clothes. As a further "bonus," I received a Christmas package of beauty products.

Once in a while, I agreed to be a guinea pig for the beauticians who practiced hair removal on me using wax, and I got new hairdos from prospective hairstylists. I learned a lot from my supervisor. She was generous to a fault and a very classy lady. I worked at Elizabeth Arden until Karl went to seminary.

Grandmother's Death

One evening, several years after we were married, we went away for the weekend to Ocean City, Maryland. We were sleeping, when Dale woke me up and said, "Karl, my grandfather just came to me and told me that my grandmother has died. She's gone to be with him, and she is fine."

Again, my grandfather had come to me, but I still wasn't sure if it was my imagination or if it was really happening. I knew Grandmother suffered from Alzheimer's, but she hadn't been ill, that I was aware of.

The next evening, when we returned from our trip, the phone was ringing. "That's my mom," Dale said. "She is going to tell me my grandmother died."

I don't know what prompted me to say this to Karl, but I knew in my heart of hearts that my grandmother was no longer on this earthly plane. My grandfather had come to me after his death to reassure me that he was okay, and he was back to reassure me that my grandmother was okay now, too. It was time for me to trust these visits.

Just as Dale said, the phone call was from Dale's mother telling us that her grandmother had died.

Integrity on the Math

One day, Dale and I went to the store and bought a few items. The cashier gave me back too much money! I tried to explain that she had made a mistake, but she insisted that she did not make any mistakes.

It was such a heated argument that the manager came over to find out what was going on. We went over the receipt carefully, only to prove that I had, in fact, received too much change. Meanwhile the checkout line was getting longer behind us. The manager then realized that I was trying to give them money back, and explained this to the cashier in detail, so that she finally understood. After I returned the money, her whole demeanor changed. She thanked me and, with an enlightened look on her face, she said, "That's the first time anyone ever gave me money back."

Coca Cola Bottling Company

I was searching for direction in my life, and wanted to find an honest job. A friend of mine was working for the Washington Coca Cola Bottling Company and suggested I give it a try. The job would be what I made of it. I explored the company's ethics and found that they wanted honest people to work for them. I reasoned that I would take the job until I figured out just what I really wanted to do with my life. It would only be temporary; however, this time, I mentioned that I was interested in advancing to a leadership position within the company. The hiring representative said this could be a real possibility because of my background. All their leaders started out at the bottom and had worked their way up. "Fair enough," I said. "I'm not afraid of hard work."

As I worked for the company, I gained many friends. This job was different, because it could become whatever I made of it. I was on a commission basis, and earned what I sold. Dale and I moved into an apartment at Villa Del Sol, in Silver Spring. It was not far from the Coke plant. We located ourselves not too far from Columbia, Maryland, where we planned to build a house and live.

I remember driving to downtown Washington, D.C. on the way to my route. I soon discovered it was one of the roughest areas in D.C. at the time. I was assigned to 10th & W, Mt. Pleasant Street. Many of the businesses were "shoeshine stores." The Coke distributor next to me had been robbed three times. It was the route no one else wanted because it was so dangerous. Besides, it was difficult getting the truck down the narrow alleys, maneuvering around all the traffic in the streets, and it was almost impossible to find a place to park.

I was living on faith, and I believed God would show me what He wanted me to do. I prayed every morning as I drove my route. I prayed for the people who lived on the streets downtown, and I prayed that God would watch over me.

It was a tense time after the riots in Washington, D.C. when Martin Luther King, Jr., had been shot. There was a lot of mistrust and racial hatred. The city still bore the scars with many burned out buildings and there were plenty of drug dealers, prostitutes, and illegal numbers games on the streets. This was my assigned area.

After a week of training, I was on my own. I recall my mother saying, "Fools will go where angels fear to tread." She said this to me many times. I was fearless, and unafraid of going anywhere.

I prayed that I would make a difference wherever I went. I was soft spoken, unassuming, and I didn't appear to be a threat to people. I was short, and in my Coca Cola Uniform with a jaunty white hat, everyone knew who I represented. And, everyone called me "Coke."

As I got to know people, they began to realize I was not like the salesman before me; I talked to people, instead of always being in a rush to leave. I was usually one of the last drivers to arrive back at the plant, and still had to reload my truck for the next day's delivery.

I was very generous to my customers, and I gave out free Coke or Sprite to the people I met. I liked to bring in a six-pack of Coke and put it on the counter of one of the small Mom and Pop stores I delivered to and I would tell the owner, "Here's a free six-pack, take it home to your wife and children." I did this all the time and I paid for every can! Sometimes, on a hot day, and when I was filling a Coke machine, I would take a cold soda from the machine, and replace it with a warm one from my truck, give it to a customer and say, "Here, enjoy a cold one." In the summer time, I would easily give an equivalent of a case away each day. Yes, it reduced my profit, but I was not so much concerned about the money as I was about creating good will. The storeowners came to know me as honest and hard working.

The local people were all getting to know me, and once a very large and angry man in one of my stores said rather loudly, "You know white people don't come in here," and gave me a mean look with a scowl.

"Oh great, what do I say now?" I thought. Everyone in the store looked at me, and it became so quiet you could hear a pin drop. I felt the Spirit was with me, and as I opened my mouth I said with a loud voice, "It's not my fault! It's not my fault!"

The man looked at me with a frown on his face and said, "What?"

I said, "It's not my fault I was born white! I can't help it! It's not my fault I'm white."

The owner of the store and the people in the store broke out laughing!

So, I said again, "I can't help it. It's the way I am!"

He looked at me and smiled and said, "Coke, you're all right."

The people came to know me as their friend, and more importantly they came to accept me as I was, and they knew I accepted them without any sign of prejudice. I was like family. I know it seems odd, but I became friends with the corner prostitutes and the palm readers. I gave them free drinks, but I kept my personal distance from them. I could be a friend, and talk with them without accepting any of their offers.

"Anytime, Coke!" they would say.

And I would tell them, "No thanks, I'm married." Thank God, I was very happy in my marriage.

As I walked and talked with God each day, I was given the words to say that would help me defuse situations that could have otherwise become explosive. My intentions were to help people more than to make money.

Man in the Gutter

Early one morning, as I arrived at my first stop, I noticed a man lying asleep in the gutter right in front of where I would pull up my handcart. I could have yelled at him to move, but instead, I leaned over to the man and shook his arm.

"Are you hungry?" I asked him. "Would you like something to eat?"

I helped him up, and I could tell by his breath that he had consumed a lot of alcohol the night before. "Let me take you over to get you something to eat," I said.

I helped him to a little breakfast shop, not far away, and told the owner to give him something to eat and get him some coffee. I would pay the bill. I then returned to make my first delivery. I was learning to do what God wanted me to do. I believed that was what Jesus would have me do. I was starting to feel like I was part of the community where I worked. They were my friends, and I felt compassion for their plight.

Crossfire

It was the middle of the day and I was preparing to deliver to a liquor store downtown on one of the main streets. I was pushing the limit to get as many cases of soda cans as I could on to the cart. More than I should have, actually. As I started to wheel the huge stack, about 13 cases, into the store, I had one arm on the cart and the other was holding the top of the pile. As I got in front of the store, I saw RC, the Royal Crown Cola distributor and he was yelling at me, "Get down! Coke, get down!"

I suddenly noticed the police cars pulled up at an angle, and the policemen with their guns out crouched down next to their police cars.

There was another policeman with a bull horn in his hand. I had walked right into the middle of the action, and I just froze there, balancing the 13 cases of Coke. The liquor store was in the process of being robbed! RC yelled at me again to get down and rushed over and tackled me to the ground. 156 cans of Coke went flying everywhere. At that the police rushed the store, dodging the cans of Coke scattered all over the side walk. Where all the policemen came from I couldn't say, because I hadn't seen them from where I stood. RC worked for a competitor, but he was still a friend. We started to argue with one another.

"Why did you knock me over?" I said. "Now I have cans everywhere!"

RC said, "Coke, I was trying to save your life. The police were ready to start shooting!"

The police were angry with me because there were soda cans everywhere, and they were falling down over them, and the robber got away! The robber probably laughed all the way to the bank! When the news got out about what happened to me, the local people thought I was the funniest Coke salesman they ever had.

At Christmas time, the Coca Cola Bottling Company received cards and letters from the store owners I served. They were full of compliments about my service. The President of the company called me into his office to find out what I was doing.

"We haven't had so many cards about one person in a long time," he said.

Against the Wall

There were seven or eight "shoe shine stores" on my route. They were often dark and full of smoke. I was very naive about places like this, so I just went in and serviced the coke machines as usual and left.

One day I entered another shoe shine store and the next thing I knew, several guys pushed me up against the wall really hard. I heard someone yell from the other side of the room, "Hey! You leave him alone. He's my man."

And, just like that, the hands holding me suddenly let go. I walked over to the counter toward the man who had yelled out.

"Coke," he said. "You remember me?"

I wasn't sure, at first. I was still a little stunned by what had happened. "I have the store on the other side of town," he said. "And you gave me some free coke," and then I recognized him.

"Oh yes!" I said. I leaned over the counter and whispered, "What's happening?"

He said, "Those guys were going to rob you! But, I told them you were my friend." With a smile, I said, "How would you like to take a case of coke home to your wife and family?"

He laughed and said, "Just give me a six-pack."

I felt lucky that day. I could have been robbed and beat up, but God's grace was with me. I believe in that Golden Rule, "Do unto others as you would have them do unto you," and it applies to everyone.

Later, when I prayed, I thanked God for being with me that day. I learned that what you do for others comes back to you in ways you do not expect. If I had been indifferent, or even hostile to my clients, I'm convinced that it would have come back to me, and I would have been robbed. Thus, the lesson Jesus taught us, "You will reap what you sow," (Galatians 6:7) is true.

Running Numbers

I was delivering to a store on the main street, one day, when several people came up to me and said, "Coke, we have a proposition for you. We have been watching you and you're okay. We would like you to run the numbers for us."

I said, "What?"

"Run the numbers, like a bookie, people place bets with you. You are all over town, so you would be perfect."

I thought for a second and said, "You know what? I have a problem."

The guy looked at me and said, "What problem?"

I said, "I teach Sunday school."

They looked at one another. I'm sure that's not what they expected me to say. I shook my head and I said, "I can't do it. I teach Sunday School."

Then there was a big smile on one of the guy's faces, and he said, "Coke, we knew you were different. You really teach Sunday school?"

"Yeah, I sure do, every Sunday."

That was the last time they ever asked me to do that! When word got out on the street that I was a Sunday school teacher, customers began to come to me asking for advice, or wanting to tell me about their problems.

I worked for the Coca Cola Bottling Company for two years. I learned some of the greatest lessons of my life, especially when I took time from my work to help the poor and lonely people, those who needed advice or a sympathetic ear, or those who just needed encouragement. I learned to be a friend to the friendless.

I was scared sometimes, but it was just another lesson in learning to trust in God no matter what the situation.

I made many friends, and enjoyed laughing with the people, as well as helping to create a friendly environment wherever I went. I remember that many visitors to our nation's capital would get lost on the back streets of the city, and they always seemed to find me, and would ask me for directions. I could tell they were scared to death, and I would calm them down and tell them how to get to wherever they wanted to go.

Sunday School at Warner
Ministry Looming Closer

When Dale and I moved back to Kensington, I started attending my home church again, the Warner Memorial Presbyterian Church. We joined the choir and went to practice during the week. We would always visit with my mother after church on Sunday and after every choir practice.

I volunteered to teach the High School Sunday school class. Dale and I, and another couple, Max and Marge, worked with the Senior High Youth Group.

One Sunday in church, the youth group presented a drama production called "Look to the Baby," that Dale and I directed. It was our first drama about the teachings of Christ, and both Dale and I had acting parts as well. The youth group did a superb job, and I could not have been more proud of them. Even the minister was impressed.

We took them to the shore on Youth Sunday, and we celebrated an "agape meal," which is very similar to communion, but does not bless the elements. It is a "friendship meal" in the name of our Lord Jesus Christ. We provided a few mountain top retreats to help the youth to grow spiritually. It seemed as if God was leading Dale and me in the direction of ministry as we worked every week with people who were searching for God's truth. I played the guitar and Dale played the piano for the youth group songs, and they were wonderful experiences for us all. We were enjoying our time working in the Church.

When I taught Sunday school, I would share some of what God was teaching me as I worked for the Coca Cola Bottling Company. I believe we are all on a spiritual journey and are supposed to use all of our experiences to draw closer to God. At different stages of life, we learn different lessons. As we apply what we know, more is given. I keep trying to live out these teachings, and it isn't always easy.

Deacon

I was asked by the church nominating committee to serve as a Deacon of the Warner Memorial Presbyterian Church. I agreed and the congregation approved it. The date of ordination was set, and on the day I was to be ordained a Deacon, I knew I was committing my life to serving Christ in the Presbyterian Church.

I was brought before the congregation, and was asked a series of questions, which I answered in the affirmative. Then, the people laid their hands on my head and prayed. I felt a tingling from my head to my toes, and knew it was the Holy Spirit. Everything felt right and good. I pledged my service to the church and I visited the sick and took flowers to people at home. On occasion, I would help the minister by reading the scripture at the worship service.

Hymn of the Day

I remember, before going to Church on Sunday mornings, I would often sing hymns in the shower. I would then be shocked when I got to church, only to hear that the hymn I had been singing earlier that morning had been chosen as part of the worship! I never made a big deal out of it, but it happened so often that Dale would listen to the hymn I was singing in the shower, and wait to see if it was among the list of hymns that was sung in the worship service.

The Third Divine Call

Early one morning I had a dream from which I awoke shaking. I heard, "Karl, read the book of Jonah." It woke me up very early before work, so I read the book of Jonah, just like I was told to do in my dream. As I read the scripture, I broke out in chills over my whole body. When I finished reading, I had an inner revelation. I was like Jonah! I had been running from God for three years, since my first "call" in Elkins, and my second "call" in Georgia. And now it was time to stop running!

Dale and I had the blue prints for a house we were going to build in Columbia, Maryland, in a planned community on Trotter Road. I owned the land and was talking with a loan officer about securing a loan to build a house. Dale and I were both working, and we didn't have any children yet. Now it looked as though I would have to turn my whole life around and follow another path. Is this what God wanted me to do?

I was concerned about going into the ministry. I didn't want to be like some of the ministers I had seen on television. I didn't want to jump up and down and pound my fist on the pulpit, nor did I want to stand in front of the congregation, put them down, and make them feel guilty. That was not my way.

Then I heard my answer. It was while I was reading the book of Jonah. "Karl, you don't have to be afraid: be yourself," the voice said.

I realized that God could still use me, somehow, even though I was scared to death to get up in front of people. I recalled the story of Moses and how he did not want to speak before others, yet God called to him and he answered. I realized that even though I was not perfect, God could still use me. As I put all the pieces together, I realized God had wanted me to work for Him all along. Up to now, I had been running away from my call. All my life I had experiences that were unusual, but now, I could use these gifts to help God in the ministry.

I talked to Dale about selling the land we were supposed to build on, and using the money to put myself through seminary. Dale was quite agreeable. She said she was glad God was calling me, and that I should follow the call. Like the Biblical "Ruth," Dale said that she would go wherever I went.

Karl was uncertain whether to accept this third call or to continue to live the life we were leading. Even though I had always wanted to be a minister's wife, I also was afraid. I knew it would be difficult to give up all that we had, including our two cats, and my dream of starting a family. I knew that this wasn't about me, but about what we could do for God and how we could help this world become a better place. So I encouraged Karl to go right ahead and pursue his calling.

Finally, I said in my prayer, "All right, God. Take me and use me according to thy will."

Application to Seminary

After my Jonah call, I decided that I would finally apply to enter a seminary, but what school should I go to? I made an appointment to see my minister at the Warner Memorial Presbyterian Church in Kensington, Maryland. I walked into his office and was impressed by the kneeling bench I saw there. Here was a minister who prayed on his knees.

"What can I do to help you?" he asked.

I explained how I felt called to the ministry and wanted to get his advice about it.

He said, "Oh Karl, you don't want to go into the ministry. It's one of the worst professions in the world! Nobody will listen to you, and you'll be treated like dirt! You will be underpaid! And, everyone will dump their problems on you. Please rethink your decision to go into the ministry!"

Wow! His comments took me aback. I explained how I had been running from this call for several years and was just now finding the courage to answer it.

He went on, "But, Karl, there are so many other ways to serve God than going into the ministry. Do you want to preach? What is it that you want to do?"

I told him that I wasn't exactly sure, but I did know that I needed to go back to school to learn what I could about the Bible and theology, and get a degree in ministry before I could really do what God wanted me to do. Not being disheartened, I asked, "What school do you recommend?"

"Well, Karl," he said, "I feel it is my obligation to try to discourage you from going into the ministry. It is not an easy profession by any means, but if it is meant to be, then there is nothing that I can say that will stop you from going into the service of our Lord. I congratulate you if you do decide to go, but I know it will not be easy."

I was amazed that, in the midst of the conversation, he completely changed his attitude toward my decision. I believe that he was testing me, to see if I was truly called by God. My spirit was so tested and tried at that point, that I felt there was nothing that could keep me from following through with my plans to become a minister.

"Karl," he said, "There are several schools that you could apply to, both liberal and conservative schools. My recommendation, if you want to get a good Biblical conservative understanding of the Bible, is that you consider Union Theological Seminary in Richmond, Virginia, as opposed to Union Theological Seminary in New York, which is a more liberal school."

"Would you write me a recommendation?" I asked.

"Yes," he said, "However, I must ask you to seriously consider the difficult journey you have chosen."

"I will," I told him.

I had been struggling for years about this call to ministry. I knew intuitively that it was my destiny and where I had been heading all along, thus it was a relief to finally make a decision.

Psychological Testing

In order to become a minister in the Presbyterian Church, one must submit to extensive psychological testing, and a protracted process of being taken under the care of a presbytery, in my case, the National Capital Union Presbytery.

I recall missing an appointment with a psychologist. When I arrived one minute late for the second appointment with him, he was very angry that I had missed my first appointment. He told me that my procrastination was a sign that I subconsciously did not want to go into the ministry. I assured him that I had been helping someone, and had lost track of the time. It in no way changed my desire to serve God in the ministry.

It occurred to me that the psychologist was trying to test my mental stability and the soundness of my motives and intent. I was required to be interviewed by three different psychologists and several committee boards at the church and Presbytery level. I remember one psychologist who asked me how often I had sex with my wife.

"What does that have to do with my going into ministry?" I said.

He said, "I need to know this in order to properly evaluate you."

I couldn't believe it. So, I told him, "I have sex with my wife every day."

He almost fell off the chair when I said that!

I found it hard to believe that all those questions were necessary in order to make a fair evaluation, but I put myself and my faith in God's hands. If I was to be accepted and the way was made clear for me to go into the ministry, then I would proceed to the next step. After months of testing and waiting, I was finally approved to enroll in the seminary.

Telling my Friends

I told my friends, "The Crew," that I was going into the ministry, and they couldn't believe it. They said, "Karl, the kid we grew up with? No way!" I recall debating religious issues with my friends and arguing the "existence of God" on numerous occasions. Some of my friends claimed to be agnostic, and challenged me to prove the existence of God. I did my best to explain my belief that God does exist and loves humanity in spite of the cruelty of mankind. I had to admit that I had little or no proof, and could only base my evidence upon my own religious experiences.

My friends and I would often go downtown to Washington, D.C. to have a few drinks, and they invited me to go downtown with them one last time. They wanted to see if they could talk me out of going into the ministry, if they could. It was, as usual, a good hearty discussion over who could prove what was real or not real, what was good, and what was evil, and how we could understand a God whom we cannot see. We simply had differences of opinion. I wasn't going to change them and they were not going to change me. So, we simply agreed to disagree agreeably. In all, most of my friends were very supportive and wished me the best.

My Recommendations

I applied to Union Theological Seminary in Richmond, Virginia, and secured three important references. One reference was from my religion and philosophy professor at Davis and Elkins College, Dr. Phipps. I recall discussing with Dr. Phipps a book that he wrote, Was Jesus Married? Based upon the Jewish customs of the day, he thought that it was probable that Jesus was married. However, I argued that if Jesus was an Essene, and had dedicated his life to "spiritual pursuits," he may have chosen to remain unmarried. I conceded that it would not have changed Jesus' basic teaching at all had he been married, but the Bible remains silent on the issue. Dr. Phipps gave me an excellent recommendation.

My second recommendation came from Mrs. Stickley, who was my 7th grade English teacher, Deacon in the church, and a great inspiration to me. As I mentioned earlier, I was one of those students that had a hard time reading. I was always confusing words by reading ahead, and then going backwards, and flipping words around. Today they would call it "dyslexia," but back then there was no diagnosis and no name for it. You were just thought to be stupid. It never made sense to me that I could get A's in math, and barely pass English. I was placed in one of those "slow reading groups," but in spite of that, Mrs. Stickley gave me an outstanding recommendation.

My home pastor, Dr. Roth, also wrote an excellent recommendation. He knew that I had worked tirelessly as a volunteer in the church for many years. I sang in the choir, served as a deacon, and helped the youth group. I had also played the guitar during Vacation Bible School, visited shut-ins, taught Sunday school, helped to repair the church building, as well as assisted the pastor in worship.

Paying for Seminary

When choosing a new profession, the first issue to address is how to pay for your education. There were some scholarships available, but I was not an A student in College. However, I did demonstrate that from the time I entered college my freshman year, when I received C's, I had ended my senior year with all A's and B's.

My only 'ace in the hole' to pay my tuition, was the land I had bought in Columbia, Maryland, which happened to be situated in a fast growing area. Dale agreed, so we sold the land and used the money to pay for my seminary training. It became the "Lord's Acre" that we sacrificed for the Lord's training!

Through the years, I have never again owned any land or a house. However, I must say that the Lord has always provided a house or manse for me and my family to live in. I trust that the Lord will provide again in my later years.

Dale and I agreed to give up our jobs, our property, our pets, and our possessions, to serve the Lord in the pastoral ministry. It was a bold step of faith.

Acceptance to Seminary

I recall the day the letter from Union Theological Seminary in Richmond arrived, announcing that I had been accepted into the Fall class of 1974. However, I was required to take 'baby Greek' during the summer before I could enter school. Many students had already taken the course during their regular college studies. I had no idea how I would do at a foreign language such as Greek. I had taken some French in high school, and two semesters of Spanish in college, but this too would be a leap of faith for me!

Because I would be going to school full-time, both Dale and I would have to give up our jobs in Washington, D.C. and move all our belongings to Richmond, Virginia. It was the only way for me to go to seminary. It was tough for Dale to give up our cats, because no pets were allowed in the school apartments. Fortunately, Dale's parents, Ken and Ruth, took care of Cayce; and, my mother, Frances, gladly took care of Tiger. We were relieved that they both found good homes.

Chapter 9

"But this is the covenant which I will make with the house of Israel
After those days, says the Lord:
I will put my law within them,
And I will write it upon their hearts;
And I will be their God, and they shall be my people."

Jeremiah 31: 33

Seminary 1974 - 1977

The first week of seminary, I was very apprehensive. I had my first Greek test after only one week of class, and I was delighted to receive my first A.

Richmond was a new town for us, and both Dale and I had to learn where everything was located – doctors, stores, new roads, and new friends.

I prayed to God, asking Him to help me through this difficult stage of learning the Bible in a scholarly way. To become a Presbyterian minister, I had to learn both Greek and Hebrew. It was quite a challenge!

During my second week of school, I remember feeling overwhelmed, and questioned if I had made the right decision. It was not an easy transition going from the working world back to the world of books, classes and exams.

Then, Dale announced some surprising news. "Guess what Karl, I'm pregnant!"

It was fantastic news, but a huge shock at the same time. News came of the pregnancy during the greatest challenge of my life. We had no medical coverage, as the insurance from our jobs had stopped, and the new insurance provided by the seminary had not yet begun. We had no money, only our faith in God. Surely, He would help us through this trying time.

When I told Karl I was expecting, I was very happy but also filled with trepidation. How were we going to afford a baby? We had lost our insurance and the schools' insurance plan hadn't kicked in yet. Not only that, I didn't have a job and I would be unable to work a conventional job, due to my pregnancy. I wanted this baby, and had been hoping for one, but knew we would need a strong faith in God for support in the coming months.

The Second Week – Dream of Dying

It was the second week of "baby Greek" and I was learning a language completely foreign to me. Fortunately, I had a fantastic teacher! He was a man of prayer and great patience, whose skill and understanding were incredible. I found myself meeting the challenge with as much faith as I could muster. I had given up everything to pursue a new life, a new field, and a new way. I was determined to make it work.

Shortly after, I had a dream that horrified me. I dreamed that I died. I saw the ambulance drive up to the Seminary apartments to pick up my body, and I watched as they covered my head with a sheet. Dale was dressed in black standing next to my body, crying, as they carried me away. I woke up shaking.

What could this mean? I had never before had a dream in which I died. My dreams were becoming more intense. They were more vivid and clearer than ever before. Why would God give me this dream and how was I to interpret it? I woke Dale and told her my dream. Why would God show me a dream like this after I had given up everything to follow His call to ministry? How was I to make sense of this dream?

About a week later, the meaning of the dream became clear. I realized that the old Karl was dying and a new Karl was in the process of being born! It did not mean I was literally going to die. It was a symbolic dream revealing the spiritual transformation that was taking place within me.

I remembered my days at Coca Cola, the heavy lifting, the harsh language on the job, and old friends that would go out drinking and smoking cigarettes with me. The immature, carefree me was on the way out.

There was a new self that was emerging, one that was dedicated to a life of helping others, one with greater depth and maturity. A self that had chosen a path not filled with riches but with love and compassion for the sick, for the outcast, the lonely, the depressed, the abused, and the injured, while searching for its own wholeness.

Yes, I was dying, but dying to selfishness. I came to understand that there is a process by which I had to first surrender the old Karl, pick up my cross, and follow Jesus. Then the new Karl could begin to emerge. This meant a new birth for Dale, too. When one of the partners makes a complete about-face, the other partner has to change, too, or the relationship can't work.

Dale's Work

When we moved to Richmond, I got a job taking care of children. Union Theological Seminary provided childcare services, if requested, by people in the community. Seminary students and their wives would register with the office when they were available to provide childcare. We were also available for extended care when there was a need for parents to go away for a week or two on vacation or go to a medical conference without their children. They simply contacted the seminary office. Potential caregivers would be interviewed and, if accepted, the seminary couples would stay in various homes to sit with children or pets. I became a nanny to these families. This provided Karl and me with a little extra money for food and expenses while we lived there.

Food Stamps

We had very few belongings and very little money to live on. We qualified and lived on "food stamps" while we were at the seminary. However, even that ran out before the end of the month. I remember the best birthday present my parents ever sent me was a check for

$25.00, which was a lot of money in those days. They sent the check at the end of the month, (my birthday is June 3rd). We had very little food in our cupboard at that time, so we went shopping and filled it up. What a treat that was!

A Warning of Impending Danger

Dale and I were on our way to the movies to see "The Towering Inferno," when all of a sudden I felt a tingling from head to toe. I told Dale I felt that something was wrong. It was the same ominous feeling I had when I was a child many years ago, riding my bike with the dangling, noisy tin cans tied to it. Here we were on the way to the movies, and I felt it again, and now I was going to ruin the show for Dale.

"Dale," I said. "I know this feeling means that there is something wrong."

Before I could say any more, Dale said, "Let's go back, it's only a movie. We can see it another time."

I was very apologetic about having to turn back.

I said, "When I've acted upon these feelings, I've never been sorry, but when I don't act on them then, I have regretted it."

"Don't worry about it," Dale said.

So I turned the car around and headed home. Since I had the same type of tingling feelings when I was a child, I thought there must be something wrong with my mother. I hurried as fast as I could, and as soon as we got home, I went directly to the phone and called my mother in Kensington.

As soon as she answered the phone, I was relieved, "Hi! How are you?" I asked.

"Fine," she said.

Then I just stumbled for words, "Are you sure you're okay?"

"Yes, why do you ask?" she said.

"Well," again I struggled for words because I did not know what to say.

Suddenly, Dale yelled out from the other room and said, "Karl, come here quickly."

"I'll call you right back," I told my mother. "Something has come up."

Dale ran in and said, "Karl, there is something wrong in the other room." I rushed into the other room, and saw that smoke was seeping into the room from somewhere. I walked into my study, and there was smoke coming through the wall. As I looked at the cloud of smoke, I visualized the fire that was the cause of the smoke, but the fire wasn't really there, at least not yet. It must have just started because we didn't notice it when we first walked in, but it was moving fast!

I quickly got back to the phone and dialed 'O' for the operator. When she answered, I explained that there was a fire somewhere in the apartment complex, with lots of smoke although I couldn't say exactly where it was. I told her to send a fire truck, and gave her our address. She asked me to repeat the address several times, so I did. When I could finally hang up the phone, we decided to warn others and evacuate the building!

We lived in a three-story apartment building and our apartment was on the first floor.

Dale said, "I'll run and tell the people on this side, you go and warn the people on the other side." So, I ran to the side of the apartment opposite ours, rang the doorbell and knocked loudly.

When a fellow student answered I asked, "Is there a fire in your apartment?"

With a confused face, he said, "What fire?"

I told him there was smoke coming through the walls of our apartment, and his apartment was on the other side of that wall. He quickly ran back to look in his apartment and came back and said, "I don't see any smoke."

"There has to be a fire somewhere with all the smoke," I explained. His wife appeared at the door, so I suggested that she evacuate all the people on this side of the apartment building while her husband and I looked for the fire. She agreed, and went off while her husband and I went to check the laundry room that was in the basement beneath the apartments.

We ran downstairs where there were several washing machines and dryers, but didn't find any smoke. There was a closet door on the other side of the room, so I grabbed the door knob and opened the door. All of a sudden, there was a loud "Whoosh!" and a huge ball of fire was exposed as soon as I opened the door! We were both thrown back by the force of the fire, and turned to run. The whole closet room was engulfed in flames that ran up to the ceiling, and the smoke came billowing out.

Fortunately, neither of us was hurt when I opened that door. I once heard that you should feel the door before opening it, but I was in too much of a hurry to find the cause of the smoke, and hadn't thought of it. I grabbed a fire extinguisher that was mounted on the wall but when I turned it upside down, and shook it, only a small stream of water came out. It was useless!

"What good is this thing?" I said.

The smoke was starting to make us cough, and in that same instant we both said, "Let's get out of here!"

As soon as we got outside, the fire truck arrived. I warned them to get their masks on because there was a lot of smoke, and sent them to the basement. The firemen worked for some time to put the fire out. They pulled out a bunch of mattresses that had somehow caught on fire. They were able to put the fire out before it engulfed the building. Later, I asked the fireman if that fire could have burned the whole place down. "Yes," he said. "A fire like that wouldn't take long to burn the whole building to the ground!"

Dale and I returned to our apartment, and I called my mother to explain everything. I had known something was wrong, but I hadn't figured out exactly what it was.

That seems to be the story of my life. I get these tingling feelings and the dreams that mean something, but sometimes, I have no idea what they mean until much later on.

It was no coincidence that I was alerted to go back home when we did, to be the ones to discover a smoldering fire. God was warning us of some tragic event that was ready to erupt. Surely, God was watching over us.

What I can't explain logically to anyone except my wife Dale, is why I get that tingling feeling from head to toe. I know that when that happens to me, I am being alerted to a problem somewhere. It happens very infrequently, but when it does, I pay attention! Dale and I did the right thing and hopefully saved some lives, not to mention extensive damage to the Seminary housing.

Jason's Birth

Dale felt that the time was drawing close for the baby she was carrying to be born. We didn't know if it was a boy or girl, although Dale had been told in a dream in July of 1972 that she would give birth to a son on February 11th. But our doctor insisted that she wasn't due until March 3rd.

When Dale went to the Doctor on the 11th of February for her regular appointment, she was three centimeters dilated. Dale was in labor! As the contractions got closer, I played the music from Handel's Messiah, the "Amen Chorus!" We had taken the Lamaze classes together, so I could be present and supportive of her during the delivery. I remember doing the breathing exercises with Dale to encourage her. Finally, the time came for the delivery and our child was born. We had a son! We were so delighted we sang "Happy Birthday" to him in the delivery room; after all it was Jason's Birthday! It seemed that Dale and I were always singing songs together. We sang for our pets, why not our children?

Jason was born on February 12th, at 9:25 a.m., one day away from the date Dale had predicted, and it was a wonderful experience for us all. We felt God had blessed us, and since Dale and I were praying for healing to come to the world, and I was taking Greek in school, we decided to name our son "Jason," the Greek name for healer.

Of course, I was thrilled to have a son. It was fascinating to me that I had predicted that a son would be born on February 11th. I knew that our child was supposed to be due on March 3^{rd,} so it never *occurred to me to think he might be born in February. I was off by a few hours, but that's not so bad, considering I had the dream two and one half years earlier!*

A Shocking Dream of Jason that I Would Never Forget

One week after Jason was born, I had the worst nightmare I had ever had. I woke up out of the dream shaking and terrified. I was angry at God for giving me such a dream, and I couldn't believe He would do such a thing to me. I dreamt that laying before me was little baby Jason. Then for some unknown reason, I took a knife and cut the baby's brain in half. His brain was split in half! I woke up shaking.

I was scared and furious at God! How could He give me a dream like that? I would never take a knife to our new born son whom I loved. What good was the dream? It was full of violence. I started questioning whether I could ever do such a terrible thing. Did I have that much violence in me? Why would I even think of doing such a thing, even in a dream?

I didn't want to tell Dale about my dream, but I had never held anything back from her before. I was, as she would say, "honest to a fault." My heart ached and I was depressed about the dream. What could it mean? God had spoken to me before through my dreams, but this one was hard to decipher! For several days, I considered what God was trying to tell me about our newborn child. I had difficulty getting that dream image out of my mind. It was certainly a dream that I dearly wanted to forget but I knew I never would. I finally talked to Dale and we decided that God was giving me a warning dream. Not that I would harm him, but that God was instructing me to never "undercut Jason's intelligence."

I had already had a premonition that I would have a child that would be smarter than me. Is this not what every good parent hopes for? Therefore, it stood to reason that, if he did have great intelligence, I should take care not to "undercut" him or dissuade him from pursuing greater things, but be supportive of his intellectual pursuits.

I had had enough training and education to know that the worst thing you can do to another person is to discourage him or her from trying to succeed at something. It does not profit a person to tell him or her, "You are no good and stupid." I had heard that often enough from some of my teachers who did not understand how my brain worked. That simply lowers a person's self-esteem. Rather, it is better to encourage and give positive reassurance that will raise a person's self-esteem. Maybe this horrible dream was God's way of reminding me to be positive in raising my new born son, Jason.

It wasn't until many years later that I would really find out what that dream meant. Jason was a colicky baby who stayed up late, but he was very bright. By the time he was 2 years old, he could read and recite the alphabet, and he was reading books before he went to kindergarten.

Excellent Professors at Union Theological Seminary

I was honored to have studied under some of the best professors the seminary had to offer. Dr. John Bright taught me about the <u>History of Israel</u> and <u>Jeremiah</u> in a way that made the Bible come alive for me. The people of the Bible struggled just like we do every day. It was an incredible realization. I was taught Hebrew and Greek by several excellent professors. I was introduced to wonderful books that, unfortunately, were never canonized into the Bible, like the Books of Barnabas, Mary and Thomas. I enjoyed studying the Psalms in the original tongue, and enjoyed the counseling courses with Dr. William Oglesby. Dr. Oglesby, was so popular on campus that all the students I knew admired him. He was affectionately called the "Cockroach," because he was a down to earth professor who seemed to understand everyone. And it was such a pleasure to visit the Biblical library at Union Theological Seminary, which was one of the best in the world. Sometimes I couldn't believe that I was actually holding ancient Biblical documents in my hands!

Some of the other classes I enjoyed were Ethics and the comprehensive study of the Bible.

Bible Study Group

While I was in seminary, I began a Bible Study Group for people in the community. It was not composed of students, but of local people who lived and worked throughout the community, and were interested in "Spiritual Development." I led this group the last two years I was in seminary. It was based upon the Search for God books from the Association for Research and Enlightenment, the organization founded on the work of Edgar Cayce.

I discovered that the seminary provided me with a great conservative knowledge of the Bible and how to interpret the Word of God, and I was learning how to articulate that knowledge to others. However, there was little time for personal spiritual development on campus. Something was missing that I needed to help make me an effective pastor.

I decided to lead a Bible study and discuss the scriptures in light of the spiritual lessons that came from Edgar Cayce. I was in the learning mode and sought to learn all that I could from every source available to me. After all, was I not in seminary to learn and grow and deepen my relationship with God? There were several avenues that were helpful to Dale and me as we studied the Bible and its spiritual lessons.

First, Mr. Cayce was a man of God who loved the Bible, he loved the Presbyterian Church, and he also had extraordinary spiritual experiences. We could identify with the struggles he went through as he dealt with other people. There were many who doubted his abilities, and at times when he tried to help others, there were those who tried to take advantage of him and misuse his gifts for personal gain. We did not want that to happen to us.

Second, Edgar was a religious man who placed Jesus Christ in his life first and foremost. We admired this trait about him. Unfortunately, he became discouraged when people were less interested in his faith and Biblical knowledge than the information that came through him. Dale and I did not want that to happen to us either. We felt and still feel our faith in Christ is what enables us to be in harmony with our Creator.

Finally, the studies were helpful because Edgar provided a format for us to enter into dialogue with one another. It provided a guide for us and gave us hope to develop a deeper prayer life.

I learned about the Bible at school during the day, but it was this little group of people in our Bible Study who kept my Spirit burning. We grew together as we shared and prayed, and sought to be a channel of blessings for others.

Dream of the Ocean or the Mountains

I had a dream that a stranger came to me and told me I had to make a choice between going to the Ocean or the Mountains. I have always been pulled in these two different directions. I loved the idea of being at the ocean with the water, beaches and wind blowing. But part of me also wanted to be in the mountains and in the woods experiencing the trees, plants, rocks and hills. But in my dream, I had to make a choice. I realized that I was not being asked where I would do ministry; it was asking me to choose either a liberal path or a conservative one. It was a choice between new wave religion and organized religion, and I was to choose which direction I would ultimately go when ministering to people. Should I minister to people who needed guidance from the Holy Spirit, or should I minister to them through the "Word" of God revealed through scripture?

For me, the mountains symbolized the conservative path, as Moses brought down the Ten Commandments from Mt. Sinai and people were given a clear choice, "Keep my commandments" and "Choose this day whom you will serve." The Word of God is revealed through the scriptures, and teaching these principles is the primary focus in ministry.

The ocean or water can be a symbol of the spiritual path, and a ministry led by the Holy Spirit. A charismatic ministry would be one led by the Holy Spirit as one reveals God's Word through divine inspiration and revelation. The primary focus would be spiritual development through prayer and praise, spirit-filled messages, and being filled with the Holy Spirit.

For the most part, Dale and I have chosen to do ministry in the mountains, but there have been times when we've dipped into pools of God's waters to minister to others through the Holy Spirit.

Developing our Prayer Life

Dale and I continued to develop our prayer life but it seemed as if we were met with many obstacles continuously along the way. When I consulted seminary colleagues, most were curious about my interest in this form of prayer "in dialogue," yet fascinated by the concept. The Quakers wait until someone in the group is influenced by the Holy Spirit before they speak. They believe that the Holy Spirit can come through anyone. My conservative friends, who were part of the "right wing" religious community, thought there was too much room for evil to influence me, even if my intentions were good. My response to them was always the same, "How did the disciples know if evil was influencing them when they opened themselves to the Holy Spirit?" The ultimate test is to proclaim Jesus as Lord!

Finally, there were my own doubts and fears to overcome. I suppose that was the greatest obstacle of all. I knew it would take time to learn to trust in the God whom I loved, to guide Dale and me in developing our prayer life. But we soon learned that God does answer prayer.

Answered Prayer

When I was at a critical point in my seminary training, I had some very difficult tests in Hebrew, and Old Testament Exegesis. It wasn't just me, all the students found this course difficult. It was the most demanding course of all and the professors were not merciful to those who did not meet their expectations. The night before the final exam, I prayed to God. I had exhausted my mental and physical abilities to learn the information, and I asked God for help. It was a pivotal point in my studies.

Days before, I was shocked to learn that other students were dropping out of school because it was too difficult for them. These were students who had attended Yale and Harvard, and they were outstanding students. Would the same thing happen to me? I was a student from Davis and Elkins, a small college in West Virginia. I considered those who were dropping out to be much more qualified and knowledgeable than me. If they couldn't make it, how could I?

In my prayer to God, I asked Him, as I always did, to use me to help others.

My prayer was:

"If it be thy will, guide me in the learning of the knowledge that will help me to know the Bible, the Hebrew language, and the history of the people of Israel, so that I can better interpret the Word of God to others. If it be thy will, help me to answer the questions to the test I will be taking tomorrow, so I can be the minister that you want me to be for the benefit of others, not for myself. Whatever happens, lead me in the way you want me to go, so I can be a channel of blessings to others."

After the prayer, I waited in silence, when suddenly a bright light surrounded me and I was overcome by a wonderful feeling of peace and love. Then, as my eyes closed, I saw before me a list of questions written on a piece of paper. A still small voice said, "Here is a list of questions. Study them well. They will not be easy for you." I read them with my eyes closed, and studied them thoroughly. Then after several minutes, I opened my eyes. I was amazed at what I had experienced, and quickly wrote down what I had seen. They were not easy questions at all. I spent the rest of the night studying these questions, and was amazed by my own enlightenment, as they seemed to take me in a new direction in my studies. It was early in the morning when I had finished, and I had just enough time to get one hour of sleep. I thanked God and promised I would do my best.

I walked into the exam room and waited for the test to be handed out. I still remember exactly where I was sitting in the room when I received the test. I sat there in awe as I read the questions one after the other, exactly as it had been revealed to me in prayer, and, in the same exact order! Other students were busy writing, but I wanted to cry. A tear came to my eyes as I thanked God. As promised they were not easy questions, but I began writing with confidence as I understood the background for each question. As I wrote, a more significant thing happened to me. It was not the test or the information I had absorbed, but the confirmation that God was on my side, and He wanted me to do well. That day I felt so grateful to God that I thanked him and told him I would endeavor to always do my best.

I knew that I could not rely upon God to intervene for me again, and I never did need to ask for that help again. That was the first and only time in my life that God ever revealed the questions to me before a test. And, that was okay with me, because the most important thing that I learned was that God, Emmanuel, was with me.

I rarely ever tell this story to anyone, because, most people react with disbelief. I can't blame them. At first, people reject the probability outright. But, after a little thought they'll say, "I wish I could do that," or "If everyone could do that, why take tests?" However, this is the only time in my life that this sort of thing happened to me. It was an answer to prayer that strengthened my faith in God. If everything were given to us on a silver platter, how would we ever learn? But, I had learned something far more important. Without a doubt, God wanted me in the pastoral ministry.

When the results of the test came back, over half the class flunked the test and inevitably flunked the course as well. Some of the students then dropped out of school. I was grateful to God that I had passed.

My CPE Work

I enrolled in the Clinical Pastoral Education (CPE) of Union Theological Seminary and received hands-on training at the neighboring hospitals, and was known as "Chaplain Karl." There are several remarkable stories I would like to share with you that were both uplifting and educational. It was my good fortune to have studied under some of the best counselors of the day.

The Man Who Had No Arms and No Legs

I visited one patient who had no arms and no legs, and he was on kidney dialysis. He was visibly upset because a Jehovah's Witness had been in to see him earlier and had told him that, because he was neither baptized nor fully immersed, he was going to go to hell. He expressed his desire to be baptized but did not want to be fully immersed in his condition. I assured him that he would be saved by his faith and by the baptism of the Holy Spirit, not by the ritual of immersion in water. I laid my hands on his head, prayed for him, and asked that his sins be forgiven through his faith in Christ. He thanked me and asked if he would have arms and legs in heaven. "Yes!" I told him. "You will receive the 'glorified body' as Christ received a glorified body - whole and complete." Two days later, he died.

It was my desire to give this man hope that would be of comfort, and to help him in his hour of need. It was not my place or anyone else's to condemn him. I felt it was wrong for people to visit patients in the hospital only to make patients feel guilty, and condemn them to hell. Jesus would not have condemned them; he would have given them hope and healed them.

The Man who Would Not Speak to Anyone

I was at the nurse's station one day when a nurse suggested I visit a man who would not speak to anyone and refused to cooperate with the staff. So, I walked into his room, and politely introduced myself as a Chaplain of the hospital. I offered my services to him and told him he could talk to me about anything he wanted.

"Are you in any discomfort or pain?" I asked.

"No," he answered.

"Is there anything I can do for you?"

"No," he answered.

I could see by his stern look and body language that he appeared to suffer from depression and was very angry.

I walked over to the window and said, "You know sometimes it's nice to go outside and get out of the hospital for a while." I could see that I got his attention, so I continued, "How about going outside of this hospital with me? I'll wheel you around so you can get some fresh air. Would you like me to do that for you?"

He slowly lifted his head and looked me straight in the eye, "Yes, I would like that," he said.

I told him that I would make the arrangements. I then went to the nurse on duty who said it would be fine. He was unable to walk, so I borrowed a wheel chair. I proceeded to wheel him outside of the hospital where I talked with him about what a great day it was. I talked about everything except the hospital. It was then he finally began to talk to me about how he felt. We stayed outside for quite a time before I brought him back in, and he thanked me. The next day, the nurses came to me and said, "What did you say to him? He's like a different person. He is talking and cooperative."

Sometimes we have to see the beauty of God's creation on the outside before we can deal with the struggles we have on the inside.

The Man Who Smoked Through a Hole

One of the areas I was assigned in the hospital was a cancer ward. I came upon a man who sat smoking a cigarette and was exhaling the smoke through a small hole in his throat. Smoking was allowed in the hospital at this time, so there he sat. He would breathe cigarette smoke in and then out it would come through the small hole in his throat area. The nurses told me that he had had his voice box removed because of cancer, and he had smoked most of his life. As I talked to the man, he would place a little round device on his neck and make sounds so that I could understand him. I asked if he understood what happened to him.

"It's the smoking that caused me to loose my voice box," he told me.

I was a bit surprised by his frankness and asked, "Why do you still smoke?"

He laughed and said, "It's too late now. Why quit?"

I did not want to argue with him, so I said, "I was just concerned for you and your future welfare, and I hope you do well."

Some bad habits are hard to break. Even after a serious surgery, such as his, we may still find it difficult to break some habits we know are bad for us. I was a smoker myself, and began to wonder what it would take for me to stop.

As I talked to the head nurse on the cancer ward, she showed me some pictures of the lungs of both a smoker and non-smoker. What I saw frightened me. The lungs of a non-smoker were pink and clear, while the lungs of the smoker were as black as tar, which they literally were. After this experience, I decided it was a good time for me to quit smoking. It wasn't easy. I had to quit several times before I was through for good, but I finally did it.

The Paralyzed Man Who Cheered Me Up

I was walking in the paraplegic ward of the hospital and I was feeling tired and a little downcast that day when I passed a huge black man who was a paraplegic. He called out to me, "Hey Chap, come here!" So, I walked over to the gurney where he lay.

"Why are you down today, Chap?" he said.

I was surprised that he had noticed I was down.

"Cheer up, Chap," he said. "Today is a wonderful day!"

I couldn't believe my ears, so I said, "Wait a minute, something is wrong with this picture. Why is it that you who are paralyzed are cheering me up when it's me who should be cheering you up?"

That is when he taught me one of the greatest lessons of my life.

"Chap," he said. "I've learned that happiness is a state of mind. If you think you're having a bad day, you are going to have a bad day. But if you think you're going to have a good day, you'll have a good day!"

"Thank you," I said, "I won't forget what you said." It was totally mind-boggling to me that this man, with all his problems, was able to cheer me up that day.

The Young Farmer Who Lost Both Hands

I'll never forget the young farmer who was wailing and crying out so loudly that the whole floor could hear this man weeping over the loss of his two hands. He lifted his two bandaged arms and cried out, "Why, God? Why me?"

I had no idea what to say to him, and we all felt for him. So I asked, "What happened?"

As I talked with him, he told me how it happened, "One of my hands got caught in a corn picker while it was running, and when I reached into the corn picker to pull out my hand the other one got caught, and I lost both of them."

His hands were both damaged beyond the ability to save either one. He also had a family to support and didn't know what he was going to do. All I could do was listen to him and try to feel his pain.

Some days, I would come back home shaking from my experiences in the hospital. As a result, I learned to appreciate the gifts God gave to Dale and me.

The Seminary Student Who Left Ministry

A colleague of mine was so devastated when a patient he was ministering to started physically beating him and blamed him and God for his condition. This upset him so much that he not only left the program, he left the ministry all together.

Before he left, a group of us tried to convince him that the patient's anger was not directed at him personally, but toward God. Blaming God is one of the stages of grief that people go through after a loss of a limb, a loved one, or even a job. They lash out at God in their pain.

As chaplains or ministers, we represent God and can become the target for that anger.

Unfortunately, he couldn't get over it and he left the ministry.

The Maximum Security Prisoner

One day I received a call that one of the inmates who was being treated at the Hospital asked to speak to a chaplain. There was a maximum security prison next to the VA Hospital. So, sometimes prisoners would come over to the hospital for treatment. I happened to be on duty that day. As I arrived at his room, I noticed a security guard in front of the room. The room itself had a steel door with a tiny window covered with wire. "You don't have to go in there," the guard said to me.

"It's okay, I don't mind," I said. So, the guard opened the door and let me in. There was a rough looking guy sitting at a table, with a chair for me. When the door closed, the first thing he said was, "You know I could kill you before that guard could get back into this room."

I was stunned by that statement, but quickly responded, "Yes-sir, you certainly could."

I didn't want to argue with him about that. He told me that he was in for life because he had killed several people. He had nothing to lose but his own life, and that did not matter to him. He could have been lying to me, but I wasn't going to question him about that either.

Maybe I could build up his self-esteem a bit, and I said, "I think there has to be some good in you, because otherwise why would you call to see me, the chaplain on duty?"

He admitted he did not know why he called me, but he wanted to talk to someone. "Maybe you can teach me something," I said, "I'm still learning."

He told me how his family had deserted him when he was young. He did not know what it was to 'love,' nor did he know the meaning of the word. All he knew was the hatred, the fighting, the con games you played to get what you wanted, the life of crime, and then, the world of prison.

"I don't care who I kill," he said.

"What about your conscience? Doesn't that bother you?" I asked.

"Conscience, what conscience?" he said.

I was amazed at his lack of heart. We talked about fifteen minutes and I said, "I don't know if I've helped you, but you have helped me." I thanked him for sharing his feelings with me, and I left.

Naive me, I had believed everyone has some good in them somewhere but, after talking to this man, I wasn't so sure any more. His soul was dark, as if he had no conscience, and no way to determine good from evil. How can you live without a conscience? Evidently, some people do.

There is a scripture in the Bible that says that people were so bad they didn't blush! (Jeremiah 6:15) In other words, they didn't feel bad about doing wrong. They had no conscience.

The Man Who Saw His Friends at the Foot of the Bed

I walked into another hospital room one day to visit a man who was very sick. His wife was sitting right next to him. The man was very intelligent and I had an interesting conversation with him, but I could see that he was very weak. I closed my visit with a prayer and he squeezed my hand very tightly as I prayed. After the prayer, he pointed to the end of the bed and described several of his friends that were there. He thanked them for coming. His wife and I looked at one another, because we could see that there was no one standing at the foot of the bed. His wife began to cry softly and said, "Can we talk in the hallway? We left the room and she asked, "Do you think the people he described at the foot of the bed were really there?"

"Yes, I do," I responded. I told her that I believe they were probably his friends waiting for him on the other side.

I asked her about her husband's condition. She told me that he was not expected to live very long. His illness was terminal.

"Were his friends good people?" I asked.

She said, "Oh yes, his friends were all good people."

"Don't worry," I said. "He's preparing to enter the Kingdom of God and his friends are waiting for him." She thanked me, and she was glad that I had affirmed that her loved one would be fine. The next day, the man passed away.

Trying the Discipline of Fasting

While studying in seminary, I decided to go on a spiritual fast that would last for fourteen days. During that time, I drank only water, and I prayed, offering myself to help others. The important thing about a spiritual fast is, it's not so much about abstaining from food as it is putting God first in your life.

It was hard not to think about eating, but after the first week, I lost any desire for food. I began to understand how some people develop problems with Anorexia Nervosa. I was surprised by this, but I can now understand why health officials don't want to advertise this bit of information. It could be disastrous for some people, and could result in dietary illnesses.

For me, it was a religious experience. I felt closer to God and my prayers extended from minutes into hours. Time as I knew it ceased to exist. I discovered that what really matters to the soul is the process of growing closer to God. I learned that the soul does not keep track of time, but records the events that offer growth.

I also experienced a oneness with God, and this is what is really important. It didn't matter whether I got better grades than my fellow students in class. What mattered was what was happening between God and me. I was no longer in competition with my colleagues; the only struggle was within myself. Before Jacob received his new name Israel, he had a struggle with an angel. As I studied the Hebrew Massoretic text, I learned that "the man" Jacob struggled with was really a part of himself. In the same way, I too had to overcome a part of myself in preparation for the work that lay ahead of me.

Making the Decision Whether to Complete the Doctor of Ministry Degree

I was enrolled in the Doctor of Ministry program (D. Min.) that required extensive training in advanced Greek and Hebrew as well as a host of other theological courses required for my Masters of Divinity Degree. It was a new program that simultaneously trained students for regular and advanced degrees, and required a great deal of work (although the school dropped the program a few years later). I reached a crossroads in which I had to choose between graduating in my third year with a Master of Divinity degree or continuing on for another year with an internship, one more course, and a thesis due at the end. I was married, with a young child, had very little money, and my spirit was ready to serve the Lord. Therefore, I decided not to continue pursuing the advanced degree as I felt ready to begin ministry.

Avoiding An Accident

In 1977, I was driving our little Ford Capri out of Richmond, Virginia from the seminary, on my way to see Dale who was "house sitting" for a family on vacation.

I was driving down a dual lane highway when suddenly a car shot out from nowhere and stopped dead in the middle of the road! I couldn't believe it! I was traveling about 60 miles an hour on a duel highway, and the car was right in front of me. It was as if the driver was surprised to see me coming and stopped in the middle of the road. I jammed on the brakes with all my might, and you could hear the screech of the tires upon the road! In a matter of seconds, I was drawing so close to the car in front of me that I could see the terrified face of a boy who looked as frightened as I did. I was surely going to slam into him and he and I would be killed!

I'm not totally sure what transpired during those next few seconds, but I knew if I just kept my foot on the brake heading right for that car in front of me, it was not going to solve the problem. Making a quick calculation, I kept my foot on the brake long enough to get my speed down, but at the last moment, just before impact, I took my foot off the brake and quickly turned the steering wheel to the left. I could feel the tires leave the road, so I quickly reversed the steering wheel back to the right, and again the tires left the road. So, I steered back to the left, until the car spun around and finally came to a stop. I found myself on the other side of the highway, facing the wrong direction!

It was a miracle that no one was hurt, and there was no damage to either car! No one was coming down the highway at that precise time either. I didn't waste any time driving my car back to the other side of the road and to the other car that was still sitting there.

The young boy sat behind the wheel, totally in shock, and repeatedly apologized for what had happened. He explained he had pulled out on to the road without looking fully to his left. When he saw me coming, he just froze and slammed on the brake!

"I thought you were going to hit me straight on," he said.

I still wasn't exactly sure how I was able to avoid him, but it definitely was a close call. I felt there had to be an angel guiding my car that day.

Then an eyewitness came forward and said, "I never saw anything like that before." He said to me, "Your car lifted up into the air at the last second and you were riding on the two wheels of the left side of your car. You just cleared the top of the other car by inches before coming back down to the ground. You spun around in the other lane, where you were fortunate there were no other cars coming! I saw the whole thing and couldn't believe my eyes!"

I knew that my tires had to have left the ground, and it was amazing that the car didn't flip over! I was more relieved than angry with the boy, so I told him sternly, "Never do that again!"

Then, we all went on our way giving thanks to God that we were still alive. I was shaken up, but I felt God's grace was upon me and the other fellow, too! I offered a prayer of dedication to God asking Him to direct my path so that I would be Jesus' good disciple. It was for me a transforming experience and I re-dedicated myself to serving God and Him alone.

Graduation at Last

I was anxious to graduate and start ministry. I briefly considered taking a job as a hospital chaplain, and I felt exceptionally qualified to serve as such as I had helped many patients during my internship at the Medical College of Virginia and the McGuire Veterans Administration Hospital. All the reviews I received from the staff and my peers were heartwarming. They reported that they observed in me an exceptional ability to help the ill and injured. However, I felt called to the pastoral ministry, where there is a shortage of ministers and the turnover rate is very high.

The day of graduation came and my mother and father could not have been more proud. I had accomplished a graduate education in spite of my guidance counselor's prediction that I would never graduate from high school.

That day, my mother told me the surprising story of my birth.

Birthing Story

My mother had been told that she could never have any more children after Laura was born. Her blood type was RH negative and the doctors told her it was just impossible to have another child. Four years later, she was pregnant again. She remembered what the doctors had said about her inability to have another child. She went to church and kneeled before God in prayer.

"Please enable me to have this child," she said. "If you do, I will give this child to you. Take him and use him as you wish."

It was the same prayer Hannah made when she dedicated her child to God, before giving birth to the prophet Samuel. (I Samuel 1: 9-20)

This story confirmed for me the three strong calls to ministry that I had experienced. I began to understand all the more why God had called me, and why He was with me, even when others were unsupportive. It helped to explain why I had always felt that I had a destiny I must fulfill.

Finding a Church

Now that I'd chosen my path, I needed to find a church. Before graduating from seminary, I began the process of writing my resume to let the presbyteries and pulpit nominating committees know that I was available. I was contacted by several churches who wanted to hear me preach, and we arranged for me to fill a vacant pulpit so that they could hear me.

When I preached at a vacant pulpit in southern Virginia, there were two small congregations that were looking for a pastor to serve both churches at the same time. This is called a "yoked charge." After my sermon, both churches issued me a call on the spot. I was surprised, and said I needed to pray about it for at least one night, and would get back to them the next day. I struggled with that call because I could see the tension between the two churches. I thought I could help, but recalled what one of my professors had said, "Don't take a problem church as your first call." I called them on the phone the next day thanking them for the offer, but I turned them down. I gave them no reason, except to say that I did not feel called to serve them.

Another church that showed an interest in me was in Pineville, West Virginia. After we met, the committee offered me the call to be their pastor before they'd even heard me preach! They seemed to love us and were truly delightful people. I was astounded, and not afraid to admit I was a little nervous. They were very kind to me and assured me that God was with me. What incredible faith they had! After my sermon, they promised me they would be issuing a call. To think I had fears of speaking before people!

Finally, a third church in Pennsylvania, also in a yoked charge, heard me preach along with members of the other church and invited me to come and serve them. So, now I had another call, and I had to decide which parish God wanted me to go serve.

What a pleasure to know that there were people who wanted my services. I prayed long and hard for God to guide me in the right direction.

Chapter 10

"Choose this day whom you will serve…
But as for me and my house,
We will serve the Lord."

Joshua 24: 15

First Church Call
Lower Path Valley Presbyterian Church
Fannettsburg and Burnt Cabins

Moving Day

The move to our first church was exciting. It was a new beginning for us, and we were eager to explore and fulfill all the challenges of pastoral ministry. I accepted an offer to serve two churches, one the Lower Path Valley Presbyterian Church in Fannettsburg, and the other, Burnt Cabins Presbyterian Church. The Fannettsburg church was larger, and Dale and I lived in the Manse across the street. The smaller church in Burnt Cabins was on the other side of the mountain. In my first meeting with the Carlisle Presbytery Executor, he explained that the Presbytery was considering closing both of these churches and was going to keep a close eye on our progress.

God had called me here and I was going to do the best I could to follow the Holy Spirit. It was interesting that, of the three churches I was called to, this one, more than the others, was struggling financially. But this did not discourage me, because I was trusting in God to guide me in my ministry.

Just before we moved our furniture to Fannettsburg, Dale began to feel ill. She lacked energy and vitality. She went to an internist before we left who diagnosed her with a virus in the colon. She also had a pregnancy test but that turned out to be negative. The doctor advised her to rest, but she still continued to have pain in her left side. We prayed that she would feel better soon.

We rented a U-Haul truck, and loaded it with all our belongings, including some items we'd left in storage in Kensington, Maryland. When we arrived at our new home, there were many people waiting to help us unload, and it proved to be the beginning of an exciting ministry.

The ordination date was set for July 24th, 1977 and would take place in the Church at Fannettsburg with most of the area ministers in attendance. There were wonderful speeches and all the pomp that goes with such an occasion, and I vowed to do my best to serve God in this community.

At the reception, one minister we had just met looked at Dale and asked, "When are you due?"

"I'm not expecting," she said. He turned bright red and immediately apologized to Dale, but as it turned out his comment was prophetic, although we didn't know it at the time. At any rate, our new friends seemed glad to have us, as they explained that they had been looking for a long time for the right pastor.

Our first month, both Dale and I had abdominal pain and diarrhea. We weren't sure if it was because of the water, or something else in our new environment. We even drank distilled water hoping it would help. Then, it occurred to me that my diarrhea mainly came upon me on Saturday nights and Sunday mornings, before preaching. It was true, I was so nervous about preaching that for three months, I suffered from a case of the runs before I preached. I even shook a little when I preached, before I was finally able to calm down my system.

Dale, however, was another matter. She suffered from abdominal pain that was increasing in intensity. It was a Sunday morning, and it was ten minutes before the Worship service began when I found Dale lying on the bathroom floor writhing in pain. I told Dale, "That's it! I'm taking you to the hospital, as soon as I finish preaching!" I asked her if that was okay with her. "Go," she said. It was a short service, and I asked the congregation to pray for Dale.

After Karl went to church, I called the doctor that I had been trying to get an appointment with for the last week. I had an appointment for Tuesday, but I didn't think I could make it until then. I was bleeding and in a lot of pain. I felt faint and ill. Dr. Bundy called back and told me to get to the hospital as soon as Karl got out of church. We raced to the hospital where they had a wheelchair waiting for me, and took me into an examination room right away.

After the service, I explained to the congregation how sick Dale was. The people told me to get to the hospital now! I raced Dale to the emergency room, and she explained to the doctor how the pain had become increasingly more intense over the last month.

After the doctor's examination, he said, "I have to operate immediately. She has a mass inside her. Either she has a tumor or she has an ectopic pregnancy. Either way, I need to operate now, because it can become life threatening. "Okay," we said, and prayed to God. As it turned out, Dale had been pregnant, but it was a tubal pregnancy! A baby cannot develop properly in that location.

When I came out of the anesthesia in my room, I saw three figures standing at the foot of my bed. I was upset when I learned I had lost the baby I had been carrying as I wanted to have another child. As I mourned my loss, I felt the comfort not only of my husband and son, but from the three "angels" who stood at the foot of my bed.

This was the first time that Dale had become visually aware of the presence of angels. We prayed and thanked God for Dale's healing, and for helping us get the proper medical care. I later realized that my zeal for church work had nearly blinded me to the proper care of my own family.

Conversing with the Dead

During Karl's years of ministry in Fannettsburg and Burnt Cabins, he did not have to preside over many funerals. At this time, I became increasingly aware of my ability to sense the presence of an individual who had just died and passed over. I had always been able to feel the presence of my grandfather, and my great-grandparents. So it wasn't really a surprise when it began to happen more and more frequently. I could sense others who had passed over. When observing a dead body, I became aware of whether or not the soul had left the body.

I also observed that those individuals who were secure in their belief in God had no trouble leaving the earth plane and "going to God" or onto the next dimension. But those individuals who were not well anchored in their faith couldn't always leave right away. It was as if they were asleep and unwilling to go or didn't realize that they were dead.

Sometimes I could communicate with these souls. I usually could hear that they were "all right" and would communicate this to the family, carefully stating, "I know your husband is fine and he is with our Lord."

When I noticed that a soul had not yet left their body, I would pray and assure them it was all right to leave. Their work was done and they should follow the light of Christ. Usually, by the time they were buried, they had left the earth plane and gone 'home.'

Dale would "get" messages from people on the other side, whether they were members of our church or not. In fact, this has gone on all through our ministry. But, I have never felt comfortable telling people in the church about this phenomenon from the pulpit. "Oh, by the way, my wife just got a message from your husband, he's okay." However, we would reassure them that their loved ones were fine.

Learning about Country Life

Karl and I grew up in the suburbs on the outskirts of the major cities in Washington, D.C. and Philadelphia, so we were minimally aware of farming as a way of life. When we moved to Fannettsburg, a major dairy farming community, we had a lot to learn. The first day we arrived, we found a large bag of green beans in our refrigerator. There was more there than we could possibly eat, and as I didn't know how to preserve food, I gave some beans to my family who helped us move in. Members of the congregation came in and helped as well. A couple came to baby-sit Jason for the day, while we moved in. They were a great help and an inspiration to us as the years passed.

As Karl and I settled in, we learned the basics of gardening. We learned to can and freeze the vegetables we grew in our garden and we bought local corn to freeze. As the years went by, I became quite proficient in preparing and preserving food. I even made pickles and homemade ketchup. This was really a necessity, since we didn't make a lot of money in the ministry and this helped put food on the table.

My mother had taught me how to sew when I was a girl and now was the time to use this skill. I made curtains for the living and dining rooms and Karl and I re-upholstered the sofa in the living room. Whenever something needed to be done, we did it ourselves. If we didn't know how to do it, we learned how to do it from others.

Karl's Hunting Story

The two churches I served were separated by the Kittatiny and Tuscarora Mountains, all part of the Appalachian chain. There were Mennonite and Amish people who farmed in the area, and we developed a close friendship with several Mennonite families. The area was full of wildlife, covered by trees except for the tilled farm lands in the valley where we lived. This was country living! The people were down to earth and hard working. Hunting deer was a normal part of their life. Deer meat was a staple in their diet, and hunting a way of providing food for their families. Everyone had a hunting story. As soon as they could carry a gun, young children were taught how to hunt, and young women became hunters as well as the men. In the hunting season, visitors from other areas would come to the mountains where we lived, and some owned cabins just for the hunting season. Schools were even closed during the hunting season, two days for "buck," and one day for "doe."

I had some small game hunting experience in high school, but had never hunted deer before. I talked with several of the church members who encouraged me to hunt on their land, and gave me a few tips on how to hunt, what to know about the state license rules, what to wear, and how to dress a deer.

On my first day of buck season, I got up early, found a good spot up high, and waited. I could hear the sounds of nature all around me. There was a calm feeling of peace out in the woods with nature for company, even if I didn't do anything else. Then all of a sudden, I saw several deer walking over the hill from left to right. There was only farm land down below the edge of the woods, and I could clearly see that there were no other hunters within my field of vision. That was my main concern, of course, as I didn't want to accidentally shoot another hunter. The orange vest we wore for safety was very visible in the woods and for quite a distance across the farm land. There, clearly visible, two deer were walking across my field of vision at about 120 yards away. I lifted my gun, put the deer in my sights and fired one shot. I saw the deer go down, so I quickly ran down to see if I had actually hit it. Yes, I had got it, but to my surprise it was the wrong deer. I shot a doe, not a buck. Oh Great! I dressed the deer as I was instructed, tagged it, and went home to talk with the other hunters to ask what I should do.

I walked into the kitchen by way of the garage and Dale asked me, "Did you get a deer?"

"Look at my clothes, and tell me what you think?" I told her.

She looked at me and said, "Of course you did," since I was covered with blood.

But the bad news was that I had shot the wrong deer. I felt awful! I went over to the farm house at noon because I knew the hunters would be coming in for lunch at that time and I told them what had happened.

"Don't do anything! I'll take care of it," the farmer said. "It's illegal you know."

I told him, "I'm a pastor. I can't do that!"

"Well it's up to you, but I wouldn't tell anyone," he added. "People do it all the time."

"But, it's not right," I said. "I have to admit my mistakes."

I went home and called the county game warden, and I explained who I was and what I had done. He could tell I was repentant, and was very nice to me. He arranged to meet me, and told me to bring the deer to him. He didn't fine me, and said that I had done the right thing by calling him. The deer would be used to help feed the people at one of the local nursing homes. I received a call from him a few days later that the residents of the nursing home had really appreciated the deer meat.

It didn't take long for the story to get around the whole Upper and Lower Path Valley area. The minister shot the wrong deer! For several days after, everywhere I went people would say, "Oh, you're the pastor who shot the wrong deer!" There was usually a grin on their faces and a gleam in their eyes that said they were glad they could kid the pastor for making a mistake. But, I was quick to point out that, because I was honest about my mistake, others had benefited.

The following Sunday morning, the church service was full of people, some whom I had never seen before. Apparently, they were hunters who had heard my story about shooting the wrong deer. It endeared me to them, and it was as if I were now one of them.

As time passed, Dale and I gained many friends as we adopted the lifestyle of country people. We learned to hunt, can and freeze food for our family, just as they did.

The Chain Smoking Man

I visited a man at his home one day, and noticed that his fingers were very brown. He was holding a cigarette in his hand, but before the cigarette was finished, he would light another cigarette from the old one. In the course of our conversation, I watched him do this several times. He was a true chain smoker. I asked him if he had tried to quit smoking, but he said he couldn't. He admitted that he had an addiction problem, and had even gotten hooked on the Valium he had been taking for pain, and it was difficult for him to get off that medication. He just couldn't stop smoking. He even woke up at night to smoke. Here was a man who really needed help, but I didn't know how to help him.

About eight months later, I heard that he was in the Chambersburg Hospital, suffering from lung cancer. I visited him several times, and on one occasion, I heard him screaming. I asked the nurse, "Why is he screaming?" She told me he was undergoing radiation treatment for his lung cancer and they had accidentally over-radiated him and his skin was pealing off his body. He was in excruciating pain, and I was horrified! I tried to visit with him, but he was in too much pain to even talk to me. He died the next day, and it was probably a blessing that he did. In those early years of treating lung cancer with radiation, the doctors were not always sure how to proceed, and the equipment was not always safe.

It was also common for those undergoing radiation treatments for cancer, to die of pneumonia. As a pastor, I saw the results of what the medical profession sometimes did to its patients. Sometimes the medical treatments were a wonder, but at other times, they caused suffering.

Mennonite Boy

There was a Mennonite boy who would often stop by my office in the Manse to talk about God. Although he had a learning disability, he had a very outgoing personality and he liked to sing. I enjoyed our conversations. I was in one of my generous moods and offered to give him my old beat-up guitar if he was willing to learn to play it and sing. His eyes lit up! He couldn't believe that I would give him my guitar. I showed it to him, and while it did have a hole in the back, it was still very playable.

"I always wanted to learn to play the guitar," he said. "Then I can sing to the music."

A few days later, another Mennonite friend asked me, "Karl, did you give this young man a guitar?"

"Yes, I was in one of my generous moods," I told him.

"That was good of you," he said. "But we're not sure you did us any favors. He sings all the time with that guitar, and frankly he can't sing worth beans!"

Stelle, Illinois

My sister was a member of a spiritual community in Stelle, Illinois, and she invited us to come and visit her. The people in this community were expecting the end of the world and the "rapture" to happen at any time. Their leader was expecting a space ship to land in the village, and to lift the people up to safety, while the rest of the earth burned. My sister informed me I had the rare privilege of being interviewed by the leader of the community, and that it was a huge honor. I had no idea this was going to happen. I thought I was just visiting my sister.

I questioned the validity of the leaders' proposed theory of the end of the world. I found apparent conflicts between his theory and Biblical scripture. The leader believed that only a small group of people would be saved, while the Bible teaches, "Everyone who calls upon the name of the Lord will be saved." (Joel 2:32 & Romans 10:13)

Fortunately, my sister, Laura, and her husband, Robert, did not buy into the philosophy of the original founder. They liked the community which provided them with support and a loving environment to raise their children.

I told the leader that what he was preaching was wrong and unbiblical, and I declined to be part of their community. I was immediately informed that I would not be accepted anyway. My sister and I continued to be friendly, but we decided that we would disagree agreeably.

Dale and I returned home very concerned for my sister's welfare. We needn't have worried. After one and a half years, my sister and her husband became disenchanted with the community and left on their own.

The Woman Who Went to Hell and Back

There is an interesting story of a woman I visited at the hospital in Chambersburg. She was a friend of one of our church members, who requested that I visit her, so I did. I entered the room and introduced myself, and told her I was available to talk with her and help her in any way I could.

When I asked what church she attended, she told me that she didn't attend one. She said that she was not a religious woman, and had not lived a very good life. Then she said she wanted to share with me something that had happened to her, which was the reason why she was in the hospital.

"What happened?" I asked.

She told me that she had been experiencing chest pains, and she had made her way to the doctor's office where she collapsed. Later, the doctors told her that she had had a heart attack and was declared dead. It was the most horrible experience of her life. She heard people screaming. It was dark and there was fire everywhere. She was terrified.

"What do you think happened?" I asked her.

"I think I went to hell," she said.

"Do you really feel you were there?" I said.

"Yes," she said. "I haven't told anyone this story because they would think I was crazy."

I assured her that we all have our own unique experiences.

She said, "The next thing I remember was the doctor telling me that my heart had stopped for a few minutes, but I miraculously had survived."

"Wow!" I said. "Can you tell me what you think God is trying to tell you now?"

"Yes," she said, "I believe God is giving me a second chance."

"Yes, I too believe that God is giving you a second chance." I encouraged her to find a church home and to accept Christ as her savior. I never saw her again, but my hope was that she had taken my advice.

That was the first and only time I had ever heard of a near-death experience that involved so much darkness. It was obvious to me that God was giving her another chance, but what was important were the choices she now faced in making changes in her life.

Prayer Room

Dale and I converted one of the rooms of our house into a prayer room. There was a small room upstairs that was just perfect for prayer and meditation. We felt that it was important for us to be in communion with God in order to be good leaders of the Church. It was a place to pray and meditate upon what God would have us do. It was also a place in which to give thanks to God, and to seek guidance. I would spend half an hour to an hour in prayer every day. In this room, I could focus upon the things that really mattered for the church, the community, and my own family.

It was also in this room that Dale and I developed a deepening awareness of God. If we had a problem or a question and needed guidance, we would go to God in prayer and ask for his help. We would pray and then ask questions aloud. It took us some time to find a way to ask questions, and seek the answers that we hoped God would give us. We didn't use any objects, images, or spooky means, but prayer alone. We were seeking answers from the highest source, God, in Christ Jesus. We have come to call this "Companion Prayer." When two or three people are gathered in prayer, Jesus has promised to meet us there. (Matthew 18:20) When two people are of one ideal and one spirit, their energies are combined and there is an increase in high spiritual energy.

The Stranger Who Died

There was a man in the community who lived alone. He was not a member of any church, and had no real support group, so I went to visit him in the hospital. When I got there, I found that he had died only moments before I arrived.

Not knowing the man's history, I asked the nurse, "What did he die of?"

"Old age," she said. I paused for a moment in total disbelief, and thought to myself, old age? How old does one have to be to be too old? I started to walk away when something told me to go back. I

151

wondered how old he was, and if he had truly died of old age. I went back to the room where he died to look at his chart. I discovered that he was only 74 years old, and that he had died of malnutrition! I was horrified!

As a chaplain and staff member of McGuire Hospital, I had the confidential privilege of viewing the charts of patients to help assist me in treating the patient mentally and spiritually. I didn't know how the local hospital here worked with the local pastors, but I went back to see if I could talk directly to the doctor who had treated this man. Fortunately, the doctor was in, so I explained who I was and asked him if he could clarify the cause of death. He looked right at me and sighed. "Malnutrition," he said, "All his levels were low when he was admitted." I knew then that I would need to do my own investigation into this man's past, hoping that I would not discover any criminal activity. I had a feeling right from the start of my ministry that I would be called to pursue any irregularities that I found, and see that the necessary changes were made.

I learned something important about my prayer life early on as well. If I was going to pray for someone, a church, a community, or the world at large, then I also needed to do something tangible about it as well. Prayer can be a force that sometimes calls us to action. Sometimes all we can do is pray. However, I learned that when I pray, God usually gives me the means to solve whatever I am praying about. I will be led to the right person, the right resource, the right asset, and the right direction that will lead to wholeness and peace with God.

Upon further investigation, I discovered that the man lived by himself since his children were grown and had moved away. He did not adequately prepare meals for himself. The family members had little, and could not afford to get him into a home for seniors. He lived alone in a small trailer, and there were no food programs in the community where he could go to get meals, and no "Meals on Wheels" program.

I went to the Session of the Presbyterian Church I was serving, and explained the problem. "We have never had Meals on Wheels," I was told. That phrase, "We've never done it before," is always a deterrent to making changes in bettering a church, a community, or a family.

Following through on my prayers, I organized volunteers in the community and we picked up meals from another community center in a town south of our location for delivery to those who couldn't help themselves. Before long, people realized the value of this program and began to emerge to ask for help and food assistance.

The daily personal contact with the elderly in need was invaluable to them. It improved the quality of life for these people immeasurably. Eventually, the program was expanded throughout the whole valley, and the elderly in need were receiving "Meals on Wheels" regularly. Thank you, God.

Barn Raising

Early in my ministry, during one heavy snowstorm, the barn roof of one of the church members caved in. People responded quickly and saved the livestock, but the barn was a mess. The owner did not have much money, but worked the farm and was just able to make ends meet.

"If you would like me to help," I said to the family, "I will organize a team of men to help rebuild the roof. I've had extensive construction experience." I then said, "It would be like an old fashioned barn raising."

We had some Mennonite and Amish people living in the Valley. If this happened in their own community, they would all chip in and help. Why couldn't we learn from their example to do the same for one another? At first, the farmer and his family were still in shock, but by the next day, they had agreed. The insurance adjuster had to review everything, of course, and then we had to coordinate the repair of the concrete wall and order the necessary materials. We set an appointed day, and with the help of most of the men in the church and community, we raised the roof in one day! The women cooked a fine meal for us and we all enjoyed the wonderful fellowship of one another. I began to see what it meant to be a community of caring people. I was proud of these people. They did a good job.

A Dream of Our Own Children

Dale had a dream of lights that came to her. As they got nearer she realized they represented the children that we would have. "We will be with you soon," they said.

The doctors said that the chance of Dale having another ectopic pregnancy was 27 percent, and she had lost one ovary when she had the miscarriage. However, we already had one child, and the dream indicated she was in for a big surprise. She would eventually give birth to two more children, Christiana and Julie.

Again, I had dreams of our future children. They were females and looked like twins, but weren't. I took that to mean they would be born close together, but I didn't realize how close, until later.

Christiana and Julie were Born

Dale was in labor, and the contractions were coming one after another. "She can't have this baby," the doctors said. "She's not ready." So, they decided to stop the delivery. At the time, the procedure for stopping the contractions was to give an alcohol I.V. (intravenous) in the hospital.

I stayed the night with Dale at the hospital, and I could not believe what they were doing to her. It was as if the hospital were a bartender, and Dale was being forced to have one drink after another of straight alcohol. She didn't even get a chance to enjoy drinking because the alcohol was flowing straight into her veins. It was a night like no other. I've seen Dale a little tipsy, but never like this before. They should have just told us to go straight to the bar and get drunk!

Dale was laughing and laughing and I couldn't help but laugh with her. I told her I was getting jealous, because it seemed like she was having a party without me. The sun was rising, and it was getting quite early in the morning. Dale was sick, and was about to pass out from the alcohol, but it had no affect upon stopping the labor. Another doctor we knew in the practice came into the room and said, "This is ridiculous!" He immediately stopped the I. V. himself. He said, "This baby is very determined to be born today, and there is nothing we can do to stop this child's arrival."

Our daughter, Christiana, was born the next day. Her reactions were very slow. She opened one eye, gave me a small smile, and went back to sleep. She later developed jaundice and was placed under a bilirubin lamp. They also placed two surgical masks on her that made her look like she was wearing a bikini. Another mask covered her eyes, like sunglasses, and she looked like she was at the beach.

My mother arrived the day I gave birth to Christiana. She came to help take care of Jason and me while I recuperated. Because Christiana developed jaundice, we had to wait for her bilirubin levels to come down before she came home. She stayed in the hospital one day longer than I did. I believe the alcohol I ingested contributed to her jaundice.

Christiana was considered our prayer baby by some members of the church. They knew of my difficulties with the ectopic pregnancy and felt I needed added prayers to ensure a safe delivery and healthy baby. When everything went well, we were all eternally grateful to God.

Much to our surprise, I became pregnant again. I guess the dream I'd had previously, meant I was going to have another child, a girl. This baby was due on November 18th.

Julie was born 14 months after Christiana on November 17t. Hers was the easiest birth of all our children. She seemed to be the calmest of all as well. People gradually took the two girls for twins early on, and they still are mistaken for each other, even today.

No Place for Kids

After I had been in town for several months, it became obvious to me that there was a problem in the town that needed to be addressed. There was a crowd of young people who sat on the empty steps of the church parking lot after hours, drinking alcohol, making noise, and disturbing the peace, until 2:00 a.m. in the morning. I consulted the session and they informed me that this behavior had been going on for years. The police were unable to control it, because CB's were in use by most everyone in town, so if a police car entered the valley, everyone knew it instantly and tipped off the kids. The bigger problem was that there was nothing else for these kids to do.

There were three bars in the town, one church and absolutely no place else for kids to go. So, I started visiting the church parking lot, talking to the young men who were drinking and disturbing the peace. Because I was there, the conversation always turned to religion. They challenged me to prove the existence of God. So, I would refer to Psalm 53, "A fool says there is no God." And, then I would try to show evidence of God all around us. Many of these "kids" were abused at home and were very skeptical, however. Most had been ridiculed by their parents regularly, and had low self-esteem. One told me, "I don't like being at home because all I ever hear there is that I am no good, and I can't do anything right." It was really apparent why the kids came to town to party with their friends. They wanted to feel good, but didn't know any other way. I assured them that they were God's creation and were good in His sight, and that they had great potential to do a lot of good. I listened to their problems, but I know Dale was afraid for me.

My major concern was for Karl's safety. I was concerned when Karl went out night after night to talk to the youth. You could hear them yelling, laughing and carrying on from our house. We lived three houses away, across the street from where they would hang out and disrupt the community.

We also had three children under the age of five and two were babies. I remember standing by our daughter's bedroom window facing the street, being frightened to death, holding one of my babies in my arms as they carried on. I didn't know if our children would be fatherless before the night was out. I would stay awake until Karl came home.

Dale was nervous whenever I went out to talk with them. She had heard that a Methodist minister had been killed ministering to the youth in that area. As a result, the Methodist church closed it doors for good. Members of my own church were concerned about me as well, although I did have supporters who congratulated me for being the first minister that ever tried to do anything to help the people who hung out on the streets at night. I told the elders that if anyone wanted to go with me they were welcome, but I had no takers.

I made a recommendation to the elders that I believed might help solve some of the problems for the youth who had no place to go and nothing to do. I suggested they take part of the church parking lot that was not being used and build a basketball court on that spot so the kids would have something to do. They agreed, on the condition that I raise the money for the basketball court. They also agreed to dismantle the abandoned steps which were not only an eye sore, but also encouraged the kids to sit and drink.

It didn't take me long before I was able to raise all the money necessary to build the kids a basketball court. I even solicited donations from the bars in town toward that goal. Some people criticized me for approaching the bars, so I responded, "Well the devil has had it long enough, it's about time we use the money for good." I never heard any more complaints. The young people were delighted that finally, someone was doing something for them, and I continued to talk with whomever happened to come by and play. Those who did not care to speak to "the preacher" just kept their distance. I sometimes felt like I should be wearing a Marshall's badge, because at one time I broke up a potential knife fight between the town kids and those from another town. I defused the situation by talking out a solution with them. Eventually, the night problems began to subside.

Stop Signs

On that same corner of town in Fannettsburg, where we built the basketball court, there was another potentially hazardous situation. The main intersection was dangerous to cross. Trucks would barrel through town at 60 miles an hour, when the speed limit was 25 miles an hour. Truckers would get off the turnpike and cut through our little town as a short cut. I asked the session if they had ever tried to do anything about it. "Oh, yes," they said. "We have tried for many years, asking for a street light in town, but the state officials always refused because of the expense." I suggested that the session try asking for stop signs instead. They would not cost very much, and the signs would serve to slow the traffic down. The session agreed to support me in a letter writing campaign.

I consulted a lawyer who was familiar with the history of the intersection. There had been accidents at the intersection for many years in a row. I had him prepare petitions, and I circulated them throughout the community. When I had collected a good number of signatures, I presented the petitions to the Pennsylvania Department of Transportation (PennDOT) officials.

Shortly after, a speeding truck crashed into one of the buildings at the corner of the intersection. The building was totally destroyed. Here was another example of the need for slowing down the traffic in our area. A few months later, without notice, PennDOT installed stop signs at the intersection, with warning signs further up the road. It was a long overdue victory that would save lives and provide better safety for all the people in town.

The Church Door That Would Not Open

One Sunday morning after the worship service, a curious event took place that was truly a miracle. I always ask God to guide me in the Worship Service. I prepare a sermon as I was trained to do in seminary, but then allow the Spirit to move me to preach what comes to my mind during the sermon.

I began preaching one Sunday, and felt that I should ignore what I had written earlier in favor of a simple point. I then asked the whole congregation to raise their hands into the air. This was quite unusual, as I had never asked them to do this for the benediction, and I have never done so since. But this time, I said a prayer that God would watch over us and protect us. I closed the worship service 15 minutes earlier than usual. To this day, I don't know what caused me to do this, and I'm convinced it could only have been the Holy Spirit.

I greeted people as I usually did outside on the front steps and then went into the church. I started talking to a few people who were still inside, and the doors were closed. Normally, at this time, I would be standing outside the church greeting the congregation, but this day because the service had ended earlier, I had returned into the church building. As we chatted, one member reached over to open the door and leave, and I noticed that she was having trouble getting the door open. "I can't open the door!" she said.

I was surprised because we had never had any trouble opening the doors before. So, I started walking over toward the door to help her.

Suddenly, we heard a loud thundering crash coming from outside the church. Instinctively, I ran from the front doors, as did everyone else. The church shook violently and then stopped. We all looked at one another wondering what in the world was going on. It got very quiet. I went over and opened the door with absolutely no trouble at all, only to discover a car sitting on the front steps of the church, leaning on the railings. We were all shocked!

On a normal Sunday, at that time, the front steps of the church would have been filled with people. I would be shaking everyone's hands and there would have been a crowd of people standing around talking. Fortunately, no one was there and no one was hurt. Most people had already left the church, and only a few remained inside. The lady driving the car was shaken up, but not hurt. She explained that she had lost control of the car when the accelerator became stuck. The car went up onto the church steps smashing the black iron handrails, and sending several of them shooting into the front doors of the church like missiles. Thank God the doors of the church were shut! People could have been killed! We had truly witnessed a miracle!

Dale and I, along with some members of the church, were there to witness a few seconds earlier that the door would not open. Why couldn't we open the door? What compelled me to ask the people to raise their hands and pray, and why did I dismiss the congregation early? I know it had to be the grace of our heavenly Father and the presence of Christ protecting us.

There were witnesses who saw this chain of events. Yes, it is very difficult to give proof of God's existence, but there are many witnesses to events that happen here on the earth that cannot be explained, except by the love and grace of God. Indeed, God is here!

The next Sunday, we were all thanking God for watching over us and our small church congregation.

Loaning People Money

I often found myself helping people who were traveling from one part of the state to another, as we were not far from the Pennsylvania Turnpike. All the people I loaned money to always said, "I'll pay you back." Then, I noticed over time, that no one ever repaid the loan.

I began to feel bitter about helping people. Why should I help them, I thought? They all lied to me and said they would pay me back. I prayed about it, and felt God was telling me to give without expecting anything in return. If I was going to expect something back, then it really was not "giving" to others at all. Did God call on me to be in the "loan" business?

So, I learned to modify how I would help people. First, I would no longer offer "cash" to people, because I did not want to support any substance abuse habits, but I still wanted to help them. Instead, I would offer food, clothes, and gasoline. Sometimes, I would even pay for an overnight stay at one of the local motels. When people said, "I'll pay you back." I would say, "Oh, no. Don't pay me back. This is a gift from me or the church to you. Thank God."

My whole feelings changed. I no longer felt bitter about giving to others, because it became an act of God's love. I was keeping others from sin by not accepting their promise to pay me back, and then not doing it. I would even say, "Don't you dare say to me you are going to pay me back, I don't want you to sin. This is a gift! Maybe you can help someone else."

I eventually developed a reputation in the area. At the local gas station right off the turnpike, if a traveler needed any help, the station attendant would say, "I know someone who can help you. Go down to Pastor Karl in Fannettsburg. He'll help you!"

I had a dream once warning me not to help someone I knew. I was surprised by this dream, so I ignored it and went ahead and loaned this person a large amount of money anyway, so they could buy a used car. Dale even said to me, "Don't do it." I didn't listen to her either. This person started to pay me back, but ended up getting sick, and couldn't pay me back the larger portion of the loan. I was a very trusting person, and I feel that people should always follow through with what they agree to do. So I told him he could pay me back as he was able. Years went by without me ever being paid.

It was something that was hanging over my head, unsettled. I had another dream, but this time it was God who had something to say to me. "Karl, do you not remember the parable where the King forgave the servant his debt, and then the servant went out and did not forgive another their debt? When the King found out about it, the King was angry, and changed his mind, and did not forgive the debt of his servant, but threw him in jail instead. You are that servant. I have forgiven you your sins, and blessed you, and yet you have not forgiven this man his debt?"

I woke up shaking. I realized that I was wrong holding on to this debt. I was not being forgiving. And, I must confess, I did not listen to the dream I had had years ago or to Dale. I was the one in the wrong! The next day, I wrote the person and totally forgave him of all debt, and wished him well.

When I Met Jesus

One day I got a phone call from the local gas station off the Turnpike. I answered the phone and said, "Hello, this is Pastor Karl."

"This is Jesus." the voice sternly announced.

I paused for a second, and responded, "Yes, can I help you?"

Then the voice said, "I'm on my way to meet Mary, and I need some help with transportation. Do you think you can help me?"

I asked, "Where are you?"

He said, "I'm here at the gas station off the turnpike."
I told him, "I'll be right there. I'll do what I can to help you." I was curious, naturally, and wondered what this "Jesus" had to say. I suspected he was a con artist, but then the theological side of me asked, "What if he is the real Jesus? How will you know?" As I drove up, I decided that I would not judge or condemn him, but rather ask him questions, and see how I could best help him within my means.

I pulled up and identified myself and he quickly jumped into my car. I did not expect that. He immediately started telling me that he was Jesus. He wanted me to believe he was "The" Jesus of Nazareth on his way to meet Mary, his mother. I wanted to be fair to him, so tactfully, I asked, "Okay Jesus, tell me what you believe." He started to tell me all kinds of things that were not consistent with the Bible.

I smiled knowing that he was by no means Jesus of Nazareth. He was either someone trying to con me or he was mentally ill. He did not appear to be a threat to himself or others and he was cooperative and coherent. It was just that what he was saying was weird. I was able to discern, without condemning him, that his theology revealed he was not the Jesus of Nazareth that he claimed to be. He assured me that, if I put him up in the local motel for the night, he would be on his way the next morning. I told him I had an agreement with a local motel, if it was available, and that I could give him only one night's stay. I would even throw in breakfast for him the next morning. Fortunately, there was room for him in the Inn.

Dream of the Man Lying Down

I had a dream of meeting a man who was only comfortable when he was lying down; he couldn't stand up for very long. Then I woke up, and told Dale my dream.

At this point, I was learning to work with my dreams, as Dale worked with her dreams. We were seeking to follow what God wanted us to do. Our dreams had a way of providing guidance and help to us, as long as we could figure them out.

I told Dale that I thought the dream was a warning about someone I would meet. But I was confused by the part that he was only comfortable when he was lying down.

About two weeks later, I met a person who was renting a cottage in the area, and who needed help. I proceeded to help him with clothes and food. I talked with him at length; and he told me many stories about being in the military during Vietnam. He always told stories about how great a person he was, and all the things he had achieved, but now suffered from back problems. I told him, "I had a dream about someone I would meet. I wonder if the dream I had was about you?" He looked at me with dismay. He and his girlfriend were obviously poor because they had so little.

Then, I got a phone call from a man who claimed to be his landlord. He desperately wanted the man and his girlfriend out of his house. I was told, "You can't trust him," he said. "He is always lying."

I suddenly realized that, indeed, this was the man my dream was warning me about. He was only comfortable when he was "lying," not lying down! After meeting him on several other occasions, I was able to catch him in his lies. I picked up his girlfriend as I saw her walking along the road and gave her a ride. She and I talked and she would tell me one thing while he would tell me something quite different. Their stories were never the same. I helped him only a few more times, then decided to stay clear of him.

The next thing I heard, some of the town's people were very upset with him, and wanted him out of town. Then his girlfriend disappeared. Some of the villagers thought that he had killed her, and they wanted vengeance upon him. Some even said, "We can take care of him." I was horrified. Was this a wild western town where people took the law into their own hands? Sadly, I was seeing this happen before my very eyes. I asked the townspeople to give me one more day to try to locate the missing girl before they did anything.

The police had already been contacted, but had no knowledge of the girl's whereabouts. All the couple's friends and family were contacted, and no one knew if she were even alive. And now the townspeople were really fed up with this person, and they wanted him dead. The man said he was innocent. But, being a known liar, who could trust him? No one believed him.

I went to the prayer room and prayed. God had helped me before, but would He help me find a missing person? People's lives were at stake. Would the Lord be gracious to me and guide me in order to help others? Could I truly be a channel of blessings for others? In prayer, I recalled the biblical story where Joshua uses the Urim and Thumin to locate the missing items that were stolen from Israel. The Urim and Thumin have been a mystery to scholars and most religious leaders because they do not understand how God can use prayers and dreams to reveal the truth. Yet, Joshua's intention was good and honorable, so Joshua found his answer. Would God allow me to use such methods to discover the location of this missing person?

I was nervous, but felt confident that God would not let me down. I talked with Dale about my situation and she suggested that we use Companion Prayer. Perhaps, God would allow us to help these two persons and the townspeople as well.

Dale and I prayed often together, and decided that it was time to ask God directly for help. We had often consulted God using Companion Prayer, a form of prayer that we were developing between ourselves and God. We would pray and ask for guidance. We trusted in the promise that He would send the Counselor, the Holy Spirit to teach us.

So, we prayed again, and this time, we opened ourselves to the Holy Spirit. Then gradually the information came: "She is alive and well, and we should seek to find her in a safe haven of protection for people who have been abused."

I thanked God for his guidance and the presence of Christ who is our rock and shield. I asked that I be of help to the people of this community and truly be a spiritual leader and channel for others to follow Christ, our Savior.

I immediately got on the phone and started calling the "safe houses" of people who needed protection from abusive relationships. All I needed was to confirm whether this person was alive, but not where she was hiding. I recalled that she had lived in Pittsburgh at one time, so I called a few places there, and Bingo! I found her within twenty minutes. The spiritual guidance we had received in prayer had led us right to her.

Greatly relieved, I informed the townspeople that she was in a safe house. The people of the community were glad, but still unhappy about this lying man, and demanded he get out of town. He finally left.

Dale and I were able to defuse a potentially disastrous situation, and I learned something else very important. I learned that I could go to God in Companion Prayer with Dale and He would not forsake us, but would guide us in the right direction in answer to our prayers.

Missing Person

Both Dale and I were using our prayer room on a regular basis to pray and meditate upon God so that we could be the best channels of blessings to others. Prayer had become an important part of our ministry.

I was running two prayer and Bible study groups that met regularly all year long, and I helped other pastors begin prayer and Bible study groups in Mechanicsburg and Chambersburg. I was excited about teaching people spiritual principles through basic Bible lessons. In the process, I had been giving counsel to several individuals in the group, as to how they could become even more spiritual as they prayed and meditated upon God. One person came to me and asked if I could help locate a missing person. She had been missing for several weeks. The family was deeply affected and had consulted several psychics, to no avail.

They knew that I had always encouraged people to consult God in prayer, and that as we do, miracles can happen. I agreed to pray to God and see if I could find any answers, but I made no claims. I didn't promise anything nor did I charge any money. Dale and I would just pray to our Heavenly Father. Could we find out where she might be or even if she was alive or dead?

Dale and I learned to set a time aside for what we called "Companion Prayer" with God. It was usually a time after the kids were in bed, when we could pray without interruption. Dale would ask any question to which we were searching answers. I would lead us in a time of prayer for 15 to 20 minutes. Then we would be silent. Dale would follow the silent prayer time with questions we wanted to ask.

Later that evening, during our prayer session, I began to speak to Dale about the missing daughter. Our prayers were rewarded, and I got the answers to the mystery of the girl's disappearance. Dale grabbed a pen and paper and wrote down what I said. I spoke in detail about what had happened, how the girl had died, what weapon was used, who had killed her, and where her body might be found. It was incredible to say the least! How could we have gathered such information, and from where?

The next day, several members of the missing girl's family came to our house, and they questioned us about what we knew. Karl and I were not prepared for this meeting, and we were hesitant to reveal any of the knowledge we had obtained. At one point, the dead girl tried to enter my body so she could speak to her family, but I wouldn't let her. We sent them away, their questions unanswered.

We went to bed that evening when suddenly, I was awakened by a voice that called my name, "Dale!" I saw a man. He was dressed in brown robes with a brown turban, and he had a dark beard and dark eyes. When he spoke to me, his voice was clear and strong, "You are in grave danger," he said. "You must destroy the information you have received." Then he disappeared.

This woke me up, of course, and I was visibly shaken. I woke Karl and we immediately burned the information I had received earlier.

Why were we told to do this? It would have been too easy, with our detailed information for the family and police to point the finger at us. The information we received confirmed that the girl had been murdered. People may not have believed that our information came through prayer, and knowing so much made us look guilty.

Perhaps our whole family would have been placed in danger, and God wanted us alive rather than dead. This was one of the few times that we would ever agree to find out any information about a missing person. Karl and I decided that our gifts were better used in the life of the church.

Life or Death Flashback

I knew a woman who was a wonderful church member. She had some Castor Oil plants in her yard, and one day, I commented to her how beautiful the plants were. The plants are gorgeous, and have a strong Christian significance. The Palm of the leaf resembles the hand of Christ, as if it were His hand, pierced in the middle with five red strands or fingers. The reality is that the beans are highly poisonous and can be lethal. She graciously offered me a plastic bag filled with Castor Oil bean seeds, so I could plant them. I accepted them gratefully. "I will plant them in the spring," I said. So I took the beans home and placed them on one of the top shelves in my study as a precaution. It was a shelf up high with books I rarely used, and only when preparing my sermons.

One day, I was typing my sermon on the old typewriter in the Pastor's Study, and our one-year-old daughter, Julie, was playing on the floor at my feet. Dale was out at a community chorus Christmas Cantata practice. I turned around in the swivel chair only to find Julie eating a Castor Oil bean. I was horror stricken! "Oh, My Heavenly Father, what have I done?" I thought, as I snatched the bean out of her mouth.

Had she eaten more than this one? I couldn't tell by looking at the plastic bag, and Julie just smiled at me. My heart sank. If I only knew if Julie had eaten any beans, I thought. Had it been one bean, or a bunch of beans? Then I would know if her life was in danger. I prayed to God and closed my eyes, and in my mind I had a "flashback." It felt like a movie being replayed slowly. It went like this: "I saw myself typing the sermon on my typewriter; I could distinctly hear the sound of the typewriter as it went click, click - click, click, and click. I could also hear another sound, crunch, crunch, crunch- crunch, crunch, and crunch. I put those pieces together in my mind, and realized that was the sound I heard when I turned around and saw Julie with the bean in her mouth! She hadn't eaten just one bean; she had eaten a lot of beans!

I began to panic! I was shaking, because I realized that my daughter was sitting there smiling at me, but she'd just been poisoned!

I had to act and act quickly. I remembered Dale had stuck one of those "Mr. Yuck" labels on the phone, so I dialed the number of the poison control center. The call was answered immediately, "How can I help you?"

"My daughter has just swallowed a bunch of Castor Oil bean seeds!" I yelled.

"How many?" She asked.

"A lot," I gasped.

She quickly explained, "Three beans can be fatal to a child because it breaks down the blood."

"Is it okay to make her throw up?" I asked.

"Yes!" She said.

I told her I had some ipecac syrup that I would give her immediately.

"Good, then get her to the hospital as soon as possible," she said.

I hung up the phone and immediately dialed for an ambulance. Then I rushed to the medicine cabinet for the ipecac syrup. Dale always kept a bottle of it on hand since we were 45 minutes away from the hospital.

I gave Julie the required teaspoon of ipecac, and plenty of water. And I prayed! Within minutes, Julie was throwing up. I was relieved that she was getting them out of her little body, but I watched horrified to see that she had eaten at least ten beans! Only three can be fatal! I prayed that she had gotten them out of her system in time.

The ambulance arrived shortly after, and I rode to the hospital with Julie, where the doctors were waiting when we arrived. They said, if I had not done what I did, she would most certainly have died. After close examination, they declared all her blood levels were normal, and she was out of immediate danger. It was getting late and the physician said he wanted her to stay in the hospital overnight. I agreed, only if I could stay with her. So, I stayed with Julie all night giving thanks to God for putting up with my foolishness. I vowed never to keep Castor Oil beans in the house again.

I was at the Community Chorus rehearsal when I was notified that Julie was having trouble breathing and was taken to the hospital in an ambulance. To me, breathing trouble meant the difference between life and death. So, I didn't know if my baby was dead or alive. I went home where our neighbors were watching Jason and Christiana. Upon further questioning, I realized they had gotten the information wrong. Finally, Karl called from the hospital, and told me what had happened. I couldn't go to the hospital that night because I needed to be with Jason and Christiana. But, I knew Karl was there and would watch over Julie. I went to pick them up at the hospital the next day. I was very relieved to see that Julie was all right. I can only thank the Lord, his angels and his guides for his help, and for saving my baby.

Thinking back over what happened, I was amazed that I was able to have such a clear flashback of the incident. Somehow, I was not conscious of what was going on at the time, since my mind was on the sermon. I was writing, but when I closed my eyes, and listened to what my subconscious mind had heard, and transferred that to my conscious mind, it was as if I tuned in to what had happened as it was stored in my subconscious. While I was typing, my mind was focused upon the message of the sermon, not on my immediate surroundings. Yet, I vividly recall being able to flash back to recall everything that was going on while I was typing. It was then that I recalled the strange crunching noise that I'd heard coming from behind me. Sometimes I believe God gives us abilities we aren't aware of to get through the trials and tribulations of life. The mind is a vast, wonderful instrument, and truly a gift from God.

Cable TV Ministry

When I prayed, I asked God about the direction He wanted to take the church. I knew that there were some people who could not come to church because of a physical handicap, which made it difficult for them to climb to the church sanctuary up on the second floor. The church was uniquely hidden in a valley between two mountains. The TV reception was generally poor, so the community formed a co-op and chipped in to pay for an antenna to be placed on top of the mountain for better reception. I was praying and it came to me that the church might consider having its own channel on the local cable network. I presented this idea to the Board of Directors, who were also the elders of the Fannettsburg Church. They promised that if I came up with the money to install the equipment, the co-op would allow the church to cablecast on its own channel for at least 10 hours a week. The board and session unanimously approved.

I went to the Synod of the Trinity and asked for assistance. After a long and protracted process, we were to be the first church in Pennsylvania to broadcast on cable TV, and we were granted money for the equipment we needed.

It was an ambitious project that required a great deal of technical know-how, but we eventually figured it all out, and soon we were cablecasting the Worship Services on TV that reached out to about 4,000 homes throughout the valley.

I was touched by how a girl who had cerebral palsy would watch the worship service faithfully, and was delighted when I came to visit her. She remained a fan of mine from then on. It was incredible how this little TV broadcast of the church could bring the community so close together.

The choir would watch the rebroadcast every Sunday evening to hear how they sounded and critique their earlier performance. Sermons I had preached were replayed over and over again, as members of the congregation requested specific services be rerun. Special community choir concerts were also broadcast throughout the community, and we even aired a local exercise class! I also used it to air daily devotions throughout Lent and Advent. I recall one church member who said in the beginning of the project that it was a terrible idea for the church and would never work. Yet, one year later after we began broadcasting, that same person said to me, "This was one of the best things this church has ever done." The church was alive, and able to reach out to many people in need.

Asking God for Help

After we began the TV ministry, I quickly became overwhelmed by the added duties. I prayed to God to send me someone who could help me, someone who could help the church with the television ministry, the programming, the electronics, even the "grunt" work - all those little things that are important to achieving any goal.

About two weeks later, we had a visitor who came to our house, walked into the study and said to me, "I've come here to ask if I can be of service to you and the church. I'm not sure why I'm here, but I feel led by God to do something to help others."

"You are not going to believe this," I told him, "but you are an answer to prayer! I do need help in the church, setting up a TV ministry that will be a profound change for the people in this community, and a wonderful outreach program."

He was just the right person. I thanked God for answering my prayers and sending someone to help. I found this had happened to me on several occasions. When I had exhausted my resources mentally, physically and needed help, I prayed to God to send someone to help me achieve the goals of the church. It often took a great deal of patience, but through the grace of God, the right person always showed up, and offered to help do the work of the Lord.

Dream of Falling Through the Roof

I had a dream that woke me up and left me shaking. I always paid special attention to these dreams because they always turned out to mean something important to me. It could be a dream guiding me in ministry, or a warning dream about the future. It could even be a teaching dream. I'm not always sure, but I try to figure them out, because they definitely mean something.

I dreamed about falling through the roof of the church. It was scary and it woke me out of a sound sleep. I told Dale about the dream, and said to her that it was probably a symbolic dream warning me about falling down on the work of the church. If that were true, however, I couldn't understand what I was doing wrong. I had developed the TV ministry, which was going well, and we had more people than ever coming to church. We had accomplished a great deal to secure the future of both churches. What was it that I was not doing right? If the dream were precognitive, I knew I would figure it out eventually, because my dreams tended to precede events by one or two weeks.

Later that week, the church was hosting a community concert and choirs from different churches were invited to sing Handel's Messiah. On the day of the concert, I received a phone call from one of my technicians; he was sick and would not be there to adjust the lights and set up the video system for broadcasting the concert. I told him to stay home, get well, and I would get everything ready.

I went into the church before 12:00 noon and started working on the equipment. Lights had been installed in the ceiling, but they still needed to be adjusted properly for the concert. So, I climbed up into the attic of the church to adjust them. As I walked across the attic floor, my foot suddenly slipped and I fell feet first through the ceiling of the church! Fortunately, I was able to grab the beams on either side of where I had fallen, but my legs were dangling through the ceiling. I looked down and saw the church pews 30 feet below me. Thank God I was able to pull myself up and climb back to a safe platform.

I was very upset with what had happened. Several ceiling tiles had gone flying and there was loose insulation that seemed to go everywhere. I went back to the house and called the property chairperson, and he brought his scaffolding over to repair the ceiling tiles. I then called everyone I could find to help clean up the insulation that covered the whole church. We finished cleaning up just in time for the concert. As the last person put the vacuum away, our first guest coming to hear the concert walked through the door.

After the concert, I finally sat down in my study chair to rest, because I had been working nonstop since the accident occurred and I was exhausted, and then it hit me - the dream! I had been warned that I might fall, not through the "roof," but the "ceiling" of the church. And, it was not that I was doing something wrong, but that I was being warned to be careful or I could physically fall down and get hurt. This came as a shock to me. Most of my dreams are usually symbolic, but this dream was clearly a precognitive warning. It's always a lot of work to figure out what your dreams mean. I've been learning how to interpret dreams all my life.

Out of Body Experience

I recall two separate times in my life when I have had what I would call an "out of body experience." For my first experience, I was a young boy living in Kensington, Maryland. I was very sick and sleeping in bed. Suddenly, there I was, looking down at my own body! I was afraid and didn't understand what this meant.

This happened to me again when I was at my first church in Fannettsburg. Again, I was lying in bed, recovering from a serious illness. I remember feeling listless. All of a sudden, I heard a whirring sound, and once again found myself looking down from the ceiling, and watching myself lying in bed. I was terrified! I'm not sure why I was so scared except that it was frightening to feel so disconnected from my own body. I tried to move my body but I couldn't. It was like I had no control at all. Then I heard the whirring sound again, but this time I could move my eyelids and open my eyes. Gradually I was able to move, but I was very weak. My body felt like a wet dish rag. I was already sluggish because of the illness and loss of sleep, but I got up and told Dale what I had experienced. I didn't know what this all meant or if it meant anything at all, but this was the second time in my life that I felt like I was dead, and looking down on my own body. And while true that I was very sick, I wasn't dead, I was alive! So, why was I having this experience? I have read that people have sometimes had this same experience during surgery. Perhaps God was preparing me somehow to help others in ministry.

Using Dreams in Ministry

Using the dreams that come to me has always been a big part of my ministry. I heartily recommend to anyone, that they record their dreams and try to make sense of them. I recall having one dream about a family in the church I was serving. There was nothing specific about that dream that I can remember, but somehow I knew that God was telling me to visit them. I called on them the next day. The man of the family laughed as we talked and he seemed very glad that I had come. He showed various crafts he had made and told me stories about his life. The following day, he suddenly died. He was 88 years of age. I conducted his funeral and was able to include in the eulogy much of what we had talked about several days before. His wife came to me after the service with tears in her eyes. She told me that she was happy I had spent time talking and laughing with her husband before be died.

She asked, "How did you happen to come over for a visit? There was nothing wrong with my husband."

"I had a dream," I told her. "In my dream, I saw your husband and his family. I believe it was God's way of letting me know to support you."

There were many times I have followed up on my dreams in ministry. It was as if God had given me another tool to use to fulfill what He wanted me to do. I prayed for God to show me the way and to guide me in serving others in my ministry. Then the dreams would come about people in our church, showing their hopes and struggles. I realized that it was an opportunity for me to minister to others in another way. When I dreamt about a family in a train wreck, it usually meant that the family was on a collision course with family conflicts. I would try to put them on the right track that would lead toward peaceful resolutions to overcome their struggles. Other times, if a person is in a dream and there is nothing specific, I feel they may need some encouragement and support as they go through the trials and tribulations of life. I have found it to be a challenge to be open to God's guidance through dreams, and then help others wherever I can.

Dinner with Hugh Lynn Cayce

I was invited to meet with Edgar Cayce's son, Hugh Lynn Cayce, at an Inn near Hershey, Pennsylvania around 1980. He was giving a speech at a meeting and after speaking, he joined a number of us for dinner. It so happened that I was right next to him at the dinner table. I asked him, "What was it like being the son of Edgar Cayce?"

So he told me a story about going for a walk by the river. As he was leaving the house, his dad told him to walk up the river, not down the river. As he was young at the time, he did not always listen to his father. Why should he walk up instead of down the river? So, he and his friends ignored the warning and walked down the river. As they walked, they trod on the stones in various places, when all of a sudden, splash! Hugh Lynn stepped on a slippery rock, and fell into the water. He quickly recovered his balance and realized that he could have been seriously hurt had he hit his head on the rocks. As it was, he hurt his leg.

When he came back into the house, his dad said to him, "You went down the river didn't you?"

"Yup," he said.

Then he said, "You fell in didn't you?"

"Yes, I did," he said.

"You didn't listen to me," he said. "Had you listened, you would not have gotten hurt."

Hugh Lynn went on to explain how difficult it had been growing up because his dad always knew if he had been good or bad. This story warmed my heart because it made me feel there were others in the world with gifts and experiences similar to my own, and I was not alone.

Learning How to Give

There were two devoted members of the Fannettsburg Church that were always a delight to visit. They had one precious quality about them that really stood out. Every time I stopped for a visit, I would receive a gift. If Dale and I both visited, they would give each of us a gift. They would always ask about our children, and if we brought our children with us, which they requested at times, the children would each receive a gift as well. It was amazing to me to see how generous they were.

These gifts were not fancy, and they were usually something small. But it was the thought that made them special. I asked them about this curious habit of offering gifts to everyone who graced their home. "It's my way of giving thanks," the wife said. I was astounded by how much I learned from them. One day when I stopped by, she apologized to me and said, "I'm sorry Karl, I don't have anything to give to you today." I just smiled and said, "You have already given me something far more important than any gift. You have taught me how to give."

I have discovered through ministry that there is something I can learn from every person I meet. Some are small lessons, and others are big lessons. I learned from these friends how important it is to give, and it could be something small or large. Since then, I have tried to give something to anyone who visits our house. It may be a pen, a magnet, a picture, a church brochure, a book, a word of advice, a piece of candy, whatever I can find that fits the occasion. We can all learn how to be better givers, of our time, our talents, our love, our peace, our patience, our kindness, our listening ears, or our simple understanding. There is so much we can give to one another.

No One Died at Burnt Cabins

The Burnt Cabins Church was a small congregation that sometimes only began when enough people got there. Many of the people were dairy farmers, and often we didn't start the church service until the milking got done. They were a delightful group of laid-back people who became my teachers and my friends. I learned a great deal from their down-to-earth nature and simple ways. During the six years I served at the Burnt Cabins Church, no one died. Many people were in the hospital, but our prayers were always with them, and they always got well.

Every Minister had Chicken

A member of my congregation invited my family and me to dinner one evening, as it was her family's custom to invite every minister who had ever served the Burnt Cabins Church. She enjoyed a tradition of always serving the Pastor chicken for dinner. She explained how the tradition started when a pastor many years ago would travel by horseback over the mountain and, after preaching on Sunday, he would enjoy dinner at one of the parishioner's homes before heading back over the mountain. And they all served chicken! This is how my family and I came to be here. As we were eating, little Jason, our son, blurted out, "This chicken is tough!"

"Yes, I plucked him this morning, and I believe he was on the older side," our hostess politely said. She explained how they always killed a chicken, plucked its feathers, and cooked it for the preacher. Sometimes, that was the only meat her family ate for the week.

Substitute Teaching

While ministering in Fannettsburg and Burnt Cabins, Karl did not make a lot of money and with a growing family we needed to supplement our income some other way. I thought I should apply for a substitute teaching position, since I had a degree in Elementary Education. It was a brave step for me because I was "afraid of my own shadow" at that time. I put my name in with great trepidation, and was eventually offered a position. I'll never forget my first day as a sub. Thank goodness it was for only half a day and it was a 2nd grade class. The teacher I was subbing for was great and gave me a lot of encouragement. After my first day, I was relieved that I had done it! For years I had been afraid of teaching and I finally had managed to do it. I was proud of myself and so began a three-year period in which I was a substitute teacher in the Fannett-Metal and the Armstrong County School Districts.

Team Ministry at its Best

There have been times when I felt like leaving the ministry, because it seemed like I was beating my head against a brick wall. But during all those times, Dale remained supportive and encouraged me to hang in there. In fact, I told Dale that if at any time she felt that my ministry was getting in the way of our relationship, to tell me and I would leave the ministry. I know this might shock some people, and they may say, "You're not putting God first!" But this is not exactly true. You see, I am putting my love and my relationship with my wife first, because, if I can not first demonstrate my love and trust for someone whom I can see, then, how can I love, and teach others how to love our heavenly Father whom we can not see? I believe the two go hand in hand. Did not Jesus teach the same when he said, "He who does not love his brother whom he has seen cannot love God whom he has not seen." (I John 4:20)

At times, I have asked Dale whether I should leave the ministry, especially when I felt I was not doing a good enough job. And, was she happy? I always valued her opinion and I believe that the ministry we do is a "team ministry." Even though I am the one doing the preaching, teaching, or counseling, it is still a team effort, because I know I would not be as strong if it were not for the love and support of Dale. That's a team relationship. It also works the other way too. She could not do all the things she does if it were not for my support and encouragement. This is the power of two working in harmony. There is strength in numbers when gathered in His name.

There have been many people who have often commented on how well Dale and I work together as a team. Sometimes we work together in a complementary way. There are often times when Dale will relate to the women in the church in a feminine way, while I relate to the men in the church in a masculine way. Then, we try to unite people together whether it is a marriage, a community, or a church.

The Hard Job of Ministry

A man in our church committed suicide by shooting himself. He had been suffering from depression for a long time, and had been under a doctor's care. His wife was distraught, and called me and explained what had happened. She asked me to go to the grade school immediately, to tell their young son what his father had done. She didn't want him to hear it secondhand. She wanted me to bring her son home.

"Of course," I told her, "I'll help you anyway I can." It was one of the most difficult jobs I have ever done in ministry. I got to the elementary school and walked into the school office requesting to see the principal because of an emergency. I was immediately ushered into his office where I explained my purpose, and requested permission to drive the ten-year-old boy home and tell him what had happened to his father. Without any questions, I was given approval. The school staff knew me as the pastor of the local church, and their hearts sank to the floor for the family when they heard the tragic news.

I'm not exactly sure what I said or how I told the boy about his father, but I know I tried to handle it with great care. I explained that his mother loved him so much and was in so much pain that she wanted me to tell him the news and bring him home. When we got back to the house, the boy greeted his mother with open arms and both were able to grieve.

The community rallied around her and her family and the church members all supported her with great compassion. We helped to clean up the stains on the rug so his wife would not have to do it. She was very grateful to the community, because we all understood that her husband was suffering from a neurological medical condition that was beyond his control.

Smoke Detectors for Everyone

After discovering some local people had died because they did not have smoke detectors in their homes, I proposed a project to the church that would provide smoke detectors to any family who did not already have one. We would give each family one free detector and encourage them to buy another at the manufacturer's cost. It was a project that the deacons undertook and we purchased and installed detectors for a number of families throughout the Path Valley area. I kept saying, "If we helped save one family, it would be worth it." We were grateful to the many people who donated to this project.

Mary Viernstein Tragedy

My father and stepmother, Mary, were coming for a visit with us on Saturday. However, we got a phone call from my father on Friday evening saying that Mary was in the hospital and he asked us to pray for her. She was very sick, so they were unable to visit us. Soon after, we received another call on Monday that Mary had undergone surgery and was unconscious. It all happened so fast, we were shocked.

We later found out exactly what had happened. Mary had been complaining about severe pain in her abdomen and when she got to the hospital, they said she had "female" problems. They gave her a heavy pain medication and then sent her home. After several days of severe pain, she developed a temperature and went back to the hospital. Her condition deteriorated rapidly and she went into a coma.

After many tests, the doctors discovered that her colon had ruptured and peritonitis had set in and infection was spreading throughout her body. Unfortunately, they did not discover it in time, and her brain was affected by the infection. She was declared brain dead. It was tragic and we were horrified. The doctors had misdiagnosed her condition the first time she sought help. Now, the best we could pray for was that God would let her body die, so she would not remain on life support. Three days later, she died. It was tragic because Mary was young, only 48 years old. She had completed her doctoral degree in Psychology just a few years earlier.

My father was devastated. Grief has a way of affecting us in strange ways, but my father told me he felt that Mary had come to him after she died. She wanted to reassure him that she was all right.

Then Mary told him, "If you think the politics on earth are bad, it is also difficult here on the other side." She said it took a lot of work just to communicate to him that, "She was all right."

The point of this dialogue experience was for me to realize that my father, the scientist and engineer who taught me to question, also had a spiritual side. He wasn't sure if it was real, but I believe with all the detail he shared about the experience, it was certainly authentic. Hearing from Mary herself that she was all right, was not only a comfort to him, but it also sounded exactly like what Mary would do.

Ecumenical Worship

Serving in Fannettsburg and Burnt Cabins was very fruitful and ecumenical, as well. It was the first time our Presbyterian Church had worshipped with the Mennonite Church in a joint "Foot Washing" ceremony. Yes, even Presbyterians were washing the feet of others in a symbolic act of humility. There were many Amish and Mennonite families that we became friendly with, and we became accustomed to seeing the buggies traveling back and forth.

The Over-Affectionate Wedding

One of the first weddings I performed was for a young couple who were very much in love, and wanted to get married in the church. Members of the church were invited to attend as there were not many members of the bridal couple's families that would be attending. It was obvious to me how much the young couple loved one another, and I thought that it was a good sign to see two people in love.

The wedding plans went well, as it was a simple wedding. The couple did not have much money so members of the congregation donated flowers. On the day of the wedding, many members of the church came to support this young couple. However, there was something different about this ceremony compared to any other I had conducted thus far. The couple was "lovey, dovey" throughout the whole ceremony. From the moment the service began, the two of them were in each others arm's the entire time!

As I was speaking, most people tried to listen to what I had to say, but I got the distinct feeling that the bridal couple just wanted to get the ceremony over with. In fact, the congregation noticed how the couple was so deeply immersed in the eyes of one another that they barely glanced at me.

I resigned myself to simply finish the service and pronounce them husband and wife as quickly as possible. I remarked to them that "they had plenty of time to be 'lovey, dovey' after the wedding" to no avail. After the pronouncement, I said, "You may now kiss the bride," not that they needed much invitation. It was the longest kiss I have seen in my entire ministry. They just wouldn't stop kissing! Even the congregation was feeling uncomfortable, and you could hear the murmurs throughout the church as people were leaning over to make comments to one another. I heard someone say, "You can do that later!" They soon after came to be known as the affectionate couple.

This comes in stark contrast to another wedding I officiated over, when I noticed in the middle of the wedding ceremony that this older couple showed no emotion at all, and weren't even holding hands. Not even during their vows did the couple hold hands. As a Pastor who noticed these subtle differences, I decided I would instruct future couples to at least hold hands during the wedding ceremony. When I said, "You may kiss the bride," he pecked her quickly on the cheek. Believe me, I was not the only one to notice this. I don't doubt the couple was in love, nor would I prefer a public display like the "affectionate couple," but this couple offered nothing. I was beginning to learn that no two weddings are ever alike.

The Wedding Reception Cake

Dale and I usually like to attend the wedding receptions after the marriage ceremonies because we can get to know some of the family as well as the bride and groom better. However, there was one wedding reception where I was sorry that I went. The couple was unique. The bride was a very large buxom woman and the groom was a very small thin man. I didn't think much about the difference because they seemed to be in love with one another.

The wedding went well, and the reception was in a small building that was rented out for occasional family gatherings. It was very crowded. I didn't know any of the people on either side of the family, but it was obvious that it was not the most organized of wedding receptions. The DJ never showed up, so someone went home to get their stereo.

A few family members brought different types of food and the meal was sort of a covered dish dinner reception. All the food was homemade, and had we known, we could have brought something - at least a pot of beans. There were hot dogs, hamburgers, potato chips, potato salad, and coleslaw for dinner.

The one outstanding thing about the whole reception was the cake, it was huge! You could tell that it was by far the most expensive item of the whole dinner. However, when the couple went to cut and feed the cake to each other, it was a sight to behold. This huge bride was towering above her smaller husband, and she was determined to smash the cake in his face!

Now, how this custom ever got started, I'll never know, but let me tell you it has to be the worst thing a bride and groom can do to one another on their wedding day, to shove the cake into each other's faces! Well, the bride took off after the groom and he ran! At that moment, the bride hit the table the cake sat on and the whole cake started to fall on the floor. Fortunately, three people were sitting nearby, because it was so crowed in that little building, and they were able to catch the cake with their bare hands before it hit the floor. Meanwhile, the bride still chased the groom around the room, totally oblivious to what was going on with the wedding cake. She was determined to smash the cake in his face! I thought, "I hope he doesn't mind being dominated by her, because it sure looks like that is what will happen."

"Let's go," I told Dale.

We were not the only ones leaving at this point, because streams of people were also walking out of the building. Several older folk who left, commented that smashing the cake in each other's faces just ruins a wedding. I was in total agreement.

"Get the Soap!"

I recall another wedding ceremony in Fannettsburg where the unexpected happened. When we got to the part of exchanging rings, the groom stuck out his right hand instead of his left, and the bride put the ring on the groom's right-hand ring finger. I didn't realize this until later, but a man's right-hand fingers are usually larger than on his left hand, if he is right-handed.

The bride immediately realized her mistake, and proceeded to take the ring off his right hand so she could put it on the left hand. The problem was it was stuck. She kept tugging and tugging on the ring until it was obvious to everyone in the church what was going on. Someone yelled out, "Get the soap. Get the soap!" I made a brief comment to the congregation that we were working on getting the ring on the right finger. I felt sorry for the guy because he was just about getting his finger ripped off. "Don't worry about it," I told her. But she insisted that the ring be on the correct finger. Finally, the ring came off and, after placing it on the correct finger, we were able to complete the ceremony.

The bride blamed the groom for holding up the wrong hand which I'm sure the groom was so used to doing being right handed. However, had she done nothing at all, I doubt if anyone would have ever noticed it was on the wrong finger. I hadn't realized it and I was standing right in front of them! Sometimes, it's better to just let some things go and continue with the ceremony, because I don't think there is a single marriage ceremony that ever goes off the way you plan it. Sometimes we get so caught up in the ritual that the true meaning of love gets lost.

The Mixed Match Wedding

There was another wedding in Fannettsburg that was a total mixed match. A young couple wanted to get married in the church and after attending one of the Church Worship Services, asked the choir to sing at their wedding. They were honored and agreed to participate. Other members of the church were also invited and were happy to be present. As the wedding day approached, the choir had their robes cleaned for the occasion; the church was spruced up and spotlessly cleaned. Everyone, including myself, were all dressed for a King and Queen to enter the church.

Finally the wedding party arrived, and they were all dressed alike. You could almost hear the gasps of the choir and guests. In came the bride and groom dressed in "hippy" styled clothes. The bride wore a denim skirt, and a white blouse with big flowing sleeves. She had beads around her neck and a flower garland around her head. She was also very pregnant. The bridesmaids were dressed to match.

The men all wore jeans and white shirts with puffy sleeves. I could see the looks of confusion on the faces of the congregation, who looked at one another as if to say, "Are we in the right place?" The wedding itself wasn't bad, just different. We were shocked because we didn't expect the couple to dress down at their wedding when we had seen them dressed up at the Church Worship earlier. The wedding was fine and the couple seemed to enjoy the relaxed wedding style.

Called to Serve Another Church

I had served in the Fannettsburg and Burnt Cabins churches for six years, and I had prayed to God to ask how long He wanted me to be there. Most pastors only serve three years in their first church. It is there where most ministers make their mistakes, learn from them, and then, with the greater experience, move on to another church.

The people seemed to love Dale and me, and we were having a fruitful ministry. No one wanted us to leave. Yet, I felt God was calling me to move on to a charge where I would serve one church instead of two. I always had two session meetings a month, two deacon meetings a month, two Bible studies a week, and was constantly traveling between two church services a week. It was difficult to combine the activities of each church as both wanted to have their own separate events. However, I loved serving small churches, and learned a great deal from everyone. Still, I had a feeling that God was calling me to a larger church, where I would be presented with other responsibilities.

I was confident that I was leaving Fannettsburg and Burnt Cabins in a much better condition than when I had arrived. A private donor had donated a great deal of money to the churches, and their finances were the best they had been in years. I was leaving with the knowledge that I had made a difference for the ministry of Our Lord Jesus Christ. Dale and I had created an atmosphere of peace and were leaving many good friends. Leaving them behind was difficult, though I knew that God's call had to come first. It was a very difficult decision for me. Who would run the TV Ministry and do it right? God would provide.

So I activated my resume at the national office, and started getting calls from churches looking for ministers. Dale and I wanted to stay in Pennsylvania because it was a wonderful place to live, and we wanted to raise our children in the country, because it was a bit sheltered from the world.

Search committees looking for another pastor started attending the church to listen to me preach, and as they entered the church, the congregational members wanted to know where they were from. Sometimes Dale and I were invited out to dinner with the search committee after the worship service.

I had a lovely meeting with the Pastor Nominating Committee (PNC) from Dayton, Pennsylvania. I had judged the quality and personality of the Church based on the members of the PNC. "If the people I met are truly representative of the people of the church at Dayton," I told Dale, "then I could serve them and be their pastor."

The individuals on the PNC can usually give a minister a good preview of the people in the church they represent. But, if the composition of the congregation is drastically different from those on the PNC, then that can lead to disaster. I asked as many questions of the committee as they asked of me. I prayed to God, and took the next step. If the doors remained open, then I would continue to proceed with them. I was not under any pressure to leave and, I could take my time to find the place where God wanted me to serve.

I talked with the Executive Presbyter and other key people in knowledgeable positions and got positive feedback. The church really seemed to want me and that was a good feeling.

My sermons were simple and down-to-earth. This was just what they wanted to hear. It was a farm community, and the Manse was across the road from a field of cattle. The church was in a very picturesque location on top of a hill, and one could see the most beautiful sunsets ever.

It wasn't long before Dayton issued a call, and now I had to tell my people I was going to leave.

The Farewell Sermon

It was not a day that I was looking forward to because I knew it would be a shock to many people. Things were going so well for the two churches, and I was sure they would be disappointed.

I preached with great compassion to a wonderful group of friends. During the service, there were tears in people's eyes and afterward some of us cried quite openly and freely. Some pleaded with me to change my mind, although they realized that it would be a good move for me and my family. I put my faith in God's hands, and tried to follow his guiding Spirit, which has never let me down. I felt that God had other plans for us now, and our lives would be filled with wonderful surprises.

Chapter 11

"I was glad when they said to me,
'Let us go to the house of the Lord.'"

Psalm 122: 1

The Call to Dayton 1983

On the day of my installation, people seemed happy to have a pastor again. The previous pastor was accidentally killed when he was out cutting wood for the fireplace in the manse. A tree had fallen on him. I spent our first year consoling and ministering to the people who were still grieving the loss of their previous pastor.

Moving Can Be Difficult

The move was difficult for our children. Christiana would draw pictures on the wall of children with tears coming from their eyes. There were some temper tantrums. There is no doubt that taking children out of their happy, safe community of friends, takes its toll.

Bessie Irene Bates Ditmars

In the late summer of 1983, my grandmother started to fail. The doctors and other health care professionals were uncertain what was wrong with her. She was admitted to the hospital, where they ran some tests. There was some concern that she had suffered from a mini-stroke. My dad and mom were upset of course, as was the rest of the family. My grandmother was well-loved for her sense of humor and good nature.

My mom took time off from work and flew down to help with the situation.

As the second oldest grandchild, I was close to my grandmom. I talked with Karl about going to see her in Sarasota, Florida, as I feared I might never see her again. Unfortunately, Karl was the pastor of a church, and his income did not provide unlimited resources. I told him it had been awhile since I had seen my grandmother and I wanted to see her one last time before she died.

Karl and I figured that we had just enough money for me to fly to Florida to visit once. I had the choice of going while she was alive or for her funeral. It was a difficult decision for me to make, as I was close to my family and would have loved dearly to have gone both times. I much preferred to see my grandmother alive. So, I made the decision to go immediately.

Our children were young, ages 8, 5, and 3 at that time, and we had just moved to a new home. We were still getting used to the area, but Karl unselfishly agreed to care for the children for nine days so that I could have a long visit with both my grandparents.

During my visit, I stayed with my grandfather, who was 84 years old and still driving. We worked out a schedule where I would go to the beach for a short time in the morning and then visit with my grandmother after that. I needed the time at the beach as a break, because it was so difficult seeing the grandmother I knew and loved so ill.

While I was there, the doctors determined that my grandmother had a cantaloupe-sized tumor in her uterus, and that it had metastasized. My grandfather grew despondent. I tried to cheer him up, but it was difficult.

When I visited my grandmother, I would get her up and out of bed, take her around in her wheelchair, and try to get her to talk as best I could. Unfortunately, Grandmom thought I was her niece. I understood because I had spent time with my mother's mom who had Alzheimer's, so I took it in stride. I did want my grandmother to be the best she could be with the remaining time she had left, so every time I visited her I performed the laying on of hands. I believed that the energy within me could give her strength and improve her health.

And it worked! By the time I left my grandmother could recognize me, and she was doing much better. A short time later, she was able to go home. She even made it home for Christmas! She was able to stay out of the hospital and nursing home for over two months, and when I spoke with her at Christmas time, she sounded good.

It was more than I could have hoped for. I believe prayer and the laying on of hands had helped rally my grandmother so that she lived another four to five months. It was long enough for her large extended family to gather around her and say their goodbyes.

The Holy Land Trip

One of the first events I planned at the new church was a trip to the Holy Land. I invited people who were interested and able to go with us, to visit the holy sites in Bethlehem, Jerusalem, Capernaum, Jericho, and the pyramids in Egypt. It was the greatest trip I had ever planned for a church group. The congregation even chipped in for Dale to go along.

The Holy Land trip was outstanding, and those of us who went along really bonded. We continued to be close friends the whole time I served as the pastor of the church. Dale and I had a good spiritual experience with these people of faith for over thirteen years.

A certain member of the church said, "If you want to get to know your pastor and his wife, go with them to the Holy Lands." During the tour, I was like a shepherd watching over his flock. I recall two people who got locked in their room in the hotel and couldn't get out, and the phone did not work. They pounded on the door until someone finally heard them and let them out! Many of the hotel facilities we stayed in were not in the best condition, yet they were the best available at that time. Our eyes opened wide when we saw soldiers with machine guns patrolling in the lobbies of some of the hotels where we stayed.

I took with me a huge amount of chewing gum to hand out to children. I had heard that there were many people, mostly children, always looking for handouts. It was true. The children were delighted when I gave out sticks of chewing gum, and these were children who wore shoes with the backs cut out, because their feet grew too big for their shoes and they could not afford another pair.

Sea of Galilee

It was a beautiful sunny day, as we all boarded the boat that would take us across the Sea of Galilee to Capernaum. The boat reached the middle of the "sea," which is only six miles wide and 13 miles long. The captain stopped the engines and we had prayer.

Suddenly, something unusual happened. It seemed as if, out of the middle of nowhere, dark clouds began to form in the sky, and the wind started to pick up. The captain quickly started the engines and headed for Capernaum. As we traveled, the wind began to blow harder. The sky was now completely covered in clouds and it began to rain. The boat began to sway violently as the wind blew harder and rocked the boat. The boat was being tossed back and forth by the wind and the waves.

Oddly enough, it was only a few minutes earlier that the sky had been clear! Everyone in the group was questioning what was happening with the weather. It was like the story in the Bible when Jesus was sleeping in the boat and a storm suddenly came upon him and his companions. The disciples woke Jesus because they thought they were going to die.

We questioned the captain of the ship for an explanation. He said, "Oh, the wind comes ripping through the 'valley of the winds,' and it is not unusual for storms to come upon us quickly."

I felt like I was reliving some of the Bible stories I'd read all my life, and at this moment the Scriptures really came alive for me, and this was only the beginning!

Acoustics at the Mount of Beatitudes

When we reached the "Mount of Beatitudes," I was amazed at the natural amphitheater that we found. I could talk to Dale without raising my voice when she was 100 yards away! I always wondered how Jesus could speak to over 5,000 people without a sound system. God had provided a natural environment for the Word to be spoken and heard by all, it seemed. To this day, I still do not fully understand why the acoustics were so remarkable there. God must have allowed it to happen to be sure people would hear Jesus' words.

Bethlehem

One of the most moving events we experienced was in Bethlehem, the birthplace of our Lord, Jesus Christ. When we arrived, people were singing and celebrating the birth of Christ on January 18th. The Armenians had chosen this day for their traditional Christmas celebration. We climbed downstairs because the church had been built on top of the site, and we saw the cave, which could have easily been the manger, the site of Jesus' birth. I was moved. Many places we had visited seemed artificial or had been commercialized, but this site seemed authentic, a beautiful location for the simple birth of the Messiah.

Kidron Valley

While passing through the Kidron Valley, I was impressed by the ancient cemetery. People who had to walk from Jerusalem to areas outside the walls of the city would have to travel through the "Valley of Death" to reach their destinations. I could well imagine Jesus and his disciples traveling through this valley on numerous occasions, a true "Valley of the Shadow of Death." And, I could also envision Jesus teaching the disciples to fear no evil, as they traveled through this same valley, for God would be with them!

The Upper Room and Other Interesting Sites

We were one of two groups traveling together and my group got briefly separated from the other, while we were in Jerusalem. Unfortunately, the tour guide was with the other group. It fell on me to keep the group together, and to find our way to our destination, the "upper room," and join up with the other group. Following my intuition, I led the group on a path that eventually led up some steps. When we reached the top, we found that the wall was sealed shut, yet we could hear the voices of our fellow travelers on the other side of the wall! Some of us called out that we were not far away. We went back down and walked around to the other side to find another way up. We found out later, that the original entrance to the upper room was exactly where our group had tried to get in.

I had developed quite a reputation for bartering with the local merchants, and when Dale and I would return to the bus, the others would ask us, what did you get this time? We were known for getting some of the best deals. I told them to go to the stores around the corner from where the bus stopped, because the tour guide was getting a cut of the action by stopping the bus at certain stores. I saw money exchanged "under the table" several times.

In Bethlehem, there was a merchant who offered to sell us a nice fabric bed spread at a good price. I was not going to buy it because it was too expensive, but he eventually came down on the price, and made us a reasonable offer, so I bought it. It was amazing to see the merchant turn on the tears just to make a sale. I was convinced merchants were trying to manipulate us, so we had to be careful. The bad thing about our purchase was I used my credit card when I should have used cash. When we got home, we discovered that one merchant had double swiped our card and charged us $50.00 on another item several days after we left! I filed a complaint with Visa that my signature had been forged and advised that I was not even in the country at that time. I could prove it, so they deducted the charge from our balance.

Dale and I had a terrible feeling when we were on the top of Masada. We felt such incredible sadness that it brought tears to our eyes. Many Jews had lived on the top of Masada to avoid becoming slaves to the Romans. Eventually, when the Romans built a ramp and were close to the top, the Jews committed suicide to avoid their fate. Men, women, and children died because they wanted to be free.

In Jerusalem, while at the "Dome of the Rock," peddlers were trying to sell us umbrellas because it was raining slightly. The peddlers had made their way into the holy site in order to sell their wares. Suddenly, you could hear the screaming and yelling of the officials charged with protecting the site, who were angry at the peddlers for entering the holy site to hawk their goods. It reminded me immediately of the scripture in which Jesus was angry at the moneychangers and peddlers who defiled the temple. They were kicked out, too. The scripture was coming alive again right before my eyes!

When we traveled along the Gaza strip, we were warned by our guide and by any local Arab to whom we spoke that the land was "occupied" territory. We were also warned that it was not a matter of whether the people would fight again, but when.

I couldn't help but feel that if Jesus returned today and saw the Middle East in its present condition, he would weep and say, "Jerusalem, Jerusalem, how I would have gathered your children together as a hen gathers her brood under her wings." (Matthew 23:37)

Later, as we traveled in Cairo, Egypt, I was amazed to hear from the locals how little meaning their lives held for them. One mother said to us, "I don't worry much about my children because if one dies, I'll just have another one." I felt sad because I believe every life is precious.

I had a bad feeling while visiting the "Step Pyramid." It was very disturbing. It felt like a bad dream and I envisioned that I had been a slave in a former life and had been cruelly persecuted by guards with whips. This was an unusual experience for me, but I was convinced that I was picking up on some of the events that had taken place many centuries ago!

Pyramids at Giza

The Great Pyramids at Giza were truly magnificent! As we entered the great pyramid, our group walked up the narrow passageway to the Empty Tomb. We marveled at just how the builders of the pyramids managed to fit all those huge stones so closely together that you couldn't even slide a piece of paper between them. It was a special

191

moment for Dale and me to stand in the upper chamber of the empty tomb of the Great Pyramid and gaze down on the open sarcophagus. It seems every culture has an understanding of the afterlife and there in Egypt, we saw proof of their preoccupation with life after death, as it was reflected in these ceremonial sites.

After traveling in the Holy Lands, Dale and I shared our experiences with others, and explained how the different places made a strong impression upon us. The Bible Scriptures came alive, and we now had a better understanding of the setting in life in which much of the Bible had been written.

The Man with One Arm

There was a faithful member of our church who had one arm. He lost the other arm in a machine accident while working with a wire cable, which accidentally snapped and wrapped itself around his arm, severing it. Handicap aside, I came to know him as one of the most faithful helpers in the church. "Anytime you need anything, Karl," he said, "Call me, and I will be glad to be of service to you in your ministry." I was thankful, but apprehensive at first because he had only one arm. It did not take long for me to realize that not only was he a very enthusiastic worker for the church, but that he could do more with one arm than most people could do with two. He never let his disability discourage him, neither physically nor mentally. He attended church every Sunday, and had a wonderful attitude about life. He was truly an inspiration to me.

Good Friday Services

This was our first Easter in Dayton and there was a community worship service scheduled at our church. My parents came for a visit and volunteered to watch the children while we attended worship. Karl and I were the host church and I was singing in the choir.

My grandmother was back in the nursing home at this time and she was not expected to live much longer, so Dad warned that if they got the word, they would have to leave immediately for the drive to Florida.

During the service, I was mindful of my grandmother's impending death, so I asked the guest minister to pray for her. As he was praying, I looked at my watch. It was 8:30 p.m. As we prayed for my grandmother, I suddenly felt lighter. I visualized my grandmother leaving her body and a sense of peace settled around me. I felt her pass over to the other side. When I spoke to the pastor after the service, I told him what I had felt and thanked him.

When I returned home, I saw my parents and told Dad my impressions. He confirmed that he had received a telephone call from his brother and it was expected my grandmother wouldn't live much longer. A short while later my father got another call from Florida. My grandmother had died at approximately 8:30 p.m. during the exact time we were praying for her. I would like to think that our prayers helped to ease her way over to the other side. I was glad that I'd had the chance to see her alive, and now it seemed I was with her both times.

David and Goliath

Dale and I had grown close to another wonderful couple we met at our new church. They were antique dealers who ran a shop out of their home in Dayton. People from all over the state, including the Amish people, would visit the shop to buy old used items for their homes. They were a good honest couple and everyone loved them. The husband taught me how to use wood and coal to heat the house we lived in efficiently. The manse had wood/coal stoves in the basement, and in the family room. It was necessary to keep them going during the winter or the pipes would freeze.

The antique dealer said he would help keep us supplied with wood or coal, because he didn't want me to use the chain saw I had purchased during my first pastorate in Fannettsburg. Understandably, he was concerned because the pastor before me at the Dayton Church had been accidentally killed cutting wood for the manse stoves. So, he and other members of the congregation asked me not to use the chain saw because they did not want the same thing happening to me.

I told them I would consider it, but there was one large tree in Kensington, Maryland that was leaning toward my mother's house that needed to come down, and my mother did not have the money to pay a tree service to cut the tree down.

While Dale and I were visiting my mother during our vacation, we attended church on Sunday, as we usually did. I heard the minister preach his sermon on David and Goliath, and it was during this sermon that I realized that the tree in my mother's backyard, which was looming over her house, was my "Goliath" that I needed to overcome.

I did not want my mother to be hurt by that tree, and should it fall during a strong windstorm, it could come down right on top of her bedroom where she spent most of her time. It was a tulip poplar tree that is known to grow fast, and can be very brittle. I had faith that God would guide me on how to bring down that giant of a tree. I told Dale after the sermon, "The tree in my mother's backyard is my Goliath!" The tree was twice the size of her two-story house and approximately 100 feet tall, and I had to bring it down!

Both Dale and my mother were fearful about my desire to cut down the tree by myself. They said, "You've never done anything like this before."

"I know," I said, "But you know I have never been afraid to tackle any project and this is my Goliath!"

As long as I believed that God wanted me to do something, no matter how huge or difficult the task, I knew I would do my best to accomplish it. That "David" spirit has been with me all my life. I believe we should "Trust in the Lord with all your heart." (Proverbs 3:5)

So, I consulted a dear friend about how to take down the tree. He explained, in detail, just how I should cut it and get it to fall just where I wanted it to go. I suspected this might be the last tree I would hew down. Armed with my faith in God, and using all the knowledge I had gained from my friend, I planned just how I would hew down that tree.

At its base, the tree was almost four feet in diameter, so I started at the top - the most dangerous part. I climbed as high as I could to top the tree off. I had tied several ropes on the tree to lead it in the direction I wanted it to fall, and I tied a safely line. I also wore my repelling gear so that if I needed to get down quickly, in an emergency, I could do it. Then I proceeded to cut the top off, just the way I was told by several tree experts I had consulted.

There was a loud cracking sound! I had to get down quickly, because it didn't seem like the tree was going to fall away from me, and instead, it actually fell toward me! Within seconds, I repelled down to the ground and ran in the opposite direction of the falling tree. To my horror, the top of the tree changed direction and was falling in the direction I was running! I was still ahead of the tree, but the most unimaginable thing happened to me. Somehow I got hung up in the rope that I had repelled down, and I fell to the ground with the top of the tree chasing behind me! Dale was standing by watching the whole thing unfold. There I was lying on the ground with the tree coming toward me, so I did the only thing I could do and rolled my body away. I started rolling in one direction, but it seemed that the tree was tracking me, so I rolled in the other direction and suddenly, the tree stopped in mid air about 15 feet away.

I stood there with my heart in my throat as I watched the tree top follow Karl down the tree. It looked as if it would crush him at any moment. At one point, it appeared the tree was overtaking him. But then, miraculously, the tree stopped in midair, suspended there. I gave a big sigh of relief that the hardest part of the job was done. I was not happy that Karl had undertaken this project, but I understood his need to do it. I was just grateful to God that all was well and Karl had made it safely through another day.

What caused the tree to stop just 15 feet away? At that point, I untangled myself and moved away from the tree. Boy was I humbled, and I thanked God that I was all right. It didn't take long for me to discover that the reason why the tree stopped only 15 feet away from me was because I had tied off a safety rope at the last minute before I cut the top of the tree down. It was a last minute decision. If the tree did fall in the wrong direction, the rope would limit how far the top of the tree would go. I was fortunate the rope had held, but I believe it was God that slowed the progress of the tree that seemed to be chasing me all the way down. The rest of the tree was cut down according to plans and it took the next three months to completely cut up the rest of that huge tree.

I was grateful to God that I was able to complete the task, providing safety for my mother, but most of all I thanked God for watching over me and protecting me. I overcame my Goliath, but I was also humbled. I could easily have been killed, and I was only 15 feet away from death!

When the congregation in Dayton heard my story, they pleaded with me, "Karl, stop using your chain saw!" I prayed about it and agreed; I was not invincible. God had been with me and saved me. The next day, I sold my chain saw.

Dale's New Job

The choir director of Dayton Glade Run Church was leaving to go to college, so her job was now available, and I was offered the position. I wasn't sure I could do it, but I finally agreed that if I could get some training in choral conducting I would do it. Fortunately, a workshop was being offered at Chautauqua, New York in conjunction with the State University of New York (SUNY) where I would receive credits. The workshop was under the direction of Dr. Paul Christiansen, a great choral conductor and composer. The church paid my way and I learned choral conducting basics. It was a wonderful experience and I learned a lot.

Karl was enrolled in a writers' workshop in the afternoons, and because the classes were at different times, Dr. Christiansen asked if Karl would also sing in the choir as there was a need for more male singers. It was so much fun!

I was the director of four different choirs while at Dayton: two children's choirs, the adult choir and a hand bell choir that I had started. I directed a large patriotic cantata in 1991 during the Gulf

War, in which many community members participated. I was the director of the adult choir for 11 ½ years while in Dayton.

Exploring New Job Possibilities

One day while we were visiting Karl's mom, I had a talk with her about my job options. I told her I didn't feel comfortable teaching and I had really wanted to be a nurse when I was a little girl. Mom said it wasn't too late for me to go to nursing school if I really wanted to. She suggested I work in a nursing home or some other facility as an aide first to see if I liked nursing well enough to go back to school. My mother had suggested the same thing when I discussed this with her. Later when the children were older, I took their advice and went back to school.

Visiting in the Poconos – Take Me to the Doctor!

For vacations, we would often go to Dale's parents' home at the Paradise Falls Lutheran Association in the Poconos. The kids were young and I wanted to give them an experience they would never forget - fishing with their dad! I took the kids to a Fish Hatchery where you can fish from a stocked pond. There we were all sure to catch a fish! I explained about the fishing rod and demonstrated how to put the worm on the hook and then how to cast the line into the pond. I did this very carefully. I was careful to explain that they needed to pay attention that no one was behind them when they cast the line. So, we thought we were ready and Jason cast his fishing line out into the pond. But, unfortunately Julie was standing behind him and I heard this scream coming from Julie. I couldn't believe it. Jason had caught Julie's ear with his fishhook!

She screamed for us to get the worm off of her ear. She seemed more concerned about the worm wiggling against her ear than the hook that was embedded in her skin. I pulled the worm off the hook, and reassured her that the worm was gone, and she seemed relieved at that.

The ear is made up of soft tissue and the only way to get the fishhook out was to finish pushing it through, since it was already half way through her skin. But as I started to push the hook through, Julie started screaming, "Take me to a doctor! Take me to a doctor!" I told her all I needed to do was to push it through her ear and she would be fine, but she continued to scream, "Take me to a doctor!"

Other people were now gathering around us so I acquiesced. "Okay," I said. I'll take you to a doctor!"

I took Julie to a local emergency center, and they did exactly the same thing I was going to do. The only thing they did differently was to numb the area first before pushing the hook through. I agreed that it did make her more comfortable, and she felt more confident in the doctors than in me. It was a fishing experience we will never forget!

What makes this story even more interesting is that the next day, Jason and I were playing outside in a water sprinkler with our bathing suits on because it was hot. As Jason leaned over the water sprinkler, I followed him and leaned over too. Suddenly, Jason stood up quickly banging his head against my head, right on my eyebrow. The next thing I knew, blood was dripping down my face onto my hands. Jason was fine, but I had a deep gash on my eyebrow.

So, back we went to the same local emergency center where the same doctor had to put several stitches in my eyebrow. The doctor was quite amused and, knowing we were visiting in the Poconos asked, "When is your family going home?" I wasn't so amused, and was glad when our vacation was finally over. I went home thinking I needed a vacation from our vacation!

Gas Well at Dayton Glade Run Church

The Dayton Church was considering drilling a gas well on the church property. I discussed the matter with the Elders and agreed it was a good idea, if managed properly. It turned out to be a rather lengthy and involved project that took years to complete. The first issue to resolve was the contract. The church would receive free gas to heat the three buildings on the church property, and would also receive royalties from selling natural gas to People's Gas Company. It sounded like a sweet deal, but to execute it and make it work was a challenge.

Not many churches have their own gas well. We needed to get people who owned adjacent property to deed over underground gas rights to the church in order to make it work. Fortunately, the landowners generously agreed to deed over their underground acreage and set up the church to receive free gas for the next 50 years.

After the well was drilled, we ran into problems keeping it running. Often, I woke up on a winter morning to find it freezing cold in the house. For whatever reason, the gas pressure had dropped, and the supply of gas to all the church buildings, including our house, was shut off. I remember many times having to march up to the wellhead or gas meter to reset the pressure pin. Then, I had to go around to all the furnaces in all the buildings and relight them.

I questioned the safety of the church furnace being relit, because there was no automatic shutoff valve. If the gas came back on after the pilot light went out, gas would fill the furnace room until it was manually shut off. At times I would open the door to the furnace room and be greeted by the smell of gas. I didn't turn on the light switch for fear that one little spark and the whole place would blow! I manually shut off the gas valves while working in the dark. The next day, I implored the session to install automatic shutoff valves on the furnace. They all agreed, realizing that I could have met my maker before my time.

It took some time to get things working correctly and Dale and our family endured a lot of inconveniences so that the church could eventually benefit from a working gas well. It was a difficult well to maintain the way it was set up, but eventually, the gas well was dedicated to the church buildings exclusively, and a better setup was designed. It took a lot of work, but saved the church a great deal of money.

Judy

Judy was a devoted church member and good friend during my ministry, but her life was not an easy one. Soon after I arrived, Judy came to me and told me of being diagnosed with cancer and how she struggled to live with her terminal illness. She told me she wanted to commit suicide, but, before she did, she came to talk to me about it. "I have a feeling about you," she said. "You are different from some of the other ministers I have known, and I can talk to you." I could tell she was serious about wanting to commit suicide.

I was shocked, but understood her despair with her illness. I decided to pull out all the stops and go for broke. I would give her my best and most precious gifts of knowledge and wisdom. I taught her the best prayer I knew, and asked her to say it everyday. I promised I would help her get through this and help her realize her final goals in life.

Soon after, I had a vision from God about how long I would stay at the Dayton Glade Run Church. I asked God, "Lord, how long do you want me to do ministry in Dayton?" God answered, "You will stay there as long as Judy is alive." I awoke from my dream and told Dale what I had experienced. We both agreed that I couldn't tell anyone that dream.

I still was not confident enough in the result of my dream study to know if they were for real or not. I thought it was strange for God to link another person's life to my ministry. Why would He do that? It was a mystery to me because Judy told me herself that the doctors had given her only a short time to live. Did that mean my time in Dayton was going to be short? I finally decided that it was a test of faith, for me as well as for Judy.

The time could be short, or it could be long depending upon the application of the Spirit of Christ in me, and through me to others. Time would really confirm the truth of my visions. God had called me to ministry and wanted me to use my gifts to serve Him, and I would do so, even though I did not fully understand, and would not until much later. Judy lived for twelve more years, and I then left the Dayton church a year later.

Judy taught me a lot in the twelve years I knew her. She helped me to organize our home, and our children adored her. She would care for them from time to time and she taught them different crafts. I was amazed at her resilience in the face of her illness.

Judy had mesothelioma, which is a cancer of the lining of her lungs generally caused by exposure to asbestos. She believed that she had contracted the cancer from an old hair dryer that she had used to dry her hair every day.

Judy later said of her illness, that although it was the worst thing that had ever happened to her, it was also the best thing that had ever happened to her. While dealing with her cancer, she was able to draw closer to God. She hosted weekly Bible Studies in her home, and tried to do one thing for someone every day, no matter how small it was, or how ill she was feeling. This certainly prolonged her life for fourteen years after her initial diagnosis. The doctors were amazed that she lived this long with this virulent form of cancer.

Marriage Enrichment Group

I started a Marriage Enrichment Group with the help of a Methodist minister. It turned out to be a time of reflection and counseling that was very therapeutic and supportive for all of us who attended. Many people were struggling with one problem or another and this time together provided a means of support from two Christian pastors, working together to help others.

When the Methodist minister left the community, for another position, I continued to counsel and provide guidance to the group for several years. During this time, I learned a great deal about how to help people improve their marriage skills to enhance their relationship. The best part was that the people in the group became so confident in their relationships with one another that they did not feel the need to meet any more as a group.

Teaching Computer Classes

Because of popular demand, I began to teach computer classes. I later taught two classes as computers became more advanced. The Pittsburgh area was depressed because steel production was being lost to overseas companies, and many people were having trouble getting jobs. Since I had some technical knowledge of computers and I knew that those who had such skills would have a competitive edge, I encouraged people to learn as much as they could about computers. I was glad to teach my secretary and others how to use basic computers, and they went on to get better jobs in those areas. I was also able to help a local tax collector to use her computer in order to improve her job performance.

We finally upgraded the church office from the typewriter to a computer and were now able to get both the bulletins and newsletter done in a more efficient manner.

Learning about Mission

I was grateful for the prevailing attitude at the Dayton Church that "mission giving" was the emphasis for helping people both at home and abroad. There was an outstanding Sunday school teacher at the church, who taught the importance of setting aside a portion of your money and giving it to mission. He was one of the best Sunday school teachers I'd ever heard in my life.

From the Dayton Church, many missionaries were sent out into the world to preach and teach the way of Christ. The general plan, which I supported, was that we give 50% of our tithing to support the local church, and 50% to support the mission of the church. Donations to the endowment funds also supported both. In fact, I was able to encourage many people to donate money to mission in their wills. During my 13 years serving in Dayton, we had increased our mission giving through endowments to several thousand dollars each month. We established a Mission Committee that would distribute money to local residents in need, local mission projects, world mission projects,

World Hunger, and Habitat for Humanity. The committee would make decisions each month on a variety of mission needs as we identified them. One remarkable way we raised our awareness to these needs was to expose ourselves to people throughout the world.

I thought it would be a good idea to be a host church and learn about the people doing "Mission" work in the world. In order to accomplish this, I would invite people who lived in other countries, but were traveling in the U.S.A., to stay for a week with Dale and me, in order to teach the congregation of our church about the mission work they were involved with. I arranged this through the Synod of the Presbyterian Church and the "Church World Organization" which invites pastors from other countries to come to the U.S.A. We learned a lot about the actual state of affairs in other countries: their customs, ideology, health, infrastructure and economic status.

Poland

I remember standing at the Pittsburgh Airport with a sign that read "The Hudek family," and they were due to arrive shortly. Our church at Dayton Glade Run had agreed through the Presbyterian Church (USA) and the Church World Service to host a family from another country. It was a huge undertaking to be responsible for a family who wanted to immigrate to the United States of America. We were responsible for making sure the family had temporary housing, food, clothing, and other basic needs to help them to integrate themselves into the United States.

This family originally emigrated from Poland, but had been detained in Germany for more than a year before finally being allowed to come to the United States through our church sponsorship. They were Roman Catholic in faith, but that did not matter to us. We wanted to help someone truly in need, regardless of their religious beliefs, customs or nationality, and this was truly a family in need. They had a one-way ticket out of Poland because Peter Hudek was "blackballed" by the communist government. He had protested against workers drinking alcohol during work hours. This was back in the early 1980's, before Poland had become free of communist rule, and dissenters were severely punished.

Our congregation felt we could help this family immigrate to the United States for a fresh start. Both Peter and Ana Hudek were well educated people with the equivalent of a Master's degree, although neither spoke English. We taught them as best we could, and then signed them up for courses in English as a second language. We provided a small house for them to live in for one year until they could get on their feet, thanks to the benevolence of Mabel, a saint in our own church. This went a long way toward helping them get established.

I helped them both find jobs, and Peter bought his first car in America with our help. It was tough because he had no credit history, held a "green" card, and they spoke little English. It was very difficult for them because they were forced to leave all they had in Poland in order to come to America. They left their family and friends behind so we were their family now. We cared for them, and helped them get established, and learned as much from them, as they learned from us. It was an amazing experience!

In less than a year, after working very hard to learn English, adapting to new customs, and a new environment, they bought their first American home with a garage and small swimming pool! Ana gave birth to twin girls shortly after, which automatically made the babies American citizens. It was a remarkable success story! The family rejected in Poland because of their beliefs, came to this country, worked hard and made a good life for themselves without having to forfeit those same beliefs!

After two years, some of their family members traveled to America for a visit and Peter and Ana were allowed to travel back to Poland on occasion. "Why don't you come back to Poland?" the family would ask. "It's different, now that we are no longer under communistic rule."

But Peter said, "In Poland, we could never have been able to get what we have now! We have a house, a good job, and I'm making good money. If we go back to Poland, what kind of job could pay me what I receive now?" Later, Peter and Ana became citizens of the United States.

I'm proud of the church and especially for Mabel, who offered her little house so that the Hudek family could get their start. Mabel was truly a saint, because she gave so much of herself to others. Just to visit Mabel or speak with her was a blessing! You couldn't help but be humbled by such a wonderful person. I recall on a visit to her house one day, that two of the burners on her stove did not work. I offered to fix them for her, but she shooed it away. "Why should I have them fixed? She said, straightforwardly, "I have two burners that work!" Amazing, and she was serious!

Mabel lived a very humble life, and gave most of what she had away to others. She had been a missionary in Taiwan for six years, and understood how people could live with very little. She always said she wanted her home to be a Mission house for the Lord, and she really meant it! She invited our confirmation classes to stay at her house for weekend spiritual retreats. So, Dale and I took this opportunity to teach the Bible and tell spiritual stories to the youth that would show them how to follow the way of Christ in the world today. The youth would often talk about their retreat experiences at Mabel's house years later.

When Mabel was in the hospital and was very sick, she told me to pray for her because she could not pray for herself. She was near death, and didn't know if God wanted her to get well. I prayed for her and gently kissed the side of her face. I felt as if I were kissing a Saint. Her soul was so pure, that I could actually feel it in the kiss! She soon recovered and was back to her old self. But I know that even if she were in pain, she wouldn't have complained. I learned a lot from Mabel, especially how to be humble, more giving, and how to be faithful to the church.

Malawi, Africa

Rev. Harvey visited us from Malawi, Africa. He was a joy to have during his week-long visit, and he spoke English very well. We learned how various charitable organizations were not always

208

welcomed by the Malawi people. Harvey explained that most of the donations and money intended for the people didn't always get to them. He encouraged us not to waste our money on certain charitable organizations, because their leaders took the money meant for the poor and bought expensive cars and other luxuries instead. And this wasn't the only problem. Because of the warfare underway in neighboring countries, Malawi was being swamped with refugees who streamed into the country by the thousands all of the time. The Presbyterian Church in Malawi was doing everything possible to help the homeless, and those with no clothes, food or water.

Harvey explained that his church was very large and each worship service was packed to overflowing with thousands of people wanting to be part of this caring church family. Deacons were appointed to oversee and actually "take care" of every new group of refugees who arrived at the church.

Harvey also explained that the average life span of a native of Malawi was 45 years old. If you were older than that, then you were considered very old! Medical care and medicines were not available to everyone. Yet, even in his country, there were many citizens who were very rich. He also explained that Malawi is blessed with a beautiful lake which is the main water source for his people, and has fish for food, but it needs to be carefully managed in order to maintain the natural resources. Harvey loved our church, the choir, and the friendly people who listened so intently to his preaching.

South Korea

Another visiting pastor from South Korea had served briefly in the Department of Intelligence for his government before going into the pastoral ministry. He was now serving the Lord in Christian ministry in the Presbyterian Church. He was very well educated and spoke excellent English. He was very impressed with the size of this country and the number of resources. He was also awed with the patriotism of the people, and those citizens who flew the American flag!

He explained that for people in his country, it was important to keep up with the latest technology so that they would be able to compete with other world powers throughout the world. He believed that education was the most important thing for his people, especially the young.

It happened that our church had scheduled a Mother-Daughter banquet where the men were charged with preparing the food for the women. It was a grand old tradition in which everyone chipped in and helped cook, serve and clean up. I personally enjoyed being right in there cooking and serving the women, and our visitor was amazed at how we treated the women in our church with great respect, but I was unpleasantly surprised when I asked if he would like to help with the dinner, and he flat out refused. "No! I would rather preach," he said. It was very clear that he would have felt demeaned to have served women and do the messy job of cleaning up.

He was grateful for our hospitality, and I found it interesting that he commented over and over again how wealthy, prosperous, and vast the land was in America. He called attention to the time when this country was attacked at Pearl Harbor. He said that some foreign officer who had visited America, had said that the spirit of this country was great, and given enough time, America would be able to gather her resources, and fight off any adversary. He confessed that he now understood this in a way he had not before.

Northern Italy

We had another visitor from Northern Italy who was a "Waldensian." He was officially connected with the Methodist Church, but was traveling throughout the U.S.A. visiting Presbyterian Churches with special permission.

However, this pastor was very anti-Catholic. He argued that the "reformed faith" of the Waldensians was the correct way, the only way. He said, "The people should have the control of self-government within the church." He explained that where he lived in Italy, the "Waldensians" were in the minority and had developed some strong theological arguments to enable their church to survive through the years.

He couldn't understand how our church members did not feel threatened by American Catholicism or any other religion for that matter, until we explained that in America, all were free to worship as they wished, and that we were more concerned about living in unity with one another as human beings and finding our common ground, rather than stressing our differences.

Going to a Baseball Game?

One of the funniest things that ever happened to me was when I took my son Jason to a baseball game. We were in Pittsburgh so I asked him, "How would you like to go to a Pirates baseball game?" He was all excited and said, "Sure!" I thought it would be a cool thing to do as father and son.

We were not far from the Three Rivers Stadium and joined the flood of fans heading for the game. I found a place to park the car and as we walked to one of the gates to buy tickets, to my surprise I was told, "We're sold out." I couldn't believe it! They were sold out to a baseball game at Three Rivers Stadium! I had been to baseball games before, but they were never sold out.

Disappointed, we slowly started to walk back toward the car when we heard, "Do you want to buy tickets?" A scalper had come up behind us.

"Yeah," I said. "How much are they?"

"Forty-six dollars for two tickets," he said.

I was shocked! I knew it had been a while since I'd been to a baseball game, but I thought it would cost about $8.00 a ticket. Boy, these scalpers were really making a profit! I shook my head no, it was too much money, but as I stood there with Jason, he said he wanted to go to the game. After all, we had already parked the car, and we were standing in front of one of the gates. A loudspeaker inside the stadium announced that the game was about to begin.

It was a little cloudy and it could possibly rain at any time. I wondered if I could talk the scalper down on the price. Then the scalper came back to me again, because he could see I didn't know what I was doing. "Look here," he said. He showed me the tickets again. "I'm giving them to you at face value, $23.00 each," he said. Wow! I thought. What could I do? I had to pay the price if I wanted to go to the game with Jason. "Okay," I grumbled. I just wouldn't tell anyone what I paid for the tickets.

As we finally walked into the stadium, I got the shock of my life. It was packed and there was hardly a vacant seat in the whole place, not because of the baseball game, but because it was a football game! Apparently, we were just in time for the Steelers first game of the season! Jason was confused because I had been talking about baseball earlier. I said, "I'm sorry Jason, we're not going to a baseball game. We're going to a football game!"

I couldn't believe I had gotten that far without realizing what was going on. We weren't disappointed to see a Steelers game. In fact, we had a great time, and then I felt fortunate to get the tickets at face value. It was just one of the strangest things that had ever happened to me, and I was glad I could laugh at myself!

The PennDOT Battle

There was a traffic problem near our church that was not a laughing matter. People were hurt at the intersection every year because one could not see clearly enough when pulling out into the intersection. If another car or truck was traveling at the usual 55 miles per hour, they would most likely crash into you. The speed limit was posted at 35 miles per hour, but no one paid attention to the speed limit. The solution was obvious to everyone who lived in the town, but nothing had ever been done about it.

The intersection was close to the church and I asked the session if they had ever tried to have the intersection changed. I was told that every pastor before me had tried to change the intersection, and every single one had failed to get it done. "Forget it!" I was told. "It will never happen because it would take too much money to correct the problem." I asked the session if they would mind if I tried anyway and if they would support my cause. "Go ahead," they said. "Try, if you must, but you're wasting your time." I told them that in good conscience I had to try, because people used that intersection all the time. I did not want to preside over a funeral knowing I hadn't tried to fix the problem in the first place. So I developed a strategy, and did my research into the whole matter. I talked to as many people as I could about the history of the intersection, and got the same response from everyone, "We've tried, and the Pennsylvania Department of Transportation (PennDOT) won't do anything."

I called PennDOT directly and asked them about the intersection. They said they had reviewed the situation many times and were aware of the problems, but it would be too costly to correct the problem and do all the other scheduled projects that needed to be done at the present time.

"If I raise the money to get the intersection changed, will you do it?" I asked.

"Oh, it's not that simple," they said. "The intersection is already planned for reconstruction, but it is about ten years away." I told them that I knew for a fact that people had wanted a change for at least 20 years! He said, "Well, yes, but you see what happens is that every year the projects on the list get re-evaluated and quite often the projects on the 10-year list can easily get pushed back another ten years! I sympathize with you, but there is nothing I can do."

I was not about to give up. I've never liked to hear, "It can't be done." I will always come back with the statement, "Why not?" And, immediately try to figure out the next step.

I just couldn't believe that, if I could raise the money, whatever it took to pay for the change of the intersection, PennDOT would refuse to make the necessary changes. So, I started a letter writing campaign. I got letters sent by the hundreds, and started a petition for people to sign. I went to all the adjacent landowners and spoke to them face to face, and asked if they would mind the reconstruction of the intersection in order to make it safer, because I knew it would have to be enlarged. All of the landowners agreed they would cooperate with

PennDOT if they were to reconstruct the intersection. I felt like I was doing PennDOT's work for them, preparing the way as much as possible for the job to get done. However, after all my efforts, I was met with a nice, "Thank you for your concern, but we are unable to do anything at this time. We will consider it in the 10-year plan." Well, I knew what that meant. It would never get done.

Then it happened! Tragically, another car accident occurred at the intersection and someone died. I was sick about it, so I prayed to God. God knew that I had been trying to get the intersection changed, and now I was angry! I was more determined than ever to get something done. How could PennDOT look the other way? How could the loss of a human life be ignored? Then, a light bulb went off in my head. I got it! I would argue the reconstruction of the intersection on moral and ethical grounds!

I researched the history of the intersection and discovered that there was on record one major car accident each year, with at least one fatality at that intersection about every other year! That was it for me! I decided to consult a lawyer about launching a class-action lawsuit against PennDOT for negligence on behalf of all the victims who had lost loved ones at that intersection through the years. To put a price tag on the cost of human loss and suffering would certainly be in the millions! Fortunately, I already had it on record that PennDOT was aware that the intersection did not meet their own standards for safe intersections and was in need of reconstruction. All I needed to do was to file a class-action suit against them, and notify the Press.

I prayed about it night after night, and decided I would give them one more chance, and let them know my intentions. I called PennDOT the next day, and asked if they had heard about the accident at the intersection where someone had died. "Yes," they answered. "Good, you can expect a letter in the mail of my intention to file a class-action lawsuit against PennDOT on behalf of all the families who have lost loved ones at that intersection." By now, PennDOT knew I was serious. I had had it with their run-around answers, and had gotten the support of everyone in the town, and they knew it. I told the representative that he could certainly expect to read about it in the local newspaper as well.

Within a few a days, I got a call that PennDOT officials wanted to meet with me to present several proposals they had in mind. "That would be fine," I said. However, "I would prefer you present your ideas to the community at a 'town meeting' that I would set up in the Church Christian Education building." It would be an informal meeting for PennDOT to explain their proposed plans. They agreed and I was ecstatic, because I'd finally made some progress. I invited the local newspapers to be present, and after the meeting, they promised there would be complete coverage on the proposed projects.

It was amazing how my prayers had been answered and now that the project was taking on a new dimension, there were some big players coming out of the woodwork who wanted to be recognized. I didn't mind that they were receiving the limelight as long as the intersection was going to be corrected. There were several other stumbling blocks to overcome and we still needed to settle how much would be spent on the project and where the money would come from, but in the end the wheels were finally rolling. The following year, PennDOT began to bring in heavy equipment to redo the intersection.

After I received a commitment from PennDOT, I graciously thanked them and encouraged others to do the same as well. They spent a great deal of money lowering the surface of the road and changing the traffic pattern so that it would be safe for people to drive through the intersection, and that had always been our final objective. By making this intersection safe, our children and youth were being protected.

Youth Group Band

Dale and I enjoyed working with the youth in the church. On one occasion, Dale and I were asked to help a group of young people in the church form a band. We promised to help them get started performing, and their parents were very supportive. Dale played the "keyboard," and I played the guitar or bass guitar. Our first performance was at the mother-daughter banquet, and we later played

215

at the high school dance. We dressed up like the group "KISS" with make-up and I wore a wig to fit in.

The youth were incredibly enthusiastic about playing, and later went on their own to play in bars and at other dances. Dale and I did not go to any of the local bars, as it was not our custom, but when we heard that the band we had helped to launch was going to play there, we made an exception and decided to go hear them.

When we entered the bar, we were greeted with a warm reception by the parents of the band members. It was good to see parents who were supportive of their kids rather than being at odds with them as so often happens. I was very proud of these kids and hoped we were a good influence on them no matter where the journey of life took them.

I was really surprised to see that a great number of the congregation of the Presbyterian Church I served were also there! Granted, many of them did not attend every single week, but there were active and inactive members who were there. It offered me a great opportunity to socialize and get to know many of them, and for them to see their pastor and his wife. They could see that we were not distant people, but were willing to meet them in a tavern and enjoy a beer.

I said to Dale, "Maybe we should come here more often and get to know more of our church members." It seemed to me that in the scripture stories, Jesus was not afraid to go anywhere! He was criticized for associating with sinners, and was called a glutton and a drunkard. Jesus attended a wedding reception and when the guests ran out of wine, He performed his first miracle and created wine for everyone to drink! (John 2:1-11)

Dale and I never minded having a drink or two with our friends, but we were certainly mindful that it was not something we wanted to overdo. We were often with people who never drank any alcohol at all. We just had to be sensible and judge for ourselves when it was appropriate and when not appropriate. I have always been fond of the Apostle Paul's advice to a fellow minister, Timothy. He said, "Use a little bit of wine for the sake of your stomach and your ailments." (I Timothy 5:23) As Dale and I got to know people and they got to know us, we saw that most of them were glad to see us and would welcome us anywhere, wine or no wine.

Working with Youth

Dale and I have a long history of working with youth. We would often go on overnight trips, hike on the Application Trail, and visit amusement parks with them. We would raise money for various mission causes with all-night rock-a-thons, mile walks, car washes, ice cream socials, and spaghetti dinners. We reached out to shut-in's by visiting and singing in nursing homes, by Christmas caroling each year, and food drives for the Presbyterian Homes. We even went to the local prison to perform a concert. The prison chaplain talked with our youth about prison life. We also visited funeral homes and had the funeral director explain the grieving process associated with the death of a loved one. We had a "mock wedding" where we took the whole youth group through all the pre-marital counseling, performed a "mock wedding," and celebrated with a reception! I thought we were quite creative in educating the youth of our church.

Verna

Verna was 96 years of age and at the end of her life. She suffered from severe arthritis and told me she had to walk from one room to the other every day no matter how painful. Unfortunately, she fell down and ended up in a nursing home. When I went to visit her, she put a question to me, "Why can't I die?"

I told her that I could not answer that question because it was between her and God's will, the author and finisher of life. She told me how much she suffered from bedsores, and complained that no one had been in her room to attend to her for a long time. So, I left Verna and headed for the nurse's station demanding to speak to the head nurse on duty. I knew Verna did not have much family or an advocate to speak on her behalf.

I asked the nurse why Verna had bedsores, and told her that if Verna had been properly moved from side to side, she would not have the sores. The head nurse apologized and promised to take care of the matter, and as I headed back to Verna's room, I heard her call the other nurses in and chew them out. I hated to get the staff in trouble, but someone needed to get them to do what was right for Verna, who couldn't take care of herself.

The Woman Who Had No Friends

I'll never forget a woman who came to me for counseling. She complained about everyone. She told me how much she hated her neighbors, and how she disliked all her relatives, everyone in the community, the business people, the customers, the people who went to the same place she went to…she could not stand them! She ripped apart everyone she talked about. In fact, she hated everyone. Then, I could not believe the next thing she asked me.

"Karl, there is one thing I just don't understand. Why is it that I don't have any friends?"

I was astounded. "Uh, let me think," I said. "Gee, what was it you said about your neighbors, family, and others?"

She said, "They are all jerks!"

"Well, do you think they know that you think they're all jerks?"

She reluctantly admitted, "Yes, they all probably know I don't like them."

"Well, do you think that might have something to do with you not having many friends?" I asked.

She paused for a moment and finally said, "You know, you're right. I have been a bit harsh with everyone. I can see why they may not want to be my friend."

"YES, YES, I think she's got it!!!!!" I said to myself. What seems clear to me is not always clear to others. There is a law of reciprocity on this earth which states that "For every action, there is an opposite and equal reaction." If you would have friends, you must be friendly.

My Winter Dreams

It was the winter of 1986 when I began to have dreams about an airplane that would explode over the state of Florida. I grew concerned as I was planning to fly down to visit my parents in Florida for a week.

As my departure date drew closer, my dreams became more frequent and vivid. On the evening of January 27th my dream was the most clear and vivid of all, and it woke me up with my heart pounding. I had a horrific premonition of disaster. I was on the verge of canceling my trip, thinking my plane was going to blow up upon take off. I turned on the TV that morning, after sending our children to school, and to my horror there was the vast news coverage of a disaster that had just taken place over Florida. The space shuttle Challenger had just exploded with all crew members perishing!

I quietly slumped into a chair with my mouth wide open, shaking my head in disbelief. This is what all my dreams had been about! The Challenger was my airplane that exploded over Florida. I confused the dreams with my own visit, when what I was seeing was actually destined to happen with the Challenger and its crew.

I did feel humbled (again) to have sensed a forthcoming tragedy. Through this, I realized that some things are meant to be.

Near Death Experience #1 with the Visit of an Angel

In 1987, I went to a medical doctor complaining of back pain in the kidney area. I had been serving in Dayton for about four years. Dale said I should go and have the pain checked out, so I was seen by the doctor who said, after examining my back, that he wanted to have an IVP dye x-ray of my kidneys to see what was going on.

"Do you want me to go along with you?" Dale asked.

"No," I said. "They are just going to take some x-rays of my kidneys to see if they are all right."

As instructed, I did not eat or drink anything before the test that was scheduled for later in the afternoon. I went to the hospital and the nurse asked if I had ever had this test before, and I told her, "No." She then asked if I had any allergies. "None that I know of," I responded.

She injected a dye into my veins and took x-ray pictures of my kidneys. Then she asked me how I felt. "Terrible, I feel like throwing up," I said.

The nurse technician said, "Breathe deeply, it will pass." So, I breathed deeply and meditated, but I still felt terrible. After five minutes, the nurse came back into the room and said, "Okay, you can get dressed and go now!"

So, I got dressed and left the hospital. On the drive home, I noticed that several cars had honked their horns at me for no apparent reason! Maybe I was weaving, or maybe I was going too slowly. I didn't understand why they were honking, but suspected I was driving erratically.

Then about 30 minutes after leaving the hospital, I became very sick. I pulled the car over to the side of the road and walked into the woods because I felt like throwing up, and I did not want to be seen by everyone passing by the road. I also felt diarrhea coming on, so I went even further into the woods. I needed to pull my pants down and quickly! It was awful; I started throwing up and needed to go at the same time. I collapsed on the ground, and continued to throw up until nothing was coming out!

I felt weird. My lips felt like they were swollen to twice the size they were supposed to be, and I noticed strange red rings forming on my arms in several places. I felt very tired. All I wanted to do was just lie there on the ground. I noticed the stillness of the forest, and I could hear how quiet it was. The sun was beginning to go down and I realized what a mistake it had been for me to tell Dale not to come with me. I felt so weak, and as I tried to get up several times I just collapsed back to the ground. I had never felt like this before.

I realized that I was in a bad position lying in the woods by myself with no one there to help me, as the sun was going down. All I wanted to do was to sleep. I had been somewhat depressed lately, questioning if I should even continue my ministry.

Then, out of nowhere, a figure appeared before me. It was a man, who looked like a warrior back in biblical times. He wore a short tunic made of metal beads, with a silver and gold helmet on his head. He carried a round shield and wore a sword at his side. He had shin guards on his legs with silver and gold shoes. He stood there looking at me and said, "You have been given a choice to live or to die." He had a peaceful look on his face as he continued, "If you want to die all you have to do is to go to sleep, but if you want to live, you must go back to the hospital!"

I thought for a second, and it seemed that my whole life passed before me. I had lived a good life, and I had accomplished a lot. There was a life insurance policy for Dale and my family. However, in my mind I thought of the theological question, "Who am I to judge life and death, only God can decide who lives and dies?"

The warrior smiled and said, "Yes, God is sovereign, but today you have been given a choice." And, he repeated his statement, "If you want to die, go to sleep, but if you want to live, you must go back to the hospital."

"Let me think about it," I said. I felt so tired and weak. Then the figure standing before me said in a stern loud voice, "No, you must decide now! Right now, decide!" One last time he repeated to me, "If you want to die, go to sleep, but if you want to live go back to the hospital." I felt an incredibly peaceful feeling of God's love surrounding me. Then, I realized it was okay for me to die. I felt God would accept me into his kingdom right then, and I experienced a feeling of much love and joy. But, I thought about my family, my ministry, and asked myself, "Have you finished what you wanted to do?" I decided, "No." I wasn't finished yet. I still had more work to do, and I did love Dale and my children and wanted to help them do well in life.

At that, I tried to stand up and I noticed a tree next to me to my left and I was able to grab it. Then, right behind that tree was another tree. I took another step and grabbed on to that tree and I leaned up against it for support. Then I noticed another tree, and took one more step and held on to that tree and so forth until I eventually made my way back to the car.

I leaned up against the car, rolled my body to the door, and opened it collapsing in the driver's seat. I managed to reach over to start the car and leaned my head up against the glass window. I was so weak. I pushed my foot against the gas pedal and turned the car around. Fortunately, no cars were in the way. I noticed that I was weaving the car back and forth so badly that I could hear the tires go off the road into the gravel and back onto the road again. I wondered if this was what it was like to drink and drive. I came upon several stoplights and thank God, every one was green! That was incredible in itself, since I did not have to adjust my speed, but kept a steady pace all the way back to the hospital.

I finally pulled up to the emergency room entrance, leaving the keys in the car. I tried to run, but I felt like I was moving in slow motion, using every bit of energy I could muster just to get through the automatic glass doors. Incredibly, a nurse rushed right up to me as I entered the emergency room, and I handed her the folded pink slip that was in my top pocket. "I believe I'm having an allergic reaction to a test," I said. And, I collapsed onto the floor! The nurse called for help and they lifted me onto a gurney. I recall someone putting a blanket on me because I began to shake violently! That's all I remember, because then I lost consciousness.

When I woke up I was surrounded by people. The doctor was instructing the nurse to squeeze the intravenous bag with her hands to force the fluids into me, and someone yelled, "He's awake." They told me it was a close call and they had to give me epinephrine to get my blood pressure up, because it had "bottomed out." I had gone into what they call "anaphylactic shock" from the IVP dye they'd administered for the kidney test earlier that day. The good news was that my kidneys were fine, but the test almost killed me!

I received a call from a nurse at the hospital and was told that Karl had experienced a problem with his test. She asked if I could come to the Emergency Room. I was quite concerned, but didn't find out the full extent of the danger Karl was in until I got to the hospital. It took me a while to get there as I had to arrange childcare and it was a 40-minute drive to the hospital.

When I finally arrived I went into the room where Karl lay, and couldn't believe his condition. He was hooked up to an IV and his face was yellow. His eyes were red and watery and he was shaking. I found out from a nurse, who happened to be a minister's daughter, that Karl had gone into anaphylactic shock from an allergic reaction to the IVP dye. It was then I realized how close I had come to losing him.

The doctors told Dale that it was a miracle I'd made it back to the hospital in my condition. It turned out that my back pain was just the result of a muscular-skeletal injury, caused by the strain of lifting something the wrong way.

It was truly a near death experience and was life changing for me in different ways. From a theological standpoint, I came to believe that God, though sovereign, will give certain people choices to determine their own destiny, even over matters of life and death. I could have died and it would have been fine with God. Instead, I made the conscious choice to live and continue with my work and ministry on this earth. This too, was fine with God.

This was the first angelic visit I can remember and it was very vivid. Who was that visitor that stood before me dressed as a warrior? It wasn't until I met June Bro and told her the story, that she suggested I study the pictures of the archangel Michael depicted throughout biblical history and make the determination myself. I agreed to do that, and discovered that it was indeed Michael.

Michael is the keeper of the way, the archangel who helps people make big decisions at a time of crisis. He protected me when I was between life and death, and he offered me the choice to sleep and die, or get back to the hospital and live. Once I'd decided to live, he helped me make my way back to the hospital.

I was honored that such a distinguished figure would defend me and that my life and ministry were worthy enough of such an angelic visit. Why did he not identify himself to me? I believe it was because it was not important for me to know at that moment, so much as it was important for me to make the decision to live!

I will never forget the feeling of being at peace in that in-between state of life and death. Had I not felt the purpose and desire to live, it would have been very easy to just fall asleep in the woods, in a state of beautiful peace. And, I am sure there are many people who have had a near death experience where the opportunity presented itself for that individual to "check out" or pass over to the other side. Although I believe God is the ultimate authority over life and death, the lesson I learned was that your faith in God along with your purpose for living are so paramount, that it can influence whether you leave or stay.

Talking with Departed Souls

I communicated with one man who had died. He was the beloved father of nine children and had a devoted wife. He developed a long illness with heart problems and eventual kidney shutdown. We visited him in the hospital and supported his family throughout his illness. After his passing, we went to the funeral home to view his body. He spoke to me. He wanted me to reassure his wife that he was fine and had made the transition without difficulty. When I told his wife that he was fine she said, "I know."

There was another wonderful man who was a very gifted furniture craftsman. He had been in Vietnam and ever since his experience there had suffered with the side effects of exposure to Agent Orange. Years later, they proved that indeed Agent Orange did affect our soldiers in a negative way, and the government finally admitted that veterans should be helped. Unfortunately, many veterans had already taken their own lives.

He had a lot of pain, especially with migraines and neurological issues. Karl was very concerned about him and took him down to Johns Hopkins in Baltimore to be evaluated to see if they could do anything for him. One day, the illness became too much for him to endure. He committed suicide. We were all devastated. We had tried so hard to help him. At the funeral, I felt his presence and he told me he was "sorry" he had done this. He said he wished he had "stuck it out." I conveyed this message to Karl who was also aware he was there. When Karl gave his message/eulogy he spoke to him, reassuring him that God loved him and would be compassionate of his painful experience in life.

Another man developed liver cancer and did not want to die. He was not very involved with the church and enjoyed things of the earth. When he died, I felt his presence almost immediately. I was traveling to nursing school and he was in the car with me. He said, "I don't want to die, I like living too much!" I told him that he was dead and he needed to follow the light to God because his time on earth was over. He stayed around me for several more days. During the funeral, I saw that he had not yet left his body. I continued to reassure him that he was okay and needed to follow the light. Within several days he left. I spoke with his daughter-in-law and she told me that she had experienced the same thing. He did not want to leave and took his time leaving the earth plane.

Mother's Last Days

The weekend I was installed as the pastor at Dayton Glade Run Church, my mother, Frances, suffered a mild heart attack. I didn't know and she didn't tell anyone about it because she did not want to take attention away from my installation. After she left us to return home, she went to the doctor and was treated. She had been suffering with emphysema, and after 50 years, she finally decided to quit smoking, which was a delight to us all. Unfortunately, much of the damage had already been done to her body.

I was grateful to my mother who took care of our children while we went to the Holy Land, and her selfless support of our family. The kids remember those times when they would run circles around her. She really could not get up and down the stairs very well, and her health had been deteriorating gradually with advanced diabetes, but she still gave her all.

In December of 1987, Karl's Mom was diagnosed with breast cancer, and had a double mastectomy. She had gone to the doctor and he had examined her to find several lumps in her breasts. She had been aware of them for two years and said to the doctor, "You finally found them!"

Mom was insistent on having the double mastectomy to encourage her children "not to be afraid" to have surgery if needed.

She stayed with Karl and me for several weeks to recover, and then Mom went on to the home of Laura, Karl's sister, for a little longer. This was the last Christmas we spent together as a family. We had a good time.

Mom eventually went home and was on her own again. She did have a cleaning woman named Margaret to clean and to keep an eye on her, and some of her neighbors stopped in on occasion as well. She also had a renter named Felix who assisted her whenever she needed it.

At Easter time, we went to visit Mom. She was having pain in her right foot, ankle and leg, so we took her to a doctor in Virginia. Unfortunately, he was unable to determine what was wrong. On the way home, Mom insisted we go to the Tidal Basin in Washington, D.C. since the Cherry Blossoms were in bloom. We had a walk, took some pictures, as she requested. Most were of Mom and her grandchildren. It was a memorable day.

Unfortunately, our visit was cut short due to the death of a member in our congregation in Dayton. As we were leaving for home, Mom said, "I'm scared," as she accompanied us down the stairs to the car. She was in a lot of pain as she attempted to walk around.

Shortly after, Mom developed a blood clot in her leg, and was admitted to a hospital. After a time, she was discharged, and went to my sister's home to recover. Unfortunately, she went back into the local hospital for other problems. The circulation in her leg had gotten so bad that she developed gangrene. The doctors said that she should have her leg amputated, but knew she would not be strong enough to make it through the surgery. She decided that she wanted to go home to die in peace. Mom waited to die until I could be there with her.

When we were all there giving her encouragement, all of a sudden, Mom pointed to the corner of the room and said, "Isn't that beautiful?" All we could see was a blank wall. Is it possible she was seeing into the next world? The next morning, she passed over.

The night before she died, the whole family gathered around her bedside, singing songs to her. One of the songs we sang was from West Side Story, "One Hand, One Heart." To this day, I usually get a little teary-eyed when I hear that song.

Dale's Illness – 1990

I started feeling pain in my back, which started between my shoulder blades, and traveled down the middle right mid-section and sometimes onto my lower right quadrant. I went to different doctors and was put through a number of tests to determine what was wrong. I had trouble eating, I had lost weight and sometimes I had difficulty functioning. Eventually, after CT scans, multiple endoscopies and gall bladder studies, a diagnosis was made. They discovered that I had a complex cyst on my right ovary. I also had a problem with my gall bladder. It was decided that I would have surgery to remove the cyst.

After the surgery, it took a long time for me to recover. Karl and I had companion prayer and received information on a recovery regimen. We followed this information and I gradually improved. One treatment involved taking a hot Epsom salt bath daily. During my recuperation, I wrote a song, "Where am I going?"

Where am I Going?
What do I care?
The pain within me is so hard to bear;
But you love me, too, and help me through each night and day.
Give me the strength
I need to stay,
I need to stay.

Open my eyes, Lord!
Help me to see
Visions of heaven, waiting for me.
For you love me, too, and help me through each night and day.
Give me the strength

I need to stay,
I need to stay.

Fill me with hope, Lord.
Brighten my day.
Lift up my spirit, take fear away.
When you love me, too, and help me through each night and day,
I have the strength
I need to say,
I need to say:

Grant me my wish, Lord;
Within your power,
Fill me with life, Lord; heal me now!
'Cause you love me, too, and help me through each night and day,
I have the strength
I need to say,
I need to say:

No matter what, Lord,
I'll always be
Grateful, that you came and comforted me.
While you love me, too, and help me through each night and day,
I have the strength
I need to say,
I'm yours!

I did have a difficult time for months because I didn't know if my illness was terminal. My faith was tested and I did the best I could to meet my fears and keep my faith in God. After all was said and done, I believe the experience made me a better person and hopefully I set a positive example for others to follow their path through life. I tried to say this in song and it certainly made me feel better.

During this time, as I gradually recovered, I began to work on two musical albums. One had a religious theme entitled, "All Life's Praises" and another was an inspirational album I called, "Uplifting

Moments." Working on music was very healing to me, and I eventually finished both albums in time for the Dayton Fair.

Musical Performance at Dayton Fairgrounds

Dale and I love music and enjoy sharing our musical talents with others. I have always been proud of Dale's voice, and when she sings, she makes me tremble. I'm not sure why, but it always happens to me, and it's wonderful.

We created a little music studio in our house and produced three cassettes of music tapes. It was a lot of work to get all the mechanical licenses necessary for all the songs, but we did it correctly. Our whole family sang on the recordings and we performed our Christian music at different churches in the area. We performed at other Presbyterian Churches, the Church of God, and even a Baptist Church.

I wrote a little booklet that went along with the "All Life's Praises" album, and in it I wrote a summary for each of the songs on the album, explaining the spiritual message behind each song and its meaning for Dale and me. I used the booklet in a Lenten study in the Dayton Church.

We named our group, "Dale Suzanne and the Four Stones." The four stones were our three children and me, and was a play on our last name, Viernstein. In German, 'Vier' means four and 'stein' means stone. Dale played the keyboard, I played the guitar or violin, and our three children sang backup. One performance was at the Dayton Fair Grounds in the summer of 1990, and we sold tapes after the concert. The townspeople said you could hear Dale singing all the way into the heart of town about a quarter-mile away.

Music has always been a big part of our family and church ministry. Dale once told me that she intends to use her voice only to praise God, and that is what she has done. She has had several offers to sing professionally, but she always turned them down. Her favorite hymn is "Take My Life, and Let it Be Consecrated." In one of the verses it says, "Take my voice and let me sing, always only for my King." That's my Dale! My partner in ministry!

Raising Children in the Country

Being the mother of children can be time-consuming, challenging and rewarding, all at the same time. To raise children in the country is even more time-consuming, especially when all their lessons and classes are 25-30 miles away. And when the lessons are in different towns at the same time, well, that can be a coordinating nightmare!

The perfect example was when Jason and Julie both took piano lessons. They were scheduled back to back for 45 minutes each. I would drive them to their lessons which were 30 minutes away from our home, and then take Christiana to her voice lesson 20 minutes from there. When her lesson was over, I would go back and pick up Jason and Julie.

The children also took dance and karate lessons, and there was also soccer practice as well as games and the Boy Scouts. The girls played in the school band and all three children sang in the school chorus.

I put a lot of miles on the car and I was certainly glad when Jason learned to drive so he could take his sisters to karate and piano lessons.

Thankfully, the Boy Scouts were located in Dayton and Karl served as an assistant scoutmaster, so he was able to take Jason, who went through all the levels in scouting and eventually met all the requirements to become an Eagle Scout.

Jason

Jason was quite an accomplished pianist, but due to difficulty with "jumping eyes," he had trouble reading the sheet music. Therefore, he was forced to memorize everything in order to play a piece smoothly. He studied each composition intently in order to memorize it.

He was invited to performed for the Monday Musical Club in Indiana, Pennsylvania. The mother of the famous actor, Jimmy Stewart, had been a member of the club and Jason won an award named for her.

He also tried out for the Governor's School for the Arts, which required a lengthy and involved audition. The day he was accepted was a momentous occasion for us all. This meant Jason would receive a full scholarship to Mercyhurst College in Erie, Pennsylvania to study piano for a five-week program in the summer. There were only ten piano students accepted from the state of Pennsylvania, and as a sophomore in high school, Jason was one of the youngest selected. We believe Jason may have had a little help from his parental grandmother Frances, who had already passed on by this time. She had been an accomplished pianist herself.

A momentous challenge for Jason was learning to play George Gershwin's <u>Rhapsody in Blue</u>. He went on to play this piece with the Punxsutawney Phil-Harmonic.

Christiana

In addition to Christiana's other abilities in karate and dance, she played the flute, and was an exceptionally gifted singer. She had always participated in school choirs as well as the children's choirs in church. She was often given solos to perform, and took voice lessons to improve her skill.

When she entered high school, she auditioned for the different levels of the State Chorus, and made it all the way to the All State Chorus's 1st chair, second Alto position where she sang in Heinz Hall, and then at the Civic Arena in Pittsburgh in the Night of 2000 Stars. This gala was comprised of 2000 voices from around the state singing with the Pittsburgh Philharmonic in honor of Henri Mancini.

Christiana had her tonsils removed the following year, which changed her voice register from second alto to first soprano.

Julie

Julie was a happy child and very well rounded in her own right. She enjoyed all kinds of music and learned to play the violin, the piano, the drums, and then the clarinet. She had a lovely singing voice as well, but didn't care to take voice lessons.

She also loved to dance and took lessons in ballet, tap and jazz, and was honored to be chosen as a prominent character in a local dance company production of the Nutcracker Suite.

Julie also enjoyed her karate lessons and did quite well.

Julie's Feet

At Dayton, we had a Concord grape arbor that we enjoyed and we would pick grapes at harvest to make grape juice. One year, we decided to make some wine with the grapes from the little arbor. We read up on how to make it and decided it would be fun. After all, Jesus made wine for a wedding at Cana.

We gathered the grapes from the vine, prepared them, and placed them into a large crock. We had our children help us. We explained how, long ago, they would place the grapes in large vats and press the grapes by walking on them. We thought it sounded like fun, so we asked the kids if they wanted to try.

First, we asked Jason if he would like to help us by stomping grapes. "No way," he said. Then, we asked Christiana if she would like to help. "Yes," she said, but she was a little hesitant. However, no sooner did she get started, then she wanted out. Julie, our youngest child, was playfully asked, "Would you help us make wine by walking on the grapes?" "Yes, I'll help!" She responded enthusiastically.

So, we went upstairs and washed her feet in the bathtub, and then I carried her down the stairs and put her into the large crock full of concord grapes. We told her to stomp her feet up and down on the grapes.

Julie was our carefree child, and was usually willing to go along with us in some of the fun things we did. After the grapes were smashed, we sweetened them with sugar as instructed, and let it ferment. I placed the large crock in an old refrigerator in the garage, and placed a small warmer in with it to help the fermentation process.

We allowed it to sit for several weeks, then strained off the grapes through cheesecloth, pouring the finished product into several old bottles. We put them into storage for several years, and almost forgot about the wine we had made, until one day I saw the bottles in the basement and decided that enough time had passed to try it out. As we tasted it, we agreed it was a very good, sweet wine. So, because of all the hard work that Julie had done to help make the wine, and because she was such a sweet child, we named the wine "Julie's Feet."

Dale Goes Back to School

In May of 1991, I took my mother's and mother-in-law's advice about making the decision to be a nurse; so, I became a Certified Nurse's Aide and worked at St. Andrew's Village, a Presbyterian Home in Indiana, Pennsylvania. I liked it so much I decided to go back to school and become a Registered Nurse.

After much discussion with Karl and our children, because it would mean a sacrifice for all of us, I enrolled at Indiana University of Pennsylvania in the fall of 1991, where I took the courses required to be admitted into nursing school. I did well and entered the Western Pennsylvania Hospital School of Nursing in Pittsburgh, Pennsylvania in the Fall of 1992.

West Penn was 1 ½ hours from our home, which meant I was on the road a minimum of three hours a day. A difficult commute, but I found I was challenged by the curriculum and enjoyed stretching my brain.

I was fortunate to find several older students with whom to share the commute. It helped to pool our resources and we gave support to one another. Some days I left Dayton at 5:00 a.m. and didn't return home until after 5:00 p.m. Then I had to study and prepare for the next day's work, while taking care of my family and doing household chores. Fortunately, I had worked out a schedule with our children and Karl and they all took turns cooking and cleaning up. They were also responsible for their own laundry, which made things much easier, and everyone pitched in to help.

During this time, I was directing four choirs at church and handling the responsibilities of a pastor's wife as best I could. I was there for weddings and funerals and the other myriad functions at the church. However, I had to give up the children's choir to other members in the church, and I had to pare down other activities where I could. It was common to see me studying during our children's concerts or at church dinners.

After three years, much hard work, and many sleepless nights, I graduated cum laude in the 100th graduating class of the Western Pennsylvania Hospital School of Nursing on June 10, 1994! What made my graduation even more special was being asked with another student to sing a song from Jekyll and Hyde, "This is the Moment." My family was there and that meant everything to me. My parents came from the Poconos, and Karl's sister Laura came with her daughter, Crystal. As a special "Thank You" to all our guests, we treated them to a ride on the Gateway Clipper, a steamboat that cruised on the Monongahela, Allegheny and Ohio Rivers.

I want to add here that Karl was supportive during those three years. He even gave up his search for another church so that I could achieve my goal. He helped organize the home front with the children and helped them get to their various lessons.

My parents were also a great help. They gave me added encouragement and assisted with some money to cover daily expenses such as gas for the car and meals away from home. My mother, herself, had gone back to school when I was a teenager and still living at home, so I was fully aware of what my family was going through. My mother graduated from college when I was 17 and I admired her for her efforts. I wanted to do the same thing, and I did!

It wasn't easy completing my RN diploma while meeting the needs of my family, but we worked together. My education was surely a joint effort with my husband, children and parents as well as members of the church.

I may have gone to school and achieved my dreams without our Moms' encouragement, but I believe that their inspiration put the idea into my head and gave me the determination to follow my heart's desire. I am forever grateful. And, I'm sure my mother-in-law was cheering me on from the other side.

Private Nurse Dale

I had been applying to hospitals for work, just as I applied for a teaching job when I graduated from college. At that time, there was an influx of teachers, and we were all competing for limited positions. Now there seemed to be an overabundance of nurses. At the same time, hospitals were trying to cut costs, so they were reducing the number of RN's on staff in favor of hiring LPN's and nurse's aides for less.

My first job was in a hospice situation where I took care of a wonderful elderly gentleman named Ralph, who suffered from lung cancer and had come home to die. I was his private nurse. His family also had visiting nurses and nurse's aides to assist. I was a companion and helped his wife around the house as well. Ralph liked music and since I was a singer, I sang for him often. He really enjoyed it.

As Ralph's condition deteriorated he required constant care, so I was left alone with him more often. One day, his wife and daughter went out to buy new eyeglasses. He appeared to be stable when they left, not realizing what would await them upon their return.

A nurse's aide arrived shortly after to help bathe Ralph. As we worked, I noticed he was having difficulty breathing. When the aide finished up and left, I took Ralph in my arms to comfort him, and I began to sing. As I did so, he quietly died in my arms. It was a beautiful, peaceful transition. I noted the time and documented the case, and when his family returned a short time later, I had the job of breaking the news to them. They blamed themselves for not being there at the time of his passing, but who could know when that was going to be? He had certainly appeared all right when they left.

As it turned out they were very grateful that I was there and since they didn't have a pastor, they asked Karl to officiate and for me to sing at his funeral. It was a beautiful service.

It was a short-term assignment, but I learned a great deal during my time with Ralph. I learned that a person could have dignity in dying, and it was wonderful to see the gracious acceptance of his illness by those who loved him. I felt privileged to have been there for him at the moment he passed on.

Chapter 12

"Be still, and know that I am God.
I am exalted among the nations,
I am exalted in the earth.
The Lord of hosts is with us;
The God of Jacob is our refuge."

Psalm 46: 10-11

The Rev. Drs. Harmon and June Bro

I first met Harmon and June Bro in 1991 at a workshop in Pittsburgh. I went first as an observer to hear Harmon and June speak, and then to ask them about their theology and to learn.

The workshop was based upon their book, <u>Growing through Personal Crisis.</u> There was a yearning inside me to find other Pastors dedicated to the ministry of Christ, who believed that God works in many ways to guide his children through dreams, clear guidance visions, and visitations. I often felt alone as a pastor with only Dale to share my deep-felt spiritual experiences. Maybe Harmon or June would be able to help me understand these experiences, and tell me if there was any value to them.

Dale and I have always shared our experiences with one another, but we are very careful who we talk to about these little understood religious experiences. I felt 'burned' a few times when I did share my experiences because I was met with disbelief and even disdain. I have been called a worker of evil who deals with the occult.

I was told in no uncertain terms, "You have no business as a Pastor having such experiences."

I could not understand why I should be condemned for experiencing something that happened to people in the Bible. Did I ask for these dreams? Did I ask for visions of angels? Did I ask God for warnings? No.

Maybe I did when I prayed to God, "Tell me what you want me to do?" Maybe I did when I prayed, "Lord, take me and use me according to thy will."

It took me a while, but I learned in my ministry not to tell people things they have not experienced. It was not that I was unwilling to teach them whatever I knew. God knows, I would be more than willing to teach others what I know and have experienced. When people cannot understand the things I do, they decide I'm just misled.

I believe most people want to understand, but they also want empirical evidence to verify the data. We live in a "prove it to me" society. They might say, "It's just your imagination," or "What do you base it upon, a feeling?" This intuitive faculty is foreign to many people. But, what if these occurrences, which have been part of my whole life, are really experiences of the Holy Spirit guiding me?

I remember when I was younger I was surprised to find out that not everyone had the same intuitions I did. I learned not to talk about it. I learned later that I did not always hear the same things that other people heard either. It was as if my hearing was tuned in to a different frequency at times.

When I counsel people, I try to listen very carefully. However, very often the things that people tell me are not what they really want me to hear. They will say one thing when they really mean to say something else.

I have learned to read the emotions that people convey, including their body language, facial expressions, and eye contact. I believe these are the levels of communication that can transcend ordinary language between us. The more sensitive you are, the more you are able to pick up on the energy that the other person puts out, and this is where you can find the truth of what they are feeling.

I was impressed with Harmon and June's experiences and wanted to share some of my own experiences with them. I was anxious to see if they could advise Dale and me on how best to use the gifts we had. It was December 1992, and I received a video in the mail from Harmon. In it he described a person he would soon meet. I could not believe my ears, I had not yet said anything to him, but it seemed as if he was describing Dale and me to a tee. It was mind-boggling!

I called Harmon on the phone and set up a time when Dale and I could meet with him and June. Unfortunately, we would have to wait until April of 1993. Finally, Dale and I traveled all the way up from Dayton, Pennsylvania to Lexington, Massachusetts, to meet them. As we sat over dinner, I told them about many of the things that had happened to us through the years, and they listened with great interest.

"I have worked with quite a few people who have been gifted in this way," Harmon said. "I have worked with Edgar Cayce and Peter Hurkos who both had psychic abilities."

I learned that Harmon had worked with Edgar Cayce and after observing his work, wrote a biography of Edgar called Seer Out of Season. Harmon also counseled Peter Hurkos who had developed a psychic ability after being hit on his head.

He asked me if we would be willing to do a Companion Prayer session for him and June.

"Sure," I said. "We would be glad to show you what we do and would be honored to have you observe us and tell us if there is anything valid in what we were doing."

I also explained to them that what I did was not exactly like what Edgar Cayce did, because I didn't completely lose consciousness, nor did I go into a hypnotic trance. "We're not exactly sure where our information comes from," I confessed.

After dinner, we returned to their home, and right in the middle of their living room, Dale and I had a prayer session. I lay on the floor and Dale asked me questions about Harmon's and June's son, who had been missing for twelve years. They did not know if he was alive or dead.

It was an enlightening session. We learned that John was alive; however, I saw bars in my deep meditative state and then the bars disappeared. There was then a vision of a radiant angel who spoke to me about their son. She was beautifully dressed and had a lovely smile. She said, "He's fine!" It was the first hope that Harmon and June had received about their son in 12 years, and it was a momentous occasion for them. They later found out that he had, in fact, spent a brief time in jail.

When the prayer and question portion was over, I apologized to them for my flickering and watering eyes. "It happens sometimes," I explained. I was surprised to hear Harmon say, "Oh, don't apologize! I saw that same thing happen to Edgar Cayce many times."

I apologized to him and explained that sometimes I had no idea what I was saying and it didn't always seem to make any sense.

Again, I was shocked when he replied, "Please, don't apologize! I saw Edgar Cayce do that same thing, and there were times you couldn't understand him at all."

I said, "What? Anything I have ever read of Edgar Cayce's work has always made sense to me."

"Yes," Harmon said. "But that is because what you read has been translated from the reading. There were times I could not make sense of what he was saying. It was untranslatable."

When Harmon said that, I sighed with relief, and felt like a huge weight had been lifted off my chest.

Dale told Harmon and June, "There are many times when Karl and I are in a prayer session where there are long periods of silence. Sometimes Karl will begin a sentence and a minute later finish it. Sometimes he may go fast and other times he may go slowly, depending upon how tired he is or how late it is."

Harmon shocked us again when he said, "The same thing would happen to Edgar."

I asked Harmon and June straight out, if there is any value to what Dale and I do. I was seriously uncertain and needed validation. Both Harmon and June were completely affirming and strongly encouraged us to keep doing what we were doing in order to help others. Harmon even went so far as to say, "If I never saw you do another reading, I would be satisfied that I had finally found someone who could approach the throne of grace."

That was the best confirmation I had ever received in my whole life! We became good friends and Dale and I eventually taught Harmon and June how to do the Companion Prayer together.

The History of Companion Prayer

It took years of practice and patience to develop the technique of Companion Prayer. Dale and I actually began praying together back in our college years, and while praying we would take turns asking one another questions while in 'the prayer' state. It was in essence a spiritual dialogue we shared with each other. It was a dialogue between two people who were seeking truth, seeking answers, and seeking to help others in need. However, it took a long time to develop our unique method of companion prayer, and there were many obstacles and bumps in the road.

At the same time, in 1971, Dale and I first began to experiment with hypnosis in search of a deeper understanding of life. We were experiencing many unexplained premonitions, dreams, and visions, and were looking for answers. The Bible does say in Joel, "In the latter days, I will pour out my spirit on all flesh; your sons and your daughters shall prophesy, your old men shall dream dreams, and your young men shall see visions." (Joel 2:28-29)

We began hypnotizing each other. When Dale was hypnotized, she described having lived before in ancient Egypt, as a servant to Nefertiti. She had known "Karl" in that land. They had fallen in love with each other and decided to run away together, but alas, they were caught and "Karl" was killed. Dale was devastated, which is why in this life, she has always feared losing me!

During our junior year at Davis & Elkins College, we were required to complete an oral exam in front of the examination board. During Dale's examination, which would ultimately determine whether she would graduate, Dale described how she had lived before in another time and place. The board members were interested and asked her to explain why she felt this way, so Dale explained how we had hypnotized each other, which had uncovered repressed memories about her past life experience.

I couldn't believe Dale would say something like that during a final oral exam! What would they think of her? I realized she was just being honest, but I was concerned about how her revelation would hurt her. What would people think? Besides, we still weren't sure what was going on, and we needed more time to investigate the merits of Companion Prayer before we revealed our interest to others.

Yet, contrary to my concerns, people started coming to Dale and me, and we began to pray for others. All the while, we continued to consult with people who could help us to understand and develop our talents in a proper way.

Dale and I would take turns in our prayer dialogue with one another. Sometimes I would ask the questions and Dale would give the answers, while other times Dale would ask the questions while I would give the answers. One of us would settle into a semi-conscious state and the other stayed conscious. For us it was a meditative state, not unconscious, and not totally awake. It was a state somewhere between being awake and asleep, somewhat closer to a dream. Eventually we began to have Companion Prayer sessions for others, usually one or two a month. But we felt there had to be a real need, if not an emergency, for us to have a Companion Prayer session to ask for healing. In the beginning, our Companion Prayer sessions were strictly for Dale and me. We were not confident enough to have a session for anyone else, and who would trust the process anyway? But to our surprise, we found that there would always be some who were interested.

We explored other models of prayer, but could not find any others that really worked as well for us. We read up on how Edgar Cayce did readings, but his ability of going into a trance state seemed to be a gift particular to him, and he could never remember anything he'd said. Our experiences were different, because we were always conscious or at least semi-conscious of our surroundings or what was being said.

We were not interested in "channeling," and we did not want to be controlled by entities or disembodied spirits. We examined various meditative techniques such as "transcendental meditation" and the like, but were not happy with the use of syllables and mantras that had absolutely no meaning for us.

Our goal was to be in a prayerful state, approaching the throne of God and the Lord's Kingdom, asking for help in matters of how to live a better life in accordance with God's will. We discovered that not only does God care for us, but our Creator will help us when our intent is pure and honest, and when two or more are gathered in His Name, God will guide them. A prayerful dialogue that seeks answers can stimulate the imaginative and creative abilities within us to solve problems and find solutions. For us, attunement to our Creator God was the key. Being in the presence of God as we seek answers was the way to achieving a good end. However, we discovered that even after the prayer dialogue, it was still up to us or the individual soul for whom the prayer was directed, to take the initiative that would lead them to a wholesome outcome.

The basic premise for our Companion Prayer is written in the scripture, "Where two or three are gathered in my name, there am I in the midst of them." (Matthew 18:20) It takes at least two people to be in Companion Prayer. The scripture says, "Ask and you will receive, seek and you will find, knock and it will be opened to you." (Matthew 7:7) This is the promise that God will answer when we call to Him. The God of love wishes good for all his children, but it is up to us to ask for help or guidance, knowledge or instruction, to do His will.

Jesus said, "If you would know the way, you must be often in prayer." Therefore, a prayer was given by Christ for us to pray, not like the heathen who lift up empty words or phrases, but to say the "Lord's Prayer" as an example of how to pray.

Dale and I had solid scientific training from our courses in college, and we agreed that we would document our experiences. We began recording our Companion Prayer sessions on a regular basis through written record and on cassette when possible. From our college years to the present, we have collected over 30 years of Companion Prayer sessions and documented records for study on ourselves and individuals, and documented prayers for situations that sought to improve our ministry of the church, and the community.

It was later that we discovered that we were not alone in our endeavors. In 1932, two people in prayer together received guidance from the Lord and published a book of their experiences called <u>God Calling</u>, edited by A.J. Russell, Jove Books, NY, February, 1978. They published it to prove that a living Christ speaks today.

You would think that because we prayed and worked together as a team, it would make things easier for us. Absolutely not! We still had tragedies befall us, and we still struggled like everyone else. We still had life's lessons to learn. The difference was, we knew God was with us, and we felt "marked" to do special tasks on this earth. But, the Spirit's gift of knowledge or wisdom of something, does not prevent you from experiencing the pain. The wisdom helps you to deal with it better. Everyone who experiences loss must go through the grieving process. It is as Harmon and June Bro wrote, "We are given an opportunity to grow through our personal crisis."

It seems to me, however, that the more you know, the greater the responsibility you have, the greater the lessons you will be given, and the greater the trials and tribulations you will experience. Before you jump up and say "I, too, want to learn how to draw closer to God, and dialogue with a companion and come to know what God wants me to do," we must ask ourselves this serious question. "Am I willing to pay the price?" "Can I endure the hardships and changes that will come?" As we draw closer to God, our lives will change in ways we never anticipated.

The reader might be wondering, "What is the price I will have to pay?" It will certainly vary with each individual as we travel through the journey of life.

As we draw closer to God, we will definitely become less selfish and more giving. We will also become more understanding of people's pain and loss, and less judgmental and less distant from what is going on in the world. As we draw closer to God, we will become more conscious of our sins and what we are doing to others, and we will become more forgiving of others. As we draw closer to God, material things will mean less, and true relationships that embody love and a closer bond of family love will mean more. As we draw closer to God and care for others in need, we will be willing to sacrifice more of ourselves. Are you willing to become a living example to others? Are you willing to pay the price?

I have found that no great achievement has ever been accomplished without some great sacrifice. There are many difficult roads to travel and where many have taken the low road, Dale and I have chosen the high road. Dale and I took the road less traveled, as difficult as it was at times. Dale and I would play music together, pray together, or work on ministry together, while others pursued more self-gratifying paths. While many rode in new cars, Dale and I rode in old cars because it was all we could afford. For us, Saturday nights were a time of spiritual reflection or sermon preparation, and Sunday a time of worship and prayer. Rarely did Dale and I ever miss Sunday Worship. Even when on vacation, we still managed to worship somewhere. Not because we had to, but because we wanted to. We never thought we were better than others, but it was because we knew we needed to work on becoming better than we were. Church for us was not a sanctuary for saints, but rather a hospital for sinners.

Working on Developing Companion Prayer

Whenever Dale and I entered a dialogue in Companion Prayer, we first humbled ourselves before the throne of mercy and grace, and we would pray together in earnest. We sought to be in the presence of the Lord who is the way, the truth, and the life. We sought to cleanse ourselves through prayers of confession and recited the Lord's Prayer. "Who shall ascend to the Hill of the Lord? And who shall stand in his holy place? He who has clean hands and a pure heart." (Psalm 24:3-4)

One day, while Dale and I were in the middle of Companion Prayer, she asked me several questions about my life and purpose. She asked a question about my life at the time of Jesus's presence on earth, and I described to Dale that there was a man standing in front of me. He was apologizing that he could not find my name on his list. He was bald and dressed in fine clothing. He said to me in a very apologetic voice, "I am sorry but you do not have the proper authorization to enter." Dale asked, "Can we get authorization?" He replied, "We will have to wait and see."

It seemed that we had ended up at what some people call the "Hall of Records" or the "Akashic Library." There is a theory that each soul leaves a record of all its past life activities throughout time. This is confirmed in our Christian Bible, in Revelations 20:12, which reads, "I saw the dead, great and small, standing before the throne, and books were opened. Also another book was opened which is the Book of

Life. And the dead were judged by what was written in the books, by what they had done."

If we had accessed this Book of Life, that would be a huge responsibility and a great privilege. I prayed to God that we would use it wisely.

Several days later, we decided to do another Companion Prayer session. We prayed together and Dale prompted me to return to the Hall of Records. Once there, the man greeted me with smiles as if he immediately knew that I had been approved. He was very gracious and gave me a brief tour. I saw many books with different people listed on them, and I spotted the book marked "Karl Robert Viernstein" and pulled it off the shelf. It was a huge book, and the binding was very old. I opened the book, but I could not read the words. They were all blurry.

"Use a magnifying glass," the bald man said out of the blue. Suddenly, I was holding a magnifying glass in my hand and I placed it upon the words. I could begin to read the words, but I could read only those sections that directly related to the questions asked about my life.

Again, Dale asked about one of my past lives as they related to the time of Jesus, but a big hand reached across the book preventing me from seeing what was written. Then, a voice said, "It is not the right time for you to know this information. Perhaps, in time you will be allowed to see it." I also learned that before I could see anyone else's book, I would need to have their permission.

Often Jesus said, "There are many things I wish to tell you, but I know you can not bear these words." Even Jesus would screen what he told the disciples for their own good.

I felt that it was possible to ascend to the hill of the Lord, but only if I were living a life in which I was applying the principles I knew to be right: "Clean hands" (righteous living) and "Pure Heart" (intentions without ego). That was the path I chose.

After Christiana was born, I didn't want to do any Companion Prayer sessions. I did not feel confident that I was interpreting the information I had received correctly. It stemmed from the prayer session that we did on Dale before we knew she was pregnant with Christiana. Dale had wanted to know if she was pregnant, and when she asked, we were told there was a light in the abdominal area. However, I did not interpret the light as a pregnancy. Dale was scheduled to see the chiropractor to get a few x-rays for diagnostic purposes. That was why we wanted to make sure she was not pregnant. It turned out, however, that Dale was indeed pregnant, and I was devastated that I had not correctly interpreted "the light" as a soul.

We wondered if part of our difficulty in interpreting this message was perhaps in the way we had asked the question. In any event, this one incident caused us to stop the Companion Prayer for a period of one year.

We discovered that asking the right questions was the most integral part of our prayer dialogue. It says in the Scriptures, "Let your requests be made known to God." (Philippians 4:6)

Pilgrim Institute

After fifteen years of intermittent Companion Prayer, I talked with Harmon Bro, who suggested that I do research on Companion Prayer with his Institute. We were delighted. I would now have the objective support of a group of people who were willing to investigate the validity of spiritual information that can come through a prayer dialogue. We hoped to discover ways of improving their usefulness, and perhaps discover better ways to improve the methodology in doing Companion Prayer. We hoped to expand our awareness of our own religious beliefs and how we might continue to grow in oneness with the Creator. I agreed to work with Harmon and sent him transcripts of our Companion Prayer sessions for evaluation.

Not only did we send Harmon and June transcriptions of our Companion Prayer guidance sessions, but they soon began referring people to us to become a part of the study. We were contributing to a better understanding of the process, and we were helping people in need as well. We wanted to preserve the anonymity of these persons and of these sessions, so I devised a system that would assure confidentiality. I devised a numerical code for each individual that only we were privy to.

We soon discovered that we could do Companion Prayer for individuals even from a distance. The quality or accuracy of the information did not change regardless of the distance. This was an incredible development!

Participants were asked to fill out an application and supply a list of questions they wished to have answered. I would go over this list ahead of time and place the questions in the best order for the session. These Companion Prayer sessions were always specific to the individuals asking the questions and turned out to be uncannily accurate. We were even able to describe features of the location where the subject sat waiting miles away. We always asked the person requesting prayer as well as all those present, to be in prayer and meditation during this time to get the most accurate picture of what was being asked. Following the Companion Prayer, I informed the petitioner, as to the results. I always phoned them personally following the session and read the information I had recorded. We initially sent written texts and tapes, but have since advanced to CD's with the improvements in technology.

Each individual case was given the results of the reading and suggestions for improving his or her life whether it was of a physical, spiritual or mental nature. Some followed the suggestions while others chose to ignore them.

One individual had a serious form of cancer and followed the suggestions to the letter. This person's medical prognosis, when she came to us for help, was very grim. Doctors gave her only a year or so to live. She was truly an inspiration to others, and her perseverance in following the suggestions was a testament to Companion Prayer's success. We were grateful to God when we learned nearly five years later, that this person was still alive because of following the suggestions given her.

We are grateful to the Pilgrim Institute, which supported and affirmed our work. It was Harmon Bro's hope that we would someday be able to teach others how to do Companion Prayer.

Finally, in a Companion Prayer dialogue that Dale and I had for Dr. Bro, he was described as being *"one of the best modern theologians of our times yet overlooked by society."* Dr. Harmon Bro was calling for people of different religions "to embrace their differences, and listen and learn from one another rather than be at odds." (The Voice of Reason: Claiming Spiritual Treasures for the Ethics of a Small Blue Planet, a lecture by Harmon Hartzell Bro, Ph.D., 1997, Pilgrim Institute).

Christmas/New Year's Eve Companion Prayer

There was a period of time that Dale and I with our three children would always have a Companion Prayer session together between Christmas and New Year's. It was a time for the whole family to review the events of the last year and look forward to the New Year ahead. Family members could ask questions about their life, their health, their purpose, or whatever concerns they had on their minds.

I remember the feeling of great joy and peace surrounding me, and the Spirit of "Christ" being present. A bright light filled the room.

One of our children asked, "What gift could I receive?"

An image appeared to me after the question was asked. A very large man in a plaid shirt with suspenders and a white beard smiled and said, "Come here and I will show you." I was taken into a giant mall with gifts as far as the eye could see all wrapped and ready to be delivered. The man turned to me and said, "Do you have any particular gift that you want? Just look around and see. The gifts are all here, all you need to do is ask for whatever you want." The man never said who he was and our children didn't dare ask, but it was easy to see that the man could have passed for "Santa." Then I noticed the gifts were labeled and in different sizes. Some were labeled "love," while others said "peace," and "joy!"

The man said again, "They are all here for you. All you need to do is ask for them, and in time, you will receive them."

We ended our Companion Prayer with hope in our hearts, and we realized that in Christ, all things are possible, and gifts are abundant to all who would sincerely ask for them. The Scripture says, "Ask, and it will be given to you; seek and you will find; knock, and it will be opened to you" (Matthew 7:7).

On that New Year's Eve, our family received a great blessing as we gathered together in prayer. We learned that no gift is beyond our reach if we truly believe in a loving God.

Chapter 13

Yea, though I walk through the valley of the shadow of death, I will
fear no evil:
For thou art with me; thy rod and thy staff,
they comfort me."

Psalm 23:4

Traumatic Times

Near Death Experience #2 with the Dream of a Relative

It was the summer of 1993 when I had another near death
experience. I had been experiencing some lower abdominal pain for
about two weeks and thought it was food poisoning, but the pain
persisted for days and got progressively worse.

I was scheduled to officiate over a funeral service one Sunday
afternoon for a church member who had passed. I wanted to support
and console the family, even though I was in a lot of pain. I wanted to
comfort the family after the funeral, but the pain became so intense
that Dale rushed me to the hospital. Doctors checked me out, asked
me lots of questions, and even though I had experienced discomfort for
quite a few days, they prescribed something for pain and sent me
home. We filled the prescription, and I tried to get some rest, but it
was difficult because I was in severe pain. This went on for several
more days.

Early Wednesday morning, around 2:00 a.m., I had a dream of my
stepmother, Mary Viernstein. She came to me and said, "Karl, go
back to the hospital now! You must go back now! Tell them you need
a CAT scan, because you have a perforated bowel!"

I woke Dale and told her my dream. Dale knew Mary very well,
and remembered she had died of a perforated bowel that had gone
undetected. Was Mary coming to me in this dream as a warning to
prevent the same thing from happening to me? Or was it my
imagination? Going back to the hospital was not what I wanted to do

because I had been there only a few days earlier. What would the doctors say if I went back complaining of the same pain? Would they dismiss it again? Dale and I discussed the dream. I reminded her that Mary Viernstein had never come to me since her death, and the fact that she had come to me now in a vivid dream was quite unusual.

Dale and I often questioned the strange dreams and events that had happened to us throughout the years, and we'd discovered that there was always some message for us to pay attention to. I really did not want to go back to the hospital, and I knew Dale was tired, but we both agreed we couldn't ignore Mary's dream. We loved her when she was alive, and I'm sure she would do everything she could to help us out even from the other side. So we decided to have a Companion Prayer session to confirm the warning in my dream before taking another 45 minute drive back to the hospital.

The Companion Prayer session confirmed that I had a perforated bowel. We were instructed to go back to the Emergency Room immediately and request a CAT scan of the bowel. This would confirm the diagnosis.

When we arrived at the emergency room, there was a different medical team on duty. I told the doctor about the pain in my lower abdomen, and about the dream of my step-mother who came to me and told me to go to the hospital and tell the doctor I needed a CAT scan. I could not eat, and I was in severe pain.

To my surprise, he listened as he examined me and then calmly said, "Well, maybe you should have a CAT scan. Wait here, I'll be right back." A short time later, he came back and said, "You're in luck tonight because things are slow and we'll be able to fit you in for a CAT scan."

It took some time, but eventually they performed the CAT scan and we waited for the results. The doctor confirmed that there was an abdominal mass there, and the "bowel doctor" would be in within the next two hours, so he was going to keep me in the hospital until the specialist examined me.

Finally the specialist arrived to examine me. "There is no doubt about it," he said. "We have to go in and operate because the CAT scan shows there is a mass in your bowel which could be a tumor or something else." He admitted me to the hospital and said he wanted me to be on a strong antibiotic before he would operate. He instructed the nurses to take my temperature every hour and if it should spike, he would come in and operate immediately. He said it was a good thing I'd come back to the hospital when I did, because the pain medicine prescribed during my earlier visit had just masked the real problem, as it had for Mary.

Six days later, the doctor opened me up and found a grapefruit size abscess caused by a perforated bowel, just as Mary Viernstein had warned. Had we waited any longer, I may have suffered her fate. She became brain dead before her body shut down because peritonitis spread throughout her body so rapidly. I felt that the vivid dream of Mary was a life saving dream!

It was a difficult recovery because they removed 18 inches of my sigmoid colon, but I was fortunate that I did not need a colostomy. I learned again to listen to my intuitive side through my dreams, and Companion Prayer. Thank you God for being with us again!

Our Son Was Missing For One Week
Fall of 1993

Jason was a bright child and he got straight A's during his senior year of high school. In fact, in his last marking period, when he took the advanced AP courses, he had a greater than 4.0 average. He was so good in Calculus, he would often correct the teacher, and other students would come to him for help in math. He had excellent teaching skills.

Jason was also a gifted pianist and played George Gershwin's "Rhapsody in Blue" with the Punxsutawney Phil-Harmonic. Some people said he was better than the orchestra. Jason received his Eagle Scout Award, after many years in the Boy Scouts, and was on the Dayton High Soccer Team.

We were very proud although not surprised when he received a partial scholarship to Carnegie Mellon University in Pittsburgh, Pennsylvania where he majored in physics.

Unfortunately, our son became ill. This happened when I was in nursing school which was located in Pittsburgh, and where Jason was attending Carnegie-Melon University. I had arranged to pick him up after my classes on Friday to bring him home for the Labor Day weekend. Several of the other women with whom I commuted were with me as well. We waited and waited but Jason never showed. I called his roommate and the residence hall director, but neither had seen him. I had to return my classmates to their homes as they had other obligations. So after a two-hour wait we finally left.

When I got home, we contacted the school security office and talked again with his roommate, and asked him to call us immediately the minute Jason returned. We called Harmon and June Bro for support because they had known what it was like to have their son disappear. We called our families and members of our church and asked them to pray for Jason. We wandered the streets of Pittsburgh looking for him and also had Companion Prayer to help find Jason.

The thing about Companion Prayer is that when dealing with another soul, a person's whereabouts will not be given unless that person wants it to be known. Just as with the Companion Prayer session for Harmon and June's son, we were told that everyone has free will and privacy is guarded. It is all a part of a soul's growth process and needs to be respected. So even though we were desperate to find our son, we realized that we had to give him his freedom and trust in the Lord that he was all right.

Finally, Jason called his cousin Crystal, and asked her to let us know he was OK. That was all he said, and we had no idea what was happening with him. When we interviewed fellow students at his school, we found out that he had not been attending classes, and was acting strangely.

One week later, security called us from the University to let us know that Jason had returned. We went down to see him and convinced him to see a psychiatrist. After his visit, he was diagnosed as having a "Psychotic Break" or schizo-phreniform disorder. Sometimes it is a temporary condition, but it can also be permanent. Unfortunately, for him, Jason's condition was permanent. For the next several years, Jason was in and out of the hospital over 25 times.

At first, it was extremely difficult because Jason did not believe or realize he had a problem. He thought that it was the rest of the world that had a problem. For some time he was extremely paranoid and felt that people were watching him, and he was finding hidden messages in their actions. It is unfortunate that approximately 1% of the population, regardless of religion, race, sex, or country of origin, suffers from this illness. It took a long time for us to accept that it was not our fault as parents. It was not something we had done or failed to do. It was a medical neurological problem.

Winter with Jason

Dale and I prayed using Companion Prayer to help Jason, and were given a plan of drug therapy, osteopathy, and holistic treatments in Virginia Beach, Virginia. We had hoped this intensive treatment at the beginning of his illness would help him to find health and wholeness.

In November of 1994, I moved with Jason to Virginia Beach to follow this intensive treatment program. Karl and I agreed that it was worth trying for several months to see if the program would make a difference with Jason. It was a traumatic time for us. Not only was I moving far from home, alone with Jason, I was also leaving behind my husband and two teenage daughters who were at an impressionable age. We all felt the pain of separation. I was particularly frightened at being alone with my psychotic son. I was so frightened that I locked my bedroom door before I went to sleep. However, I was never truly alone as I had a built-in support group that was referred to me by Harmon and June Bro and the ARE. They had doctors, chiropractors, and osteopaths, that all provided treatments for Jason and me. There was even a psychologist as well. I went to a support group meeting once a week that was a comfort. I found this group to be very giving, loving and compassionate.

I also found a great deal of support in a wonderful Presbyterian church within walking distance of where we lived. I even joined the choir during my time there. They were a tremendous help for what was to come.

I also had a first cousin, Sandy, who lived in Virginia Beach. She encouraged me through phone calls and occasional get-togethers.

We had hoped the treatments would, at the very least, arrest the disease, but we were disappointed.

During holidays such as Thanksgiving and Christmas, Jason and I would travel home. Unfortunately, it was during Christmas that we had the most difficult time.

Sunday, Christmas Day, 1994, we woke up in the morning to hear Jason yelling and screaming at the voices that were tormenting him. We then heard a loud crashing sound of glass being shattered. Jason, in an agitated state, had thrown one of the pots through the kitchen window. I was so shaken by this violent episode that I could not preach that morning. It was the first time in my life that I could not preach. Church was canceled that morning and I felt badly about it, but I was in no condition to preach and conduct a worship service. It seemed that the worst times for Jason and the illness were the holidays. It was as if he became over-stimulated during those times, and lost control.

We were so inexperienced in caring for someone with a mental illness that we didn't realize how unstable Jason really was. We kept going along not realizing the seriousness of his condition. We got a taste of that when we left a little later in the day to visit Karl's sister and her family.

As we traveled, Jason's negative behavior began to escalate. He became more agitated and tried to open and jump out the back door while the car was moving. Karl pulled over and stopped the car. Suddenly, Jason bolted out the door and dashed onto a four-lane highway. Thank goodness it was Christmas night, and the traffic was light. Julie, Christiana and I caught up to Jason first and helped to subdue him until Karl joined us. Jason pulled Julie's hair and wouldn't let go, and managed to inflict superficial injuries on Christiana and me until Karl grabbed him in a headlock and forced him back into the car. Jason was then placed between Karl and Christiana in the back seat while I drove the rest of the way to our destination. Our Christmas was filled with grief that year as we struggled to come to grips with a heartbreaking illness.

Few people realize how incredibly difficult it is for an entire family to deal with a schizophrenic person. It was especially hard on Christiana and Julie who became bitter about all the time Dale and I spent with Jason and his problems. We sought family counseling for a time, and it was also the first time in my life that I sought counseling to deal with anxiety and depression. It was a difficult time for our whole family, and Dale and I did what we could to hold things together.

I was still feeling the aches and pains of the colon surgery that I'd had sixteen months earlier. Perhaps our family situation delayed my recovery, because it took one and a half years before I fully recovered, without feeling some pain every day.

Soon after Christmas, Dale and Jason returned to Virginia Beach to continue his treatments.

One February night, Jason took a turn for the worse. As part of our treatment plan, not only did Jason have osteopathic treatments, but we took walks along the ocean on the boardwalk every day. Diet and vitamin supplements also played a large part in our program. Sometimes, Jason would walk by himself. One day he came back from his walk with a beautiful, jeweled letter opener, shaped like a dagger. Needless to say, I was not pleased with his purchase. Within a short time, he became more psychotic. He would be manic but just as quickly sink into a depression. I told the doctor I thought Jason was schizo-affective, which meant he was schizophrenic and bipolar, too. This was confirmed a short time later by the doctors.

One particular evening as I sat watching TV, Jason came out of his bedroom carrying his new dagger. I tried to talk to him, but he wouldn't respond to my comments. When he began walking faster and faster in the room and laughing uncontrollably with the dagger pointed at his own chest, I knew we were in trouble. I called David, Jason's psychologist, and told him what was happening. He came over immediately. When David took the letter opener away from Jason, he bolted out of the apartment into the cold night. It was around 8:00 p.m. David called 911 to notify the police about this situation. He told me to stay in the apartment to man the phone, and then went out to search for Jason.

The night was cold and Jason had run out without his coat. I was very worried about him and knew that he was in serious trouble. I waited alone for some word of Jason. From time to time David would stop back in to see if I'd heard anything from the police. Finally, the phone rang. The police dispatcher had taken a report about a man walking in the water at the ocean's edge. We knew it was Jason.

David said he would go to the location stated and that the police would meet him there. He wanted me to stay by the phone to relay information if needed. It was a good thing I did, too, because I don't know what I would have done if I'd been there!

As David arrived, he discovered it was Jason walking in the water. David tried to reason with him, to get him out of the water and go home. Jason was responding to those inner voices, which were encouraging him to go into the water. The police car was on the boardwalk following along. As they reached the end of the boardwalk, they knew they had to do something to get Jason out of the water, so the policemen rushed him. Jason turned and swam into the ocean for about 100 yards. The water temperature was only about 40 degrees, so hypothermia would set in quickly and death could occur within 10 to 20 minutes. They had to get Jason out of the water immediately. Fortunately, there were several officers on hand that were willing to rescue Jason. One was a former Navy Seal and another was an accomplished scuba diver. Neither of them needed to risk their lives for Jason, but they did, and they were indeed heroes. God works in wonderful ways. When they reached Jason, he gave them a hard time and fought back. He also went under several times as they brought him back to shore. They were all taken to the hospital suffering from hypothermia.

David called me from the hospital and told me to meet him there. He said Jason had been admitted. When I arrived, he told me what happened. I found Jason shivering on a warm blanket to raise his body temperature. In the next room were the police officers who had saved his life. I went in to speak with them and thanked them for saving Jason. I truly feel they were honorable men who risked their own lives to save a very sick young man.

Jason was in the hospital for several weeks until he was stable. While he was there, Julie flew down for a visit during her spring break. It was great to see her and we spent a lot of quality time together. My parents also came to visit us, and it was great to see loved ones who supported us. Karl also came for a visit and he was a sight for sore eyes. It was so good to see him.

In March, Jason and I finally went home. It was a long, difficult winter, but there were also some good times where I learned that there were good people everywhere who will step up to the plate and help their fellow man. We will be eternally grateful for the loving concern shown to us by all. Thank you, God.

Back in Dayton Again

When we returned home, it was almost Easter. I was glad to be home with Karl, my children, our pets and church family. Unfortunately, the experiences during the past year and a half had taken their toll. Shortly after our return, a letter arrived from a trusted friend who blamed Karl and me for Jason's illness, saying that God was punishing us for doing wrong. It was too much, and I broke down. I had tried so hard to do the best I could for our family and didn't know what I had done wrong. I was the last one to seek help as I had tried to hold the family together as we all went through the sense of loss we experienced over Jason's illness. I went into a major depression where I also developed an anxiety disorder. I went on medication for a time. It was difficult trying to forgive myself for Jason's illness. I know now that I was not responsible for his psychotic break. Joining the National Alliance for the Mentally Ill (NAMI) really educated me to understand that Jason's illness was not my fault, but came from a biochemical imbalance in his brain instead.

I also believe that Jason's path in life was preordained so that we all could learn and grow from these experiences. Jason said to us at the height of his illness, "The reason I am ill is for all of us to grow."

Don't think for one moment that we didn't try to find the answers to heal Jason. We called on some of the best doctors we could find and joined in Companion Prayer to access information on how to heal our son. We followed through on these suggestions. We eventually realized that the solution rests with Jason and his will to get better. He has to follow the path he has chosen for himself before coming to earth. As we learned in our Companion Prayer, "You will have grown for eons to come by going through this experience." I guess we are truly blessed to be going through these difficulties, for surely we are growing in the Lord.

Recalling the Dream of Jason

I later recalled the dream I once had about Jason when he was only two weeks old, and I wept. God had given me a dream that I would not forget. In the dream, Jason's brain was cut in two. I now realize God was forewarning me that someday Jason would become schizophrenic. It was a condition that he was born with, although it would not manifest itself until later in life. The scientists from the National Institutes of Health (NIH) were speakers at the National Alliance for the Mentally Ill (NAMI) convention in Washington, D.C., and they explained to us that it is an illness that typically occurs in the later teens with men and in the early twenties with women. It is a problem with the switching mechanism behind the pituitary gland which goes awry and can't control the dopamine levels released in the brain. It is difficult for some parents not to blame themselves for their child's illness, and we were no exception.

At first, I believed that Jason's obsessive meditation before going off to the University may have caused his "psychotic break," however, Dale felt it could have been part of the symptom. We advised Jason to stop his meditation, but he insisted that it was helping him. I don't believe it helped, but rather further isolated him from reality. I concluded that meditation is not always good. In cases of obsessive meditation, it can be harmful to some people.

Chapter 14

"The Lord is my light and my salvation;
Whom shall I fear?
The Lord is the stronghold of my life;
Of whom shall I be afraid?"

Psalm 27:1

Dayton – The Final Years

The Man Who Gave Up and Died

We learned a lesson from a man who lived in our community of Dayton. He was a very cordial person who worked in a grocery store for many years, and everyone loved him. Unfortunately, within a few weeks of retiring at the age of 65, he was diagnosed with cancer. He was devastated and he refused to speak to anyone. I visited him on several occasions although he was reluctant to talk with me, and within a few weeks he died. I spoke with his doctors and asked if he had died of cancer. They told me that was not the case. The cancer had just been detected and it was not far advanced, and he could have been treated. He had simply refused to eat, and became so despondent that he did not want to live anymore.

We were shocked because he seemed to be so affable! We thought he had a lot to live for, since he was newly married shortly before he retired, but evidently, he didn't feel the same way. For everyone in the community, it was an unexpected death.

This experience taught me an important lesson. The mind is a powerful force that can affect our physical condition. We can become our own worst enemy and will ourselves to die, or we can be at peace with ourselves and God and live. We need not be afraid. Most of the time, the choice is ours.

The Wedding with a Wardrobe Malfunction!

Some of the most unexpected things happen during weddings. Even the most well planned ceremonies can go awry. Every bride frets over finding the right dress for her wedding, and she will spend a great deal of energy searching for the right one. It may be borrowed, or it may be bought, but it is usually a brand new dress. It is one of the most important aspects of the wedding ceremony. I can't tell you how many times Dale has been called upon to get safety pins to hold up this or that on a dress. Even the guys need help with pins for corsages. However, one particular wedding had the most horrible wardrobe malfunction of all.

On this occasion, the bride had bought her dress about six months before the wedding, and it fit perfectly. However, on the day of her wedding, the bride could hardly fit into her dress. Apparently, she had gained considerable weight in the six months before the wedding, and while I wouldn't say this out loud, I had to admit that she looked like a stuffed sausage. She overflowed in her dress as she proudly walked down the aisle of the church.

The wedding ceremony was going along just fine. The bride had been presented to the groom, the appropriate prayers and scripture had been read, and I had delivered a message, as I always do, encouraging the couple to respect and appreciate one another. Then, all of a sudden, just before the vows were to be repeated, the bride's dress "popped" open in the back. The zipper had become undone and the bride turned, facing the congregation, so as not to reveal the undone dress. She began to cry and the bridesmaids immediately went into action to remedy the situation. The congregation was stunned, and we felt sorry for the bride.

As pastor leading the service, people look to me to bring order and a little levity to every difficult situation.

"We're going to take a little break for a few minutes, so everyone just relax," I told the congregation. "We're going to get everything fixed up."

It took the bridesmaids and her mother a few minutes to pin the dress back together again, and then I gave her a few minutes more to regain her composure. The groom didn't know what to do but just stand there, which was fine, because there was really nothing he could do anyway.

Finally, we continued with the ceremony. "It's what's on the inside of the person you marry that counts, not what is on the outside," I said. That seemed to calm the couple down and we proceeded with the vows, which now had a deeper meaning and really demonstrated what it meant to be married.

The Couples I Married Who Needed Acceptance

There were always couples that would come to me to be married after being turned down by other pastors. One couple came to me rather sheepishly, and asked if I would marry them even though the woman was pregnant.

I already knew the background of the couple before they spoke with me, and I'd had the young man in my confirmation class some years earlier. He was of good character. His heart was in the right place and I knew he would be very supportive of his wife. The young woman was almost afraid to tell me of her condition, but felt it was necessary for me to know. She broke down in tears and explained that when the minister of the church she had attended all of her life found out she was pregnant, he flatly refused to marry them. She was devastated.

I paused briefly for a moment and then said, "I would be glad to perform the wedding ceremony for you, because after all, did not the mother of Jesus become pregnant before she was married?" This couple, both being brought up in the church, knew exactly what I was saying. They agreed with me, and smiled. The woman's tears of sadness quickly turned to tears of joy, and they thanked me again as we set the wedding date at the church.

Another couple came to me wanting to get married, and explained that they had been turned down by other pastors. They seemed like a nice couple and they had attended the church worship services several times before talking with me. I asked them why they had been turned down, and they said it was because they were living together.

The couple was aware that they could simply go to the Justice of the Peace to be married, but they wanted a church wedding. Here was a couple in love with one another, living together, and wanting the blessing of God upon their relationship. I found no abusive relationship, no problems with alcohol, or drugs, gambling or any other disturbing red flags in their relationship. So, yes, I told them I would be glad to marry them. The day of their wedding, the church was packed with well-wishers. For many years, we have continued to keep in correspondence with one another, and they are still happily married.

The Ceiling Is Falling

It was August of 1995, the Sunday after a large wedding. I was preaching from the pulpit on Chapter I of Isaiah and raised my voice to make the point that "GOD WAS NOT HAPPY WITH THE PEOPLE." All of a sudden, there was a loud noise, "CRACK", and the people in the pews jumped. I too, jumped, pausing a few seconds. Then, not hearing or seeing anything as I looked at the ceiling I said, "There's the voice of God!" People were looking up at the ceiling of the church. There had always been signs that the ceiling had been sagging in places, but now it was clear that the ceiling had depressed two or three inches lower in one corner. I continued with the sermon and closed the worship service a little earlier than usual. We later saw the videotape of people being visibly shaken.

I instructed one of the property committee members to go up into the attic to inspect the condition of the ceiling. Upon close inspection, he informed me that one of the support beams at the front of the church had cracked. We agreed that we needed an expert to examine the support beams that held the wooden ceiling in place, before there was any further damage.

The next day I called a certified structural engineer in Pittsburgh and pleaded with him to come immediately and inspect the church building. We promised to pay any expenses. He arrived within three hours to examine the church and quickly discovered that three out of the five support beams in the ceiling were broken and the building had to be condemned for any further use until it was repaired. The building was in such bad shape that the ceiling was in danger of collapsing at any moment. Immediately, we closed the building.

We were fortunate to have a separate Sunday school building that we could use for worship until the problem was fixed. We hired a contractor to put temporary support columns in place so we would not lose the ceiling all together. While the contractor was installing the support columns, the ceiling fell another six inches. "It was amazing that the whole ceiling did not collapse," the contractor said.

God truly works in mysterious ways, and this turned out to be a wonderful time for the church to become a community. We were working together as never before; we had greater church attendance; we had fund-raising programs with good fellowship; and people were feeling generous.

One of my colleagues wanted me to come preach in his church, so that God would speak to them and draw them together. That's when I wrote the sermon, "The Two Ways People are Drawn into the Church: Disaster or Devotion."

For the next several months the session proposed three different plans for the congregation to vote on, because we wanted everyone on board to support whatever we did to solve the problems. They were as follows:

Plan One was to simply place vertical supports to hold up the ceiling. This was the cheapest solution and would cost about $20,000.

Plan Two was to tear the whole church down and build a new one, the most expensive solution that would cost about one million dollars.

Plan Three was to replace the whole upper structure, similar to the structure previously in place, but with all new electric, heat and air conditioning, windows, sound system, lights, and a new paint job that would cost about $150,000.

The congregation voted to support plan three, and that is what we did. It took nine months to complete the construction and by the time the church was re-dedicated, we had raised the money needed to cover all the expenses. This was quite a remarkable feat for a small church.

But construction was not without its pitfalls. The construction workers knew it would take several days to remove the roof of the church. There was a point when they had taken half of the roof off, leaving half of the church exposed to the outside weather. Wouldn't you know that's when we received a foot of snow? The whole community of Dayton was called to shovel out the inside of the church.

A few people in the community who didn't usually attend church said to me, "Karl, I knew you would get me inside the church someday, I just didn't know it would be shoveling snow!" We all worked and had a good time together.

I was having some chest pain, so my wife, being a nurse, insisted I go to the hospital and get it checked out. I was examined, but the doctors couldn't find anything wrong. "Do you have any stress in your life?" they asked.

"Well, I guess you could say that," I said with a grin.

"Everyday Is A Wonderful Day!"

Blair, one of our parishioners who was truly devoted to God, developed a disease called multiple myeloma. When I visited him in the hospital, I could tell he was in a great deal of pain. However, every time I saw him he would say to me, "Everyday is a good day." Whether I saw him at his home, in church, or in the hospital, he would always say something positive and inspiring like, "Today is a wonderful day!"

This was his greatest contribution to his family, the church, the community and to me. It didn't matter if he was in pain or not, to him everyday was a wonderful day. His way of dealing with pain was a wonderful example to us all. He was probably one of the few people I had ever met who understood what Paul was saying in the Bible, "My grace is sufficient for you, for my power is made perfect in weakness." (2 Corinthians 12:9) Even though there may be tragic events in our life, it can still be a wonderful day.

Cat Attack

One day something traumatic happened to my daughter Christiana, as she sat in a chair outside in the sun reading a book. Without warning, a wild tomcat attacked her and bit her on the arm. She screamed and the cat ran away. She had been sitting quietly, minding her own business when the cat attacked. Why? Was the cat diseased? We rushed her to the hospital because the bite looked bad and the teeth marks went deep into both sides of her arm.

When the doctors heard about what had happened they wanted to know if there were any signs that the cat was "rabid" such as foaming at the mouth. Christiana had no way of knowing, since it all happened so fast. Because they couldn't know for sure, they recommended that Christiana get rabies shots. If the cat was rabid, the shots would save her life. If the cat was not rabid, she would then be vaccinated against rabies. So, poor Christiana had to submit to a series of rabies shots for several weeks in a row.

I was very upset, and I asked the doctor, "What if I caught the cat? We'd be able to tell for sure, wouldn't we?"

"Yes, but how can you be sure it was the same cat that bit her?" he asked. "We can't wait to find out." Then I understood, and I couldn't take that chance with her life.

Christiana described the cat to me. She said it was a wild yellow tabby tomcat that was mean and temperamental. We had heard earlier that there was a nasty cat that had been getting into fights with other cats in our neighbors' barn. It sounded like the same cat. I was concerned that the cat would attack someone else, even children at the Sunday school building. I was determined that if I saw that cat again, it was going to be history.

Two days later, I saw a huge cat that fit the description sitting in our front yard under the birch tree. I was certain it was the cat that bit

Christiana. I quickly got my 22 rifle, loaded it, and very carefully took aim. With one shot, I killed the cat.

It says in the Revised Standard Version of the Ten Commandments, "You shall not kill" (Exodus 20:13) However, a very careful exegesis of the Hebrew text describes that the killing refers only to human beings. Therefore, a more accurate translation of the sixth commandment would be, "You shall not commit homicide."

I thought about taking the cat to be examined, but I decided against it. Christiana still had to take the rabies shots regardless, so I put on a pair of rubber gloves and buried the cat. In retrospect, I should have called the health department. They would have been glad to examine the cat for rabies at no charge.

My first and primary concern was to protect my family, and everyone else from this wild tomcat. I respect the life of animals dearly, but when they endanger the lives of people, I will act to protect and defend human life.

Talking to the Bees and the Ants

I really do not want to kill any living thing unless it is absolutely necessary. I once found that some bees were building a beehive in the eaves of our house. This could be dangerous to my family, so I decided to have a talk with the bees and explain that they were in danger, they had to leave their location, and build their hive elsewhere. I kept at this for three days in a row and by golly, on the third day, the bees were all gone. I removed the hive and there were no bees left.

Another time I tried talking to white-faced hornets, and they would not listen. That is to say, my efforts to communicate with them were unsuccessful.

I found there are times when talking to the insect or animal kingdom works miraculously well, but then there are other times when it doesn't work at all.

Every spring when the weather became warmer, the ants would come out. Invariably they would find their way into our kitchen and wander onto our countertops. I would tell Karl that the ants were back and it was time to have his talk with them. So, he would once again remind them that they did not belong in our kitchen and if they did not leave he would be forced to kill them. Of course, Karl wouldn't use insecticides due to their toxic nature. Sometimes he would have to kill a few ants to get his point across, and he would leave their bodies on the countertop where other ants would come and remove them. Usually it took only a few days before the ants disappeared, not to be seen again until a new group of ants appeared the following year.

The Wedding with an Unexpected Guest

I was conducting a wedding that had been well-planned, and the ceremony was going along without a hitch. As I was delivering my short message to the couple and the congregation, people started laughing. I couldn't understand why they were laughing because what I was talking about was very serious.

Normally, I wear my robe during the ceremony, but it was a very hot day, and because it was a small wedding and the couple wanted to keep it simple, I was casually dressed. As I proceeded with the service, I was trying to figure out why the guests were laughing. The bride and groom were looking right at me with puzzled looks on their faces. They had no idea why the people were laughing either.

I looked around to find the cause of their laughter, and I realized that they were looking down as I was talking. Suddenly, it struck me, "Oh no, my zipper must be down. That's why they're laughing!" So, I nonchalantly reached down to check my zipper, but all was as it should be. That's when I caught out of the corner of my eye, Sammy, my cat, strutting back and forth between my legs! At that moment, the bride and groom also caught sight of the cat and smiled.

"Oh, we have an unexpected guest!" I said. With that, the congregation burst out laughing. As a minister, I've learned that it's wonderful to give people permission to laugh during the service. It can put a lighthearted spin on the most solemn or unusual situations. It was hot and there was no air conditioning in the church, the windows were wide open, and Sammy, hearing my voice, had jumped onto the window sill, and entered the church. Unbeknownst to me, or the bride and groom, he was walking in the front of the church behind me where we could not see him, much to the delight of the congregation.

I explained that the couple should feel honored that even the animal kingdom wanted to bless their wedding!

Funerals That Were Difficult to Do

In my ministry, there have been funerals that I did not want to do, because I had grown so close to the family that had suffered this tragedy. Usually it was an unexpected death.

One such funeral was for a young boy who had fallen off a tractor while riding along with his grandfather, and was accidentally run over. The grandfather adored his grandson, and was devastated. It was a great tragedy for the whole family. It was a closed casket funeral. There was great grief expressed by the whole community, and if I could have raised the child from the dead, I would have done so on that day.

I presided over another funeral for a hospitalized woman in Kittanning who went into sudden diabetic shock. The nurse unwittingly gave her insulin, when what she really needed was sugar. She died instantly. It was horrible for me to learn of the terrible things that happened to people, especially when some of these deaths could have been prevented.

A nurse came to me in tears one day. She worked in a local hospital and was very upset to learn that some doctors kept ordering tests for older patients, who did not need them. "It was all done for the almighty dollar," she said. Apparently, these were not isolated incidents.

A man in another hospital pleaded with the doctors NOT to have a stress test. Even the family insisted that he not have it, but the doctor insisted that it was essential for diagnosis. The next day, the family asked me to do the funeral for the man. The stress test killed him!

As a pastor, I see how differently death comes to each of us. Sometimes the funeral is a celebration of a long wonderful life, while at other times we are mourning the loss of those who died unexpectedly as the result of a tragic event or devastating illness.

I will say in defense of the medical profession and those in it who devote their lives to saving others that the treatments for cancer and other diseases have improved greatly throughout the years. However, we still have a long way to go to provide safe medical care for so many people in need through better diagnostic methods and treatments.

Ambulance Driver

While serving as pastor in Dayton, I wanted to help provide better medical care for our community, so I volunteered to be a First Responder and drove the ambulance for three years. My responsibilities mainly included transporting patients to and from the hospital, but on occasion, I was called in on emergencies such as car accidents, heart attacks, strokes and breathing problems.

One of the biggest problems I encountered with the ambulance service in Dayton was that our response time was slow, and that was because we were out in the country and dependent upon a few volunteers.

I remember one time we arrived at a heart attack scene. When we inquired how long the person had been lying down without breathing, we were told, "30 minutes." The EMT on the scene replied, "That's too late to begin CPR."

It was so tragic that it took so long for the volunteer ambulance crew to be gathered and dispatched, that it was too late to help people. I concluded that a full-time paid staff was the only way to solve the problems of getting emergency help to the scene in a timely way, and eventually, a full-time ambulance service was established.

Greeting People after Church Worship

I have been concerned not only about the spiritual welfare of my congregation, but also about their mental and physical welfare. When

I greet people with a handshake after Sunday Worship, I generally notice their overall appearance as well. One Sunday, I saw a woman who was a regular congregant, and she looked very ill to me. She did not seem to be herself and I asked her, "Are you all right?" She gave me this indignant look and said, "I'm fine. There is nothing wrong with me." So, I apologized to her.

The next day, the same woman was diagnosed with a serious illness that almost killed her. What did I see in her that caused me to speak out suddenly? I'm not really sure, but I do know there are times when I can sense when something is wrong.

Chapter 15

"Serve the Lord your God
With all your heart and with all your soul."
Deuteronomy 10: 12

Hammonton 1996

I had been praying to God to reveal to us where He would want us to go. We had looked at several churches and talked with several pastoral nominating committees, but nothing seemed a really good fit for us. I had special skills and abilities that could be used in different churches, but I had to find the right church, one that would appreciate what I had to offer.

I was invited to preach for a church in Hammonton, NJ, and was interviewed on New Years Day, January 1, 1996. Shortly after, I had a dream that I was speaking Spanish. I interpreted this to mean that my family and I were going to live among Spanish-speaking people to whom I would be providing ministry.

Dale wanted to be closer to her family in New Jersey and my father lived in New York City; so, were we to move to Hammonton, we could see more of our families than we had when we lived in western Pennsylvania. We left Dayton at the end of July, 1996.

Dream about Hammonton

Shortly after arriving, I woke up early one morning after having a vivid dream about the Hammonton Church. Not all dreams were as clear as this one, but this seemed to be a direct message from God.

"Don't feel bad if you leave after three years," I heard God say to me.

I was aghast at such a statement, and pondered why God would say that? I had just begun my ministry at Hammonton and it was my first day on the job! I woke Dale and told her my dream. I was visibly shaken, but she said, in her calm way, "Don't worry about it." Dale always had a way of reassuring me that God was with us no matter where we were sent to serve Him. I actually served in the Hammonton Presbyterian Church ministry for four years.

Choir and Sunday School to Meet at Different Times

On the Sunday after leading my first church service, Dale was invited by some choir members to join the choir rehearsals and sing, and a few minutes later she was approached by the Sunday school teachers to participate in the morning Bible class. The problem was both groups met at the same time!

I offered the simplest solution I could think of, which was to reschedule the activities so that each group met at separate times. I was amazed that this solution had not been seriously considered before, since there had been tension between the choir and the Sunday school for some time. This simple solution helped to heal some of the inner tension, but for some reason these two groups still had conflicts.

Dale tried to participate in both groups, because she loved to sing, and enjoyed studying the Bible too, but she felt at times that she didn't fit in. For me, it was very important that Dale was happy, but unfortunately, there were times when she was very sad and felt unappreciated.

A Caring Man

The first person we got to know was a very sensitive and caring man who was a faithful deacon of the church. Unfortunately, he was diagnosed with cancer of the lymph glands and was struggling to survive. He was also the church organist, but because of his illness, he was unable to continue playing.

He lived across the street from us and having been a deacon, he was deeply interested in the caring ministry of the church. There were people he had been helping who were draining him mentally and financially, and he asked if I could continue to help these people in need. I did as he requested and helped several people get jobs to get them back on their feet. However, as he feared, some of these same people used illegal drugs, and would sink right back into financial difficulties. He had a good understanding of the homeless and their plight, and felt that the church should do what it could to help those in need. Eventually, we were able to help a few of these people by getting them into rehabilitation.

When Dale and I visited him, he would always say that he was praying for us, and hoped we could be of service to the Spanish Ministry of his church. We would often pray together for those who were sick and suffering. This was amazing to me because I knew he was suffering himself.

As the lymphoma began to take hold of him, the deacons prepared meals for him to assure he ate well. Dale, being a nurse, was able to help him some, and there were times that he was so ill she would need to help him in the late hours of the night. He had not made out a will, believing that he was going to get better.

I suggested, "You should make out a will because you never know what God may have in store."

"I'll think about it," he said.

Being a nurse, I would fix his meals and apply fresh bandages, and do whatever I could to make him comfortable.

It wasn't until I talked with him and said, "I don't know if you're going to die. We have to hope that you will get well. But, if you don't eat, and get stronger, then you could very well die."

He finally decided to write his will.

The very next day, his lawyer along with his secretary came to the house to write, witness, and sign his will. Only two hours later, he died in the arms of a church member who had come by to help. It was a shock to everyone!

The church had always been an important part of his whole life. Sometimes, he was at the church so much, he even slept in the church building on occasion.

Not having any family of his own, he donated most of his money to the Hammonton Church. He had told Dale, that because she had been such a comfort to him, he had decided to increase his bequest that he had previously considered, and would donate a greater percentage of his savings to the Hammonton Church.

Spanish Ministry

A portion of the parishioners were Hispanic, and I was charged with supporting and strengthening these people at the Hammonton Church. They were happy that I was committed to supporting their worship and pastoral concerns, and I quickly became enamored by them!

I had learned some Spanish in college, but I really didn't know how to speak the language well, so, I began taking courses at The Atlantic County Community College. I learned to speak well enough that I could say the communion service in Spanish and talk with them on a very basic level.

We had a few supply ministers each Sunday for the Spanish service, but the congregation and I agreed it would be better to have someone helping them on a more permanent basis.

There was no place for a part-time Spanish-speaking pastor to live, so we converted one of the church buildings, previously used to store clothing, into an apartment that could be either temporary or permanent housing.

The next step was to hire someone who could provide ministry to the Spanish-speaking congregation, and who would agree to live there on a part-time salary. I interviewed Sara who was recommended to me by a member of the congregation. I found her to be an outstanding individual who deeply cared for others, and had a strong commitment to Jesus Christ.

The congregation voted to have her serve, and we gave her an office next to mine, where we shared the same secretary. We worked together as a team for several years, and accomplished a great deal together. We served communion together, and while I said the Words of Institution in Spanish, since I was ordained, she did the preaching for the Hispanic Worship Service. Unfortunately, after several years, she became ill and was unable to continue her ministry.

I was always fond of Sara and her leadership in the Spanish ministry program. She trusted me and I trusted her. We prayed together for the church's joint ministry, and she gave far more of herself than her part-time job compensated her for. Sara gave of herself to the Spanish ministry and to our family, and was a good friend to us all.

Jason was Driving Us to the Ends of the Earth

Because of his illness, Jason had been living at a minimum supervision boarding home in Kittanning, Pennsylvania. The facility monitored his whereabouts, but he was free to come and go at will. Unfortunately, because we'd moved to Hammonton, New Jersey and were not there to monitor his progress, his condition started to deteriorate, and he ended up in the Clarion Hospital, Clarion, Pennsylvania.

As a result of this, we decided to move Jason to live with us in Hammonton. We thought we could support Jason better, but unfortunately, he ended up in a car accident. We covered the cost ourselves since it was a minor expense, but we really did not want him to drive at all. However, in spite of the fact that he was suffering from a mental illness, the state still allowed him to drive. I could not understand this logic. How could he be allowed to drive and not be allowed to do other things? Since he was 21, and legally an adult, he could make his own decisions and Dale and I could not interfere with his own legal actions.

One day, Jason and his car went missing. Evidently, he had taken off without telling anyone where he was going. After about two weeks, we received a call from the police who informed us that Jason was in the hospital in Worcester, Massachusetts. Jason became confused and lost his way, and he requested help from the police who proceeded to take him to the hospital. We asked a friend who lived in the area to visit him while he was in the hospital. When he was stable and ready to be discharged, we drove all the way up to Worcester to pick up Jason and the car.

Jason was unable to work and pay for his car insurance, and I was unable to pay for it either. We ended up having to sell the car to pay off Jason's debts. I thought this would be the last of Jason's wild car trips, but I was sorely mistaken!

Several months later, at approximately 1:00 a.m. in the morning, our phone rang.

"Hello? Is this Mr. Karl Viernstein?"

"Yes," I said.

"Mr. Viernstein, we have a car here that is registered in your name that may have been stolen. Do you have a son named Jason?"

"Yes, I do," I said, still trying to wake up.

The person on the phone said, "This is the Pentagon."

"What did you say?" I asked.

The person said again, "This is the Pentagon."

"THE Pentagon, in Virginia?" I said.

"Yes sir," he replied. "We are holding your son here at the Pentagon. He was trespassing on government property. We noticed that he was acting a little strangely. He said he was here to meet aliens. Does he take medication?"

I said, "Yes, for schizophrenia."

"We could press charges," he said. "But if you come and pick him up right now, we will release him to you, and we won't press any charges."

"I'll be there as soon as possible," I said.

I was a bit startled, because I hadn't even known Jason was missing. While I was on the phone, Dale went outside to see if our car was missing, and it was. Jason had left his bedroom in the basement and had taken our car all the way to the Pentagon where he was going to meet the aliens for some reason.

Dale and I had to get out maps to figure out how to get to the Pentagon, and it was not easy to figure out the route. How Jason figured it out without a map, we'll never know. To make matters worse, I had to borrow a car from a church friend because Dale's car was not working at the time.

I called Sara a little after 1:00 a.m. in the morning to explain the situation and asked her if I could borrow her car to pick up Jason who was at the Pentagon expecting to meet aliens. I am forever grateful to Sara, who loaned me her car. She loved Jason and was very understanding of the situation.

Jason Works for David

Jason got a job with David, who was an independent contractor. It was good that he was able to work two days a week, but in order to get there, Dale would drop him off at the train station and pick him up in the evening.

I am grateful to David because not only is he a long-time friend that I have known since Seminary, but he was very insightful about Jason's schizophrenia. David had experience with mental illness and he could understand and help Jason in ways I couldn't. David was able to give Jason some valuable tips on how to deal with the voices only he could hear. Somehow, he was able to help Jason discern between the good voices and the bad voices. This helped Jason to cope with the illness when the medicine was not working effectively to suppress his excessive dopamine levels. Jason worked for David for about one year while he learned some valuable coping skills.

Sign Language

Jason was able to interact socially with others to some extent, and he began dating a girl who was deaf. She suffered from hearing loss because of an illness she acquired at a very young age, and was also schizophrenic. Jason met her at "The Program," a service provided by the state, and they decided to see one another more frequently.

On her visits, we would communicate by writing her messages in a notebook. She would normally communicate by sign language, but no one in our family could sign. One day, on a visit to McDonald's, we were having a hard time understanding what food she wanted. I thought someone in our family needed to learn American Sign Language, and I decided it should be me. Over the next year when she would come for a visit with Jason, I would talk with her in sign language, learning more words, and improving my signing technique. I realized that I was talking slowly to her in sign language, but I was just learning. After a while, I felt much more confident and promised her, "If you come to church, I will sign my sermon for you."

About a month later, I found out that she wanted to come to church with Jason. So, true to my word, I began preparing a sermon that I could both preach and sign at the same time. I didn't think the congregation would mind me signing and preaching at the same time. In fact, it would be educational for them and meaningful to the girl who was deaf because I would be speaking to her as well. The spoken message would be the same.

The day of the service, I decided not to stand behind the pulpit because people would not be able to see me signing. I needed to use both hands to sign and wouldn't be able to hold my notes anyway, so I stood out in front of the pulpit.

As I was speaking and signing at the same time, about half-way through the sermon, the girl who was deaf and was sitting in the second pew, started signing back to me. I briefly paused, watched her sign, and realized she was correcting me about something I'd signed earlier. People watched curiously, and I explained that she was correcting my sign language, and the congregation enjoyed the sign language dialogue between the two of us. I proceeded to sign the corrected version, and continued the sermon with sign.

Everyone seemed to benefit from the unusual service, the difference being that I was using my hands to speak as well as my mouth. After the service was over, I was amazed that three people in the congregation thanked me for signing and understood what I was doing. They too could sign because they had family members who were deaf. Sometimes it's easy to forget that there are others in the world who suffer from disabilities, such as hearing loss, and they are sometimes excluded because they don't know what's going on and can't participate in the exchange. It wouldn't take much effort to reach out to these individuals with special needs.

Several months later, our son stopped seeing her, but I was glad that I had the opportunity to learn and speak with her to brighten her day, and demonstrate that someone cared about her.

Helping the Helpless

Because of the personal struggles we went through with Jason, we were able to be more sympathetic with others who had special needs.

There were times I was called upon to reach out to the homeless and those who had very little food. When we began our ministry at Hammonton, there were just a few people receiving help from the deacon's food pantry once a week, but within a few years, we were giving food to over 100 people a week, with the help of the deacons.

I believe there were several reasons for this. First, we rebuilt the food pantry, and adding more shelves, allowed for a greater selection of food. We encouraged the congregation to support the food pantry at least once a week, and we started buying food directly from the USDA at a discount. We actually had pallets of food delivered, and got a rolling ladder to load the food into the pantry more efficiently. It was fortunate that we upgraded the pantry when we did, soon after the government started cutting back on food stamps and welfare allocations. People did not have enough food to make it through the month, so, they came to us for help.

One woman who came to the food pantry often did not bathe regularly, and smelled so bad that she offended the others. The deacons asked me to talk with her about her odor problem. I simply told her that if she wanted to continue to receive food from us, she would have to take a bath before she came to the food pantry. We gave her all the soap she would need for a year, and she continued to visit us regularly. She was one of many people who were in need of our help.

The Woman who Needed to Come in from the Cold

There was a woman who was mentally ill and would wander around the town all day long and live from hand-to-mouth. She was an amazing piano player like our son Jason, and she too suffered from schizophrenia.

Sometimes she just wanted to come into the church building to get out of the cold, and I would let her come in to get warm. She had a hard time paying her utility bills, therefore, the church paid her fuel bill several times and even her electric bill when the electric company turned off her electricity in the middle of the winter.

She was someone who needed help from time to time, and she was most appreciative of all that we did to help her. It's hard to understand how someone who appears to be so bright and talented can be so ill kempt or disorderly. Unfortunately, it sometimes happens with mental illness.

Woman with No Home

One day, another woman came into my office asking for help because she was homeless. I told her that I would drive her to the local homeless shelter, as I did on several occasions, after I finished my office hours.

"I'm tired of homeless shelters," the woman told me. "I just need $800 for an apartment."

"I'm sorry," I told her. "We do not give money out like that. And even if we did, what would you do to pay the rent the following month and the month after that?"

So, I went to the next level in my conversation with her, and I asked her, "Where does your family live? Are they close by?"

"Oh." she said. "They are close by, but they won't have anything to do with me. I just don't get along with them."

That was the key to how I was going to help her.

"So, why is it that you don't get along with your family?" I asked her. "Why won't they help you?"

"They have helped me," she said. "But I don't like them telling me how I should live my life."

"I'm going to tell you something that is very important and can change the way you live your life," I said to her. "Do you want to know what that is?"

"Yes, I do," she replied.

So, I told her, "It's all about learning to get along with your family. That's very important! It's important for you and it's important for your family too!"

"I don't fully understand," she said.

I said, "You see, your family is the biggest support group you have. If you develop a good relationship with them, they can and will help you! But you have to be nice to them."

"That's not that easy," she said.

"It may not be easy," I replied, "but it is the right thing to do, and it will help you get on your own feet. After all, they have the shelter you need, and they are your family and you need each other."

I wanted to get a commitment from her and said, "Will you try to reconcile yourself with your family? Can you call them on the phone and tell them that you would like to get along with them, and that you need their help?"

"I'll try," she said.

Those were the greatest words I'd heard her say, "I'll try."

And try she did! About a month later, she stopped by my office, to tell me that she was now living with her family and that they were getting along.

This homeless person now had a home, but for every person who walks into my office asking for help, maybe one in ten really listens and makes a decision to change.

Julie's Cat Gets Lymphoma

Julie saw a homeless cat at the Dayton Fair, and instantly fell in love with her. She adopted her, and named her Cocoa. The cat had been with us for seven years when we noticed a lump in her neck. The vet did a biopsy and it tested positive for cancer. The vet recommended she be put to sleep, but Julie said, "No, I want to keep her as long as possible." A few months later, her condition worsened, and Cocoa started howling. Julie made the difficult decision to take her cat to the Emergency Vet Care at about 12:00 midnight. She knew that Cocoa was suffering.

After a brief examination, the doctors agreed that Cocoa should be euthanized.

I remember how much of a struggle it was for Julie to make this decision, but she did not want Cocoa to suffer any more and knew she had to let her go. I supported her and we cried together. I was proud of Julie for making the decision, regardless of her own pain, and knowing of her love for Cocoa.

Sometimes, our pets are the ones to teach us how to become more compassionate.

Working for Justice and Righteousness

Christiana had several experiences that were not only valuable lessons, but affected the direction of her life and the work that she would eventually pursue. As a result, she has become a dynamic force to help people achieve justice and righteousness.

One of Christiana's interesting experiences occurred when she was a student at Albright College. She and other students decided to demonstrate their point by sleeping outside in cardboard boxes. It was such a unique undertaking that the local newspaper sent a reporter to interview them to find out why they were doing it. Christiana explained that it was part of an awareness campaign she and other members from the Alpha Phi Omega Service Fraternity were staging to increase people's awareness of the plight of the homeless people who live in cardboard boxes.

I was glad to see Christiana developing a social conscience, and working to help desperate, disadvantaged people. As a result, residents of the area not only became more aware of the plight of the homeless, but money was raised to help support the local homeless shelters. Our daughter was learning to help others less fortunate and stand up for what was right.

Christiana was taking courses in pre-law and social justice in college, so during the summer months, she decided to find work in that area. She applied and was accepted to work in the security department at the Trump Plaza casino in Atlantic City, New Jersey. Unfortunately, she found herself being harassed verbally by a married employee while working there. She told him to stop, but when he continued to make sexual advances toward her, and propositioned her, she said, "That's it. I don't want you approaching me again." She proceeded to complain to have the company place a restraining order on him. He was transferred to another area, and was told, "Never approach her again." It was good that she stood up for what was right.

She was commended for speaking up and was promoted to a higher area of security. They liked her so much they wanted to hire her full-time with benefits, but she declined as she wanted to finish college and pursue other interests.

During her senior year in college, Christiana had the opportunity to work as an intern for a defense attorney in Washington, D.C. Her job involved investigating and gathering information that would be brought before the court. The defense attorney assigned her to interview a prison client and gather whatever facts she could to defend a man who was accused of murder. There was police testimony against him and it looked like a grim case. However, Christiana was able to piece together enough circumstantial evidence along with witnesses that eventually led to his acquittal. It was quite a remarkable turn of events for the life of this man. She was able to prove that there was no possible way he could have committed the murder based upon the particular circumstances and evidence she had gathered. The man, even though guilty of drug charges, was proven innocent of murder in a court of law based upon Christiana's work. I was proud of her accomplishments and her desire to pursue what was right and just. This was the beginning of her work to help others fight the injustice in the world.

Christiana was becoming a stronger individual and was certainly learning to stand up for what was right. She had a professor in one of her classes whose behavior and language was beyond what was acceptable and proper. All the women in the class were being subjected to demeaning language, a form of harassment. This was not an isolated incidence, but was a pattern of behavior that was embarrassing to the women, and no one wanted to cause any trouble for fear of repercussions.

That's when Christiana said, "Someone has to stand up for what is right." And, Dale and I remember how she agonized about the situation.

After another incident with the professor, Christiana filed a formal complaint to the college school board that he be removed from the school because of his improper behavior. As a result, the complaint was noted, and they decided to assign another teacher to have a formal talk with the professor about changing his behavior. That's all that the board wanted to do at the time. It worked for a while, but some of the women still noted a few digressions from time to time. Christiana felt that he must have found out who filed the complaint because he didn't mess with her any more!

It's not surprising that Christiana has championed women's rights and equal opportunities for women. Her experiences helping those who are oppressed in our society have been quite remarkable.

"Only God Knows How Long You Will Live!"

There was a woman in the church that I would visit from time to time, and she would frequently repeat the story of what her doctor told her. After examining her medical tests he said, "You have only a few months to live."

"Only God knows how long I will live!" she angrily responded.

She told me how startled the doctor was and insisted that the type of cancer she had would probably take her in a few short months.

She continued to argue in favor of her faith in God. "Only God knows how long you will live!" she'd say.

I found her to be quite an amazing lady with great dignity, and self-discipline. She had been a dancer in her youth, and still remained very flexible in her old age. She exercised regularly, and ate very well. Needless to say, she continued to live many more years into her 90's and loved to tell the story of how wrong the doctor's prediction was about her.

I believe that God allowed her to live as long as she was willing to fight to live. I have observed in my ministry that a person's faith can make all the difference in the world.

I once attended a conference on Health and Wholeness by Dr. Andrew Weil. The one story I will never forgot was about a woman who kept coming to him with one illness after another. He couldn't find much wrong with her, but it seemed that she always had a problem. Then, inexplicably, the woman stopped coming to see him altogether.

He was concerned, so he called her and asked, "What's happened to you?" He had not seen her in sometime.

"I fell in love," she said.

Apparently, she'd met someone and had developed a good loving relationship. Amazingly, her problems diminished by themselves, and her immune system strengthened noticeably! This is just another case demonstrating how a person's state of mind can have an amazing influence upon that individual's health and well-being.

I strongly believe a person's faith and willpower can powerfully influence their surroundings and affect their outcome.

A Woman who had a Serious Drug Addiction

I witnessed many instances of how difficult it was for some people to use their willpower to change themselves, especially when they were battling an addiction. My office was right in the town of Hammonton, and it was not uncommon for people to walk in right off the street and ask to speak with me.

There was a woman who came in and pleaded to see the pastor. My secretary, who was very good at screening visitors, came into my office and explained that there was a woman in tears pleading to see me. I agreed to see her, so she came in and sat down.

The woman was sobbing and said, "I had a baby a few days ago, and I had to give my child up to The Department of Youth and Family Services. My child was just born," she explained, "and I was unable to take care of him because I'm a drug addict."

I was horrified to hear her story and asked an obviously stupid question, "Why can't you stop your addiction?"

She shook her head and still sobbing said, "I can't! I can't! It's too powerful a force! It controls my whole life!"

"You mean to say that the drugs you take are more powerful than your desire to care for your own child?" I asked.

"That's my problem," she said. "I want to take care of my child, but I can't. The drugs have a greater hold on my life, and I can't overcome them."

I thought I would go for broke to help her break this addiction. "Let me call some people who can get you into a drug rehab program," I said. "I know people who would pay for it and they'll help you deal with your addiction so you can care for your child."

"No," she said. "I've tried it before several times and it never works."

I said, "Well, why not try again for the sake of your child and maybe you will make it this time?"

"No," she said. "I didn't come in here for that."

"Well, why did you come in here to see me?" I asked.

"I just needed someone to talk to," she said. "I just lost my child."

My heart sank to the floor. Here was a woman who was crying, hurting, and felt trapped by the terrible drugs she was addicted to. I got up from my desk, and gave her a hug. There was nothing more I could say. There were no programs for her to join. Not even the money I could give her could change her misery. God knows how much I wanted to help her, but the best I could do was to listen to her and sympathize with her pain. It seemed just talking helped her to gain her composure and we prayed together.

She did attend church a few times while she lived close by, and we helped her through the food pantry. But eventually she quietly disappeared, and I wonder if she was ever able to change.

The Marriage Ruined by Gambling

Addictions have a way of ruining relationships. There was a young couple that I talked to that was experiencing marital difficulties. The wife asked me to speak with them, although her husband was reluctant to speak to anyone, counselor or pastor. Therefore, she arranged to have me over for dinner as a pretense. I was glad to go and help them, but I was not sure just how much I could change their current behavioral patterns if her husband did not have a real desire to change.

We had a great dinner, and engaged in light conversation at first, but then we got around to talking about gambling. The man believed that it was his right to spend a certain percentage of every paycheck on his favorite past-time, gambling.

"It is no different than the stock market," he told me. "That is just as much a gamble as my visit to a casino."

I admitted to him that, "I own several stocks, and I am aware that I am taking a degree of risk with some of them, but they are thoughtful choices that are based upon careful research."

"It's the same as gambling," he said. "How do you know whether those stocks are good ones or may become worthless?"

"I don't know for sure," I said. "But most of them are equity stocks that should increase in value over time."

His point was well taken. Playing the Stock Market is a form of gambling, but not exactly the same as gambling in casinos. The real question that I needed to address was, "Does gambling interfere with your relationship with your spouse?" That's where the couple differed. According to the husband it did not interfere, but his wife felt otherwise. What about the children? They always seem to get caught in the middle.

The couple was stuck at an impasse, and unfortunately, there was nothing I could say to improve their situation. The couple eventually divorced.

Special People Who Supported Our Ministry

As a couple in ministry, Dale and I have had to deal with severe human problems day in and day out. Thank God that, in every church that we have served, there have been concerned people who have supported us in our ministry. In Hammonton, we had a dear friend who would ask me, "How's the cash flow in the church?"

It became a standard joke between us, but he was serious in his concern for the welfare of the church. Since he had served on the finance committee, he was interested in the success of a financially secure church. In fact, he would often give me great tips on who to see, who I should talk to, and who I should not talk to. He praised me for our accomplishments, and I considered him a great advisor. He was a small man in stature, but he had great influence upon many people. Unfortunately, he had a severe case of osteoporosis and developed an illness that became fatal. I lost a good friend.

Another person that was special to me and who often advised me on difficult matters was a man who had become legally blind. He could see only vague images, but could always recognize me by the sound of my voice. The one thing that truly amazed me about him was that even though he could not see very well, he had the best vision of anyone in the whole congregation. He was very insightful and could tell me things about people and events that would eventually come true. His mind was as sharp as a tack, and he understood the caring ministry that we were trying to create for people in need. He missed his dear wife who had been very active in the church before she died. Unfortunately, he had a stroke and died, and I was devastated to lose yet another good friend. However, our loss was his gain, for he was able to be with his wonderful dear wife again.

There were other special friends in the church with whom we could relate to because we both had children who suffered from a mental illness. We shared a certain camaraderie that only those in the same situation can relate to.

Dale and I are grateful for the support and friendships we have had because ministry can often be a difficult and thankless profession.

Christiana and Julie work at Trump Plaza

Both Christiana and Julie had interesting experiences working at Trump Plaza in Atlantic City, New Jersey. Christiana worked for the security department, and Julie worked at the gourmet refreshment store. Both got a first-hand look at how people risked their money and ruined their lives gambling. At times Christiana would be responsible for distributing thousands and thousands of dollars in chips to various game tables. She had to have surveillance follow her when she carried the chips for her protection. She worked her way up in the surveillance area and learned a great deal about other people from that experience.

Shamefully, there were many elderly people who would squander their entire Social Security money they had received for the month and then have no money left for a bus ride home. They would come to Christiana begging for money, so they could go home.

Purse snatching was another big problem in the casino. Almost every day someone would lose their purse to a thief or pickpocket.

The payout percentage is fixed electronically in the slot machines, so the house can't lose. Yet, hundreds of thousands of people flock to the casinos each year hoping this day will be the one when they will hit it big. After seeing so many problems occur in marriages as a result of gambling, I would tell people it is not wise to gamble.

I'll never forget during the 50's what my father told me about Howard Hughes, one of the richest persons who ever lived. Hughes, who owned casinos in Las Vegas said, "I am wealthy because of the greed of mankind."

There are many people in this world who want quick, easy wealth, but as Jesus said, "It is easier for a camel to go through the eye of a needle, than for a rich man to enter into the kingdom of God." (Matthew 19:24)

Profiting from people's weaknesses is not right with God.

Renewal of a Friendship

One of the all-inspiring and thrilling experiences for me was when Karl accepted the Hammonton church ministry. We would be moving to live close to my dear friend, Jane, and I was overjoyed! A minister's wife can make friends among the parishioners, but must always be objective. But my friendship with Jane goes deeper than that. Jane and I really listen to each other and we can share anything with each other. This is what being a Christian is all about, unconditional love. Jane and I don't always agree on everything, but we respect and love each other enough not to let those things get in the way of our feelings for each other. We never berate each other and only offer encouragement.

I know there are going to be some tough times ahead for us as we get older and the frailties of the human body become more apparent. I also know that through thick or thin, Jane and I will be there for each other, no matter what.

I would often go with Jane to the women's fellowship at her church, where she was the president for two of those years, and was a good leader. We were able to go shopping together, and we even went to the Philadelphia Flower Show and Peddler's Village in New Hope, Pennsylvania. What a treat!

For me, the most inspiring thing about Jane is her perseverance in the face of pain. Over 20 years ago, she injured her back and has been in constant pain ever since, and her faith in the Lord has given her the strength to live her life courageously in spite of it.

Jane's husband, Rich, suffered through a terminal illness, and he displayed courage and dignity as he "fought the good fight," something my husband always says. Rich continued to do as much for Jane as he could until his body gave out.

Jane, in turn, did as much as she could for Rich. She put her pain aside and did whatever needed to be done. She even helped to make wedding favors for their daughter's wedding, painstakingly gluing flowers and ribbons together for over 100 guests. She spent months working on those favors and never complained.

I admire Jane for her courage as she stood by her husband's side during those final days. The testimony she gave at Rich's funeral, about her love for him and her faith in the Lord, made everyone present admire her strength.

We certainly can learn from those around us, and I have learned a lot from Jane, for which I will be forever grateful.

Harmon Dies

Another dear friend that had a positive influence on our lives was Harmon Bro. Harmon had been in failing health for quite some time and we did Companion Prayer for him to help guide him back to health. One session we held in June of 1997 indicated that Harmon's health was not good and that he was close to passing over to the other side. We gave what advice we could and hoped for the best, because we were not ready to lose our good friend.

We were concerned about Harmon going back to the Association for Research and Enlightenment (ARE) for an anniversary that summer. It seemed to upset him and we felt the stress wouldn't be good for him, but Harmon being Harmon felt he had to go and he did.

We decided to visit the Bro's in Cape Cod with Jason. Harmon and June's wonderful son, John, had been reunited with them after twelve years. He has schizophrenia like Jason and the two of them seemed to get along very well. While we were there, we discussed having a seminar on Companion Prayer and set the date for September, 1997.

Harmon became increasingly ill and in the beginning of September, he took a turn for the worse. We talked with him for the last time while he was in the hospital. He was running a high fever and the doctors were trying to bring it down with ice packs. As we prayed and meditated for him, Harmon came to me and told me he was passing over. I was very upset, but realized that there was nothing I could do but pray and reassure Harmon and his family that all would be well. The great thing about the Bro's is their strong faith in God.

We lived close to Atlantic City at that time and we wanted to go to the Miss America Pageant. We had already purchased the tickets and even though we knew Harmon was very ill and I had had my spiritual "talk" with him about his passing, we decided to go. At about the time the pageant started, I felt Harmon leave this plane. We had been trying to reach his family all night, but knew they must have been by his side in the hospital.

The next morning, after choir practice, we found a message on the answering machine from June Bro. Harmon had died the night before, right about the time I'd felt him leave his body. Of course, we were devastated. We had become close to the Bro's and felt a deep sense of loss. We especially felt for June as they worked as a team doing much good wherever they could. During church, I felt Harmon's presence, comforting and reassuring us that everything would be okay. I could still hear him encouraging us to do the best we could and to continue the work he was so passionate about.

We had planned to have the seminar on Companion Prayer the third weekend in September, and June still wanted to do this in spite of Harmon's death. So, a memorial service was planned for the following Saturday. The girls and I were able to attend and Christiana and I sang. Karl was unable to be there as he had a wedding to perform. He and Jason flew up on Sunday after church to be there for the seminar, which was a touching and moving experience where our mentor's presence was strongly felt and honored.

Following Harmon's death, June decided she wanted to move to the Midwest to be closer to some of her family and friends. I volunteered to help her get ready to move, so I took several trips up to help her organize her things and to pack. Joyce, a dear friend of June's and I worked diligently to help her with the move.

While we were away, Karl woke up one morning in agonizing pain. We couldn't understand why he was in such pain on his left side. A short time later, we got a phone call that at the exact same time Karl awoke in pain, Julie had been hurt in a car accident.

Julie Gets Hurt

I woke up in the morning, while we were in Cape Cod, with the whole left side of my body in extreme pain. It was about 7:45 a.m., and I couldn't explain why I was hurting. Dale could hear me and said, "What's wrong?"

"I don't know," I groaned. "I'm just in a lot of pain."

Dale examined me, but could find no reason for the pain. She told me to take an analgesic.

About an hour and a half later, Jane, a good friend of Dale's, called. "I'm sorry to tell you this," she said. "Julie has been in a car accident."

"Is she all right?" Dale asked.

"Yes," she answered. "She's in some pain, but she did not sustain any major injuries." Jane explained that Julie was driving to school earlier that morning. It was approximately 7:45 a.m. Suddenly she was struck by a pickup truck that hit her car on the left side. She was taken to the hospital and examined, and they were just about to release her.

"Oh, thank you for calling me," Dale said. "I'm glad that you were able to help Julie while we were away."

Dale came rushing to me, and repeated the conversation she had had with Jane, and explained how Julie was hit by a car, but was all right. She was hit on her left side.

"Well, that would explain the pain I felt this morning," I said. So, we packed up early and hurried home so that we could be with Julie. Within a few hours, I was feeling fine. This type of experience did not happen to me again until September 11, 2001, when so many people died in the Twin Towers disaster in New York City.

A Series of Disappointments

Around the time Harmon was passing from our lives, we had several major life changes that occurred one after the other. My brother and his wife were having marital problems and when they couldn't work them out, he left her. This caused turmoil which eventually led to a lot of hard feelings and estrangements among family members. At the same time, there were problems in Karl's sister's marriage, which also resulted in their separation.

Jason's illness was hard for me to manage at home. Even though Karl was very supportive, the responsibility for giving Jason his meds as well as making sure he got to the train station for pickup to and from work fell on me. I am a light sleeper, and would wake to hear Jason pacing back and forth and laughing to himself night after night; there was no one with him.

On top of this troubling situation, someone had taken my choir robe and put another name on it. It was the last straw, and I couldn't take it anymore. I felt my world was falling apart. Between estranged relationships with family members, the death of my daughter's cat, Jason's continued daily illness with occasional sojourns to Massachusetts and the Pentagon, I finally snapped. The depression that I thought I'd resolved earlier, returned in full force. I was so filled with anxiety that I couldn't deal with things anymore. Thank God for a friend in church. He took me home, and at this point, I had a long trip back before I would feel normal again.

I found it increasingly difficult to function, and I cried all the time. I remember one day I was driving home after I'd picked up Julie from school, when suddenly, I started to cry uncontrollably, and I had to pull the car over to the side of the road. Julie had to take the wheel and drove us home. I felt as if I couldn't bear my life anymore. I almost felt suicidal, although I don't believe I would ever have taken my life. I did indeed feel at the end of my rope.

I cried out for help and Karl suggested a Christian psychologist who he brought in to help me through this tough time. He was so wonderful that he came to our home and we had a long first intake session there. Over the next months, I went to counseling several times a week and also took medications to assist in creating more of a biochemical balance in my brain. I also developed my own form of therapy. I played solitaire a lot and crocheted one afghan after another. I also used light therapy. A session of Companion Prayer suggested I spend time outside in the sun or use a special light bulb to expose me to more 'light.'

Several months later, Jason was re-admitted to the hospital again and when he was ready to be released Karl and I had to say "No" to his returning home to live with us. It was too hard on me and was definitely affecting my health. Turning my son away was the hardest thing I ever had to do. This was my son, whom I loved dearly, and it was painful to have to give him up, but it turned out to be the best move we could have made in regards to our health and it gave Jason a certain amount of independence. After all, at 23, he was a grown man.

After five months of treatment, I had recovered sufficiently so that I applied for a position as a nurse in the Migrant Head Start Program. I talked this over with Karl and my Christian psychologist, and we felt this might be a good opportunity for me. The position was only for a few months and would be a good chance to gain back my self-confidence.

Rural Opportunities

Rural Opportunities was a Migrant Head Start Program and Day Care Center serving migrant and under-privileged children. Dale worked as a nurse during the summer time and as a teacher for the preschool during the winter months. Enrollment during the summer months often reached as many as 90 children.

Working for Rural Opportunities was a difficult but rewarding experience. When I was hired I had to go through two weeks of training before the program began. Not only did I have to learn the regulations for the State of New Jersey, but I also had to follow Federal Guidelines because we were partly funded by the Federal Government as well. What made this program especially challenging was the language barrier I encountered. I did not speak Spanish, but thank goodness, there was another nurse on staff who could translate for me.

My responsibilities entailed making sure things were done in a healthful and sanitary manner. Changing areas needed to be disinfected after every diaper use, and health issues needed to be addressed and immunizations monitored. I was involved in several interesting cases, from trying to correct a congenital condition in a baby, to trying to stop the spread of a possible life-threatening epidemic.

Working in this environment, I was learning Spanish by being totally immersed in and surrounded by it.

I worked in this program for three summers, doing what I could to help migrant children and their families, and it was a life-altering experience.

Dale's Heart Goes Bananas

In September of 1999 I was having some gynecological problems and was scheduled to have a thermal oblation of my uterus. I was put under anesthesia and as with past surgical procedures, when anesthesia was used I often had an elevated heart rate. I returned home shortly afterward and began to recover from this procedure.

Several days later, we were asked to do a second Companion Prayer session for an individual for whom we had done a session a number of years earlier. We were pleased this individual had done so well.

Near the end of the session, I felt my heart begin to race. I wasn't too worried at the time because my heart often had an elevated heart rate. I thought my heart rate would decrease but instead it began to go faster. I asked Karl to listen to my heart, and when he heard how fast my heart was beating he said, "We need to take you to the hospital, something's wrong with your heart." My heart was beating 190 beats per minute.

Karl took me to the hospital right away, and the emergency room doctors tried to slow my heart rate. They got a crash cart ready in case my heart went into defibrillation. The doctors were able to stabilize my heart, but not correct the problem, even with medication. Several days later, they transferred me to Our Lady of Lourdes Hospital in Camden, where they performed an oblation in my heart.

My heart had produced a lot of supraventricular tachycardia (SVT's) over the years, and because I was taking a medication that was later found to cause heart arrhythmias (which they later took off the market), they found the electrical irregularity in my heart and eradicated it with the oblation. My heart stopped briefly and it took over 30 seconds to start again. I am grateful the procedure worked, otherwise I would be taking medication to stabilize my heart rate for the rest of my life.

My recovery was complicated by an infection as a result of my first procedure. After a course of antibiotics, I eventually recovered.

Through all these physical problems, I always felt the presence of God. I knew that no matter what happened to my physical body, my spirit belonged to the Lord and I would pass on to the next plane.

The Wedding from Hell

The most unusual wedding I ever performed was a series of mishaps that occurred one after another. The irony of it all was that the bride took such care to make sure everything would be "perfect" on the day of her wedding. She was meticulous about every little detail; however, even the best-laid plans can go awry.

It all began when one of the bridesmaids forgot her bouquet and purse, so the bridesmaids traveled all the way back to the house to get the bouquet. Unfortunately, the keys to the house were in her purse, which was locked inside, and they decided to break into the house to get them. By then the guests were waiting at the church with me, and we were informed that the wedding would be delayed because the bridesmaids would be late. The bride was not exactly happy, but wanted to include her friends in the wedding. After all, she had put a lot of time and effort into selecting the perfect dresses for the bridesmaids, so she agreed to wait. It was a hot day with many people in a small church sanctuary, and it was getting hotter by the minute, even though the air conditioning was running.

When the bridesmaids finally arrived, we began the service and everything was going along just fine. The session of the church was present because we were offering the Sacrament of Communion to those who wished to take part in this holy event. This wedding ceremony included many special features, so it was going to run much longer than usual.

We were passing grape juice in little cups through the second pew when suddenly the father of the groom stood up and collapsed in the middle of the church aisle. Grape juice went flying everywhere all over people's clothes.

The mother of the groom, who was sitting right next to her husband, leaned over the top of him and cried out, "I'm losing both of my Henrys today! I'm losing both of my Henrys today!" A nurse in the congregation quickly rushed over.

At that same moment, the groom collapsed on the floor right in front of me! We heard another wave of groans throughout the congregation, and another nurse in the crowd ran over to him. It appeared that he had fainted, and it was a good thing we had several nurses present.

While this was happening, the bride was the coolest one of all. She stood calmly in her beautiful gown and told her future family-in-law to get a grip on themselves! The groom tried to stand up, but collapsed again. Someone quickly brought over a chair for him to sit in.

Dale was reassuring the mother of the groom that all was going to be fine, and an ambulance was on the way. Her son was okay, too!

People were looking to me for guidance and I told them, "Everything is all right; we have an ambulance on the way. Let us take a moment to pray and collect ourselves." I then said a prayer of healing and it seemed to calm the congregation down.

When the ambulance arrived, they put the father of the groom on a gurney and rolled him out of the church.

"I'm going to the hospital with my father," the groom said.

Some people stood up to leave.

"Karl, you haven't pronounced them husband and wife yet," Dale said to me. "They can't leave."

So, I got everyone's attention and said, "Folks, we have one more thing to do before you leave the church. It is the pronouncement." I held on to the bride and groom and said, "I pronounce you husband and wife. Go in peace. Amen."

It was the shortest pronouncement I have ever made in my whole life as a minister. The organ then played and the wedding party processed out of the church.

As the people were leaving, one man told me, "Pastor, this is the first wedding I have ever attended that turned into a healing prayer service."

I went to the hospital to check on the father of the groom, and he was fine. Apparently, he had not eaten anything all day, and was suffering from dehydration and exhaustion. They were going to keep him for a while just to observe him. The bride and groom, now husband and wife, were there in the hospital along with the man's wife.

The bride said, "People are waiting at the reception hall and we must go and greet them." The reception hall was only a quarter of a mile away from the hospital, so they didn't have far to go.

The story doesn't end here, however. Dale and I went to the reception, and found the bar line was crowded with people ordering doubles. Then, there was a rush of activity and someone yelled, "Another person is hurt, call an ambulance!"

"What happened?" I asked.

"One of the bridesmaids fell down the stairs to the patio outside, and cut her head open," I was told.

Within a few minutes, the ambulance was there and it was the same ambulance crew that had been at the church earlier. One of the EMT's said, "This is the second time I've seen you people. When is this wedding going to be over?"

It was unbelievable! We'd never experienced anything like this before. Fortunately, no one was seriously hurt.

Dale and I went back to the hospital again where we found the newlyweds still in their wedding clothes, sitting near the mother and father of the groom who was still lying in bed. In the bed right next to him, was the bridesmaid and surrounding her were all her friends.

The nurses were amused that the wedding party kept coming to the hospital. It was the wedding that everybody talked about for a long time. The bride wanted a memorable wedding and it was that all right. As a footnote, the couple is doing just fine and they now have two lovely children. They laugh about the wedding and agree that it was the wedding from hell!

The Weddings at the Beach

I performed several weddings at the beach. The first was in Margate, New Jersey. It was a stormy day and there was some talk that we might move the wedding to the reception location in Wildwood, New Jersey, but the couple insisted that they get married on the beach. So, the entire wedding party and guests drove to the beach, and on the way, we traveled through heavy rain. When we finally arrived at the beach, there was a small clearing in the sky and the sun was shining through. It was as if there was an opening just for the wedding. The sand on the beach was very soft and we all took off our shoes.

It was a small wedding party, so people who were walking on the beach were invited to join in the ceremony, and several did.

I started to speak in the traditional way with the bride and groom standing in front of me and the ocean at my back, but I quickly realized that they could not hear me because of the background noise of the ocean waves. There were white caps and the water was very turbulent. Therefore, I asked the bride and groom to stand in the middle while the rest of us formed a circle around them. Our bodies formed a sound barrier as well as making the wedding more intimate. Not only could they hear me now, but we shielded the bride and groom from the blowing wind. We were fortunate that, for the moment, it was not raining. There were threatening clouds moving in from the East and I knew we had only a short window of opportunity. It was a brief ceremony with Scriptures read and the blessing of prayers.

As we were walking back to the cars, it began to rain. It was an amazing occurrence to witness. It was as if for that brief moment in time, the weather cooperated and the rain was still as we gathered together to bless this couple. Not that I stilled the water as Jesus did, but I know the scripture does tell us to "Be still, and know that I am God." (Psalm 46:10)

The second wedding I performed at the beach was in Cape Hatteras, North Carolina and it took place in front of the lighthouse. Again, the weather was rough with white caps riding in on the waves. There was no rain, but it was a very windy day. Again, I gathered the bridal party in a circle for the ceremony. However, this time my back was to the lighthouse and I was facing the ocean while the couple could see the lighthouse.

This couple loved lighthouses and had pictures and replicas of them everywhere in their home. In one interesting picture taken of the couple on the beach is of them facing one another with the lighthouse flashing between them. The wedding cake was, yes, a lighthouse.

Upgrades

The church facilities had areas that needed fixing and upgrading. Some of these had been discussed but were never acted on. One problem that no one wanted to even talk about was the presence of the underground oil tanks. In New Jersey, an underground oil tank that could eventually leak was a major problem because the surface of the ground is not far from the water table. We didn't know if ours was leaking or not, but we knew the tanks were full of sludge and had caused many problems with the heating system, which was also out-dated. The best solution that most people advised was to convert to natural gas and replace the furnace with a better, more fuel-efficient system. In the future, oil prices were bound to go up. It took a long time to convert from oil to natural gas with permits, tests, and filling the old tanks, but the issue had finally been addressed and resolved.

We upgraded to a new computer system, and created a web site for the church. We installed new church signs, remodeled several "apartments" on the church property for people to rent, and upgraded the facilities for the 'Migrant Head Start Program.

Time to Move On, But Where?

I felt my work was done in Hammonton and it was time to move on to serve another church congregation. I did not feel that I was able to use all my abilities and skills sitting in the church office day after day, but when I left, the financial officer reported that for the first time, the church was finally in the black.

Dale and I felt stymied and thought that our gifts were not being used well. We both felt it was time to move on, but where was God calling us to go? I have always felt that it was up to God to guide us, and we felt it needed to be a church congregation that was crying out for help!

Within two weeks of activating my resume on the computer database, I received 12 serious inquiries. It seemed most of the churches were large and about to begin major construction programs. My experience in construction would have been ideal for them, but beyond that, it would primarily be an "administrative" position, and not a "hands-on" ministry. I wanted a ministry working with the people.

Dale and I took on a serious search of churches. Dale dreamed that I had moved our family to the mountains, and shortly after we found a small struggling church in the mountains of the Poconos. "This is like my dream, Karl," Dale said. She felt certain that this was the church we were to serve, even before I spoke to anyone at the church about the position.

Dale and I prayed together, and in one of our Companion Prayer sessions, when we talked about where we were to go, it was suggested we look for a "community of people who worked together regardless of religion, race, or any other differences." Shawnee on Delaware appeared to be that community. We then went to the next level and contacted the search committee.

Chapter 16

"Love your neighbor as yourself."
Mark 12: 31

Shawnee Presbyterian Church 2000

Pastoral Nominating Committee (PNC)

I went to preach before the Shawnee Presbyterian Church Pastoral Nominating Committee and the evening before I lost my voice. It had happened a few times before, but why now when I was going to preach to a congregation that might be my next call to Pastoral Ministry? We had dinner with a group of the PNC the night before and I talked a little, but only in a whisper. Dale told me to save my voice for the next day when I was to preach. But it seemed that my voice was getting worse by the minute.

That night, we stayed at the home of one of the church members on the PNC. Pam told me to lie down on the couch and she would lay her hands on me and pray. Of course, I agreed, because at that point, I had totally lost my voice. Both Dale and Pam prayed and I felt a warm sensation of heat spread through my whole throat area. I was told not to say a word until the next day. I had a good night's sleep and prepared myself to preach. I was still a bit congested in my voice box, but decided to go on faith to preach the best I could. I had a hot cup of tea, prayed some more, and spoke at a whisper until it was time to preach.

I was not sure my voice would be there, but decided to put it in the hands of the Lord. Then the time came for me to read the scripture and to preach. I got up and started to speak and I was a little surprised. My voice came through crystal clear, although it was a little weaker than normal, but it was clear without straining my voice, and that was what counted.

After that experience and talking to the PNC, coupled with Dale's dream, I knew that Shawnee was where God wanted me to go. There was one woman in the church at Shawnee who always said to me, "God sent you to us!" Some time later, at her funeral, the lights began to blink on and off, and I said to the congregation, Bea is reminding me to mention that she donated the light fixtures in memory of her husband. She said to me before she died that she was going to attend her own funeral and be the "ghost of honor." I asked the interviewing Committee if they would be willing to renovate the church Manse. I told them I would help them do it, although I knew they had no idea of the skills I possessed.

George, who was a member of the PNC, asked me, "How long will you stay at Shawnee Presbyterian Church?" I thought for a few seconds and told them, "I will guarantee you at least five years." I explained that didn't mean I would only stay five years, but I knew I would be there at least that long. When I make a promise, I do everything I can to fulfill it, and everyone who knows me understands this about me. George and the others on the committee were down-to-earth people who looked me in the eye, and said they knew I could be their pastor.

The Shawnee Presbyterian Church had been about to close its doors because of poor attendance. Some of my colleagues thought I was crazy when they found out that I was going to Shawnee on Delaware. They thought we could go anywhere because I had such a good track record, and they were probably right. We could have served in a number of other churches, but Dale and I followed our intuition and went to the place where we felt we were definitely called by God. The important thing for us was to serve the church where God wanted us to be.

A Brief Talk with God

I asked God about the Shawnee Presbyterian Church and how long I might be there. The answer I received was poetic, and the message was clear. He said to me: **"You can stay a long time working, as long as you spend your time working hard."**

Renovating the Manse

We have worked hard. The first task was the extensive work that needed to be done to renovate the church manse. It was a mess. In fact, the very first day we moved in, one of the members of the church said to me, "I would never move into this house!" Another minister explained that his wife had told him, after looking at the manse, "We're not moving there."

The plumbing did not work correctly, and you had to stand in a foot of cold water in the tub while you took a shower. The old cast iron drain pipes were almost completely blocked, and there was not enough hot water to take a full bath. The furnace did not adequately heat the water. There were cracks in the walls and ceilings all over the house.

The kitchen was the worst of all. There were old cabinets that did not open or close very well, and the floor and countertops had a slope to them, so water or anything else you spilled would always run to the right. There were only three upper cabinets and three lower cabinets, nowhere near enough storage room, and there was a strong odor of "dog" in the kitchen, too.

Not all the radiators in the house worked, and in the washroom, the heater was completely broken. The water would freeze in the pipes if we did not leave the door open to the kitchen, which was always cold.

The list went on and on. But, we did not mind because we knew that in time it would all be fixed up. That's where my experience in construction came in handy.

I agreed to accept the call if the church agreed to help me fix up the manse as part of our call agreement. Dale and I worked on the design using all the experience we had gained over the years by living in many different homes. We suggested an addition that would fix and renovate the manse to be used for multiple purposes. This meant space for entertaining company, a study for the pastor to counsel people, a downstairs powder room with shower, and a full "galley" kitchen with an island and room for a table. The plumbing and heating system would also be remodeled.

Over a period of nine months, with the help of an excellent contractor, and volunteers from the church, we were able to remodel the manse. A team of volunteers would meet at the manse every Friday night to work on the inside, and Dale would fix snacks. The team worked together putting up drywall, installing the floor board by board, painting and installing the kitchen cabinets, reworking the electric wiring, and installing the tile. We transformed a house built in 1912 into a home that we could enjoy in the 21st century without changing its original character.

An Advocate for Women

After Christiana graduated from College she took a position as a legal advocate with the Women's Resource Center in Delaware Water Gap, Pennsylvania. Her job was to advise abused woman and men about the resources that were available to help them deal with the injustice of abuse. These may consist of a PFA (restraining order), going to a shelter, working things out with counseling, or even divorce. She would take photographs, and gather other evidence that would be submitted in court on the victim's behalf, and she would provide emotional support for their pain. She has also instructed new volunteers on how to answer the Hot Line at Women's Resources.

Needless to say, her knowledge and skill to evaluate and support those in need is quite extensive. One time she used her abilities to assess the character of a man that our family thought was kind and generous, but Christiana felt he was dishonest, and she warned us to be careful dealing with him. As it turned out Christiana was right and the man was very manipulative and deceitful.

If someone comes to me complaining of abuse, I immediately call upon Christiana to help that person, which she has done for me on several occasions. She has helped to enlighten me about the wide-spread problems of sexual abuse, homelessness, and oppression that still exist. I believe these experiences have made her a stronger, more dedicated and responsible individual.

Dale's New Jobs

While Karl was adjusting to a new pulpit, I was considering applying for the open position of Music Director at the Shawnee Presbyterian Church. It entailed directing the choir and playing the organ during the church service. I had directed a choir in Dayton for 11 ½ years and I was the assistant organist in Hammonton, so I had previous experience, but combining the two jobs was new to me, and I decided to go for it. I was offered the position, and soon after, I accepted it knowing full well I would have a lot of work to do to learn new music for the choir and to brush up on my organ playing skills.

Regardless, I also wanted to get back into the workforce, preferably in the nursing field, but I was uncertain as to the direction I should take. I had worked as a nurse in the Migrant Head Start Program, and also as a contracted nurse for the Sylvan Learning Center where I worked at a parochial school as well, and I enjoyed it immensely. So I thought I might look for a position as a substitute school nurse in one of the local school districts. I also considered working for a hospital, nursing home or preschool either as a nurse or preschool teacher as I had done in Hammonton.

I applied for a nursing position in the local hospital and for either a nursing or teaching position in the East Stroudsburg School District. Shortly after, I accepted the position for the school district, working in both areas, but I soon came to realize that I preferred the nursing field to teaching.

I substitute in all the schools in the district, including the local parochial schools, twelve schools in all. I'm usually called on to cover for absent nurses, but I'm also available to do hearing screenings and scoliosis screenings when needed. I love my job!

Holding part-time jobs as opposed to a full-time job are advantageous. I work with Karl in the church on a weekly basis planning worship services together, and I have the flexibility to be there for weddings and funerals as well. I am able to work my school schedule around my church schedule and vice versa. I am extremely satisfied with my working situation as it allows me the time to do extracurricular activities as well. All in all, as the expression goes, "I do what I do and I do what I love!"

Design for Meeting the Needs of the Community

There were skiers, snowboarders, canoers, and hikers who visited our village in the different seasons throughout the year. It was really apparent that our church should create a design for meeting the needs of these people and at the same time provide for better financial security for the church. Therefore, the session undertook some new projects that had only been talked about, but never initiated.

The Christian Education building was retrofitted to serve as a "youth hostel" for young people who came to the Poconos for skiing, canoeing, and hiking. We installed two showers and obtained mats for youth to sleep on. For the adults, we obtained sleeper sofas.

Another project was to provide for an emergency food pantry. This was a mission project established by the deacons to help people that are turned down for help by other agencies, for one reason or another. There are many people who often fall through the cracks and need help with food. This was another way for the church to meet the needs of the community.

Expanding the Parking Lot

As I began a new ministry at the Shawnee Presbyterian Church, I noticed that there was very little parking space. I knew from my studies of The Twelve Characteristics of Successful Churches by Ken Calahan, that one of the most important physical needs of the church was adequate parking. So, after a session retreat and a thorough discussion of the future goals of the Church, the session agreed to expand the parking lot.

We received permission from a neighboring landholder to use part of their land for parking, but we would have to do all the land preparation and use only gravel on their part of the land. We had to tear down an old shed on our part of the land first, and then hire someone to level the ground.

There was a tremendous amount of earth to move to level the land. However, I had learned a long time ago to turn stumbling blocks into stepping stones, and I believed that I could do that very thing in this situation.

The church had little usable money for the project. Therefore, I sought to see if we could sell the dirt in order to pay for the leveling that needed to be done for the parking lot, and that was exactly what we did!

The stone for the parking lot was donated, as was some of the labor.

The total cost for the new parking lot, that would fit 30 more cars, was only $1,000.00. I was told that other ministers had wanted more parking spaces, but didn't know how to go about it.

Together with the vision of the session, and thinking "outside the box," we were able to figure out how it could be done. People immediately used the lot and attendance increased.

A Blistering Experience

One afternoon, along with volunteers from our church, I helped to clear out an old shed to make way for the new church parking lot. Suddenly, I felt a stinging sensation on my right heel. It continued to burn and when I inspected the area more closely I noticed a blister beginning to form. I assumed I had been exposed to poison ivy and that was the cause for my discomfort, regardless of the fact that I was wearing long pants, socks and shoes. I thought little of it and continued on with the cleanup.

We were leaving on vacation the next day immediately after church let out, and Karl's father was coming with us since we planned to visit several of his good friends. We even took Midget with us. We started our trek across the states, intending to stop in North Carolina, Virginia and Tennessee along the way. As we arrived at the home of one of Dad's friends in North Carolina, I began to feel ill and grew more uncomfortable by the hour. The blister became larger; the area started to change color and became dark in appearance. The swelling also increased and my ankle began to throb.

By the time we reached Lexington, Virginia, my ankle was very badly swollen, and the site of the blister was an angry, open wound. I even began to run a fever. We all agreed that I should go to the hospital for evaluation.

Doctors at the local hospital took one look at my ankle and diagnosed that I had been bitten by a brown recluse spider. They administered an IV antibiotic and checked my blood for adverse reactions to my kidneys and other vital organs. Thank goodness there were none. However, it took a month's worth of antibiotics to clear up the infection, and my ankle was tender for six months.

Later, while visiting Karl's sister, Laura, in Knoxville, Tennessee, we went to the Knoxville Zoo where our niece, Crystal, worked. There we saw an actual brown recluse spider on display. The spider was dark brown in appearance and it was hard for me to imagine that this small spider had inflicted so much damage to my ankle. I was disturbed and fascinated by this spider all at the same time. The area was dark and ugly looking and the doctor said, "Unfortunately, the spider causes a flesh eating wound. It's good we treated it when we did."

The remainder of our vacation was spent with my foot being elevated, and a lot of ice packs applied. Analgesics and antibiotics were also administered. It was a very painful experience, and it took years for my foot to regain its normal appearance again. There was a darkened area around the bite, due to the breakdown of my cells, that took a long time to disappear.

This experience taught me a great deal of patience. It was difficult to be in so much pain while on vacation and to have to limit my activities with my family, but they were great! They were very supportive, kept me in plenty of ice, and helped me any way they could. It made the whole experience much easier to bear. Sometimes God uses us to give others the opportunity to help someone in need.

The Annual Christmas "Open House"

In our ministry, Dale and I have tried to be a light to the church and community in our own right. It has become a custom for us to host an open house at the manse on the first Sunday in December and invite the church family and community members to our home to enjoy good food and fellowship.

Each year Dale and I give a small token gift to every person who comes to our open house. It is our gift to them. We enjoy the company and friendships we have developed throughout the years and want to share what we have with others.

I suppose one of the strengths that Dale and I enjoy is the opportunity to work together and relate to others in a relaxed environment. This is what I believe Jesus would have us do - share what we have with others.

Golf Tournament

I was amazed that a church in a "Golfing Community" had never hosted a Golf Tournament. That quickly changed when the session realized that it could be done quite successfully with some organization and a good person leading the Tournament.

Nancy, who served on the session said, "I would love to organize a Golf Tournament," and it has since proven to be a very successful annual event.

The fellowship I have had with the golfers is as much evangelistic as it is fun. It's the one time I get to say a prayer for the golfers before all go out and golf, and I have learned that a good "Pastor" and "Pastor's wife" are not only an integral part of the community, but can be true "friends" with many people.

Jesus said, "You are my friends." So it is with us that we should love one another and be friends with one another. (John 15:12-15)

I believe the church spaghetti dinners, chicken barbecues, and all social occasions we host are for the bonding of the people in the community and with the people in the church. It's not about making money as much as it is about enjoying fellowship with the people.

Dale's Lyme Disease

Unfortunately, I contracted Lyme disease in May of 2002, and a "bull's eye" developed on my arm the day we were to leave for Julie's graduation from Rider University. I went to the doctor's to receive treatment as I was very sick with a fever and aches and pains throughout my body, but I was determined not to miss my daughter's graduation. So, with fever and aches and pains in my muscles and joints, I packed my bags and went with our family to Lawrenceville, New Jersey to celebrate! That night, before the ceremony, I was so wiped out that I went to bed early. I didn't have much energy left to gather with family and friends to wish Julie well. In order for me to see my daughter graduate from college, my faith in God gave me the strength to rise above my physical condition. The next day I was thrilled to watch Julie receive her diploma after four years of hard work.

Sinners!

How good and pleasant it was, when our whole family gathered together to celebrate Julie's graduation day from Rider University. It was a bright and sunny day when the ceremony took place outside on the grounds. There was the usual pomp and circumstance and it was a wonderful achievement for Julie. We were very proud of her!

When the ceremony was over, we lost sight of Jason. Each of us thought he was with the other. There were thousands of people milling about, and it was quite easy for him to get lost in the crowd. The family started taking pictures of Julie with her undergraduate degree, when suddenly we heard the voice of someone screaming, "Sinners! Sinners!" I immediately recognized it as Jason's voice. I was relieved that if I followed the screaming voice, I would find Jason.

On the other hand, why was he screaming "Sinners?" If you've ever seen the movie, "A Beautiful Mind," it's a good beginning toward understanding my son's torment. Jason was pointing to his imaginary people, who are very real to him, and condemning them as sinners.

You could see the horror and confusion on some of the other guests' faces. They didn't understand, and were frightened by his outburst.

I went over to Jason, put my arm around him gently and engaged him in conversation. This can sometimes break his train of thought and draw him back into the real world. I told him that we were leaving now and we had to go back to the car. He was agreeable. I also asked him if he wanted a cigarette, because I know he loves to smoke. "Yes," he said. Then he asked me if I wanted a cigarette, but I told him, "No, thank you. I don't smoke."

We joined the rest of our family, but as we were walking back to the car, Jason bellowed once again, "Shut up, sinners!"

The person walking right next to us had the most horrible expression on their face. Usually when Jason does something like this, I'm mortified, but this time I just quietly laughed to myself. These people had no idea what was happening. All they could see was someone who was out-of-control. Jason continued a few more times to shout, "Sinners, shut up!"

A campus security officer approached me and asked me, "Is everything all right?" "Everything is fine," I said.

"Okay," the officer said with a smile.

People were moving as far away from us as they could with the most disgusted expressions on their faces. We continued on toward the car and Jason calmed down. Later, Jason explained, "I was telling my friends to shut up. They were the sinners that were bothering me."

Although it was Julie's special day, she took it all in stride. "It didn't bother me because I know he has a problem," she said.

We were all glad that Jason was able to get through the whole graduation ceremony at all! Too few people understand the problems that schizophrenia can cause for both the victim and those who love and care for them. It is my hope that someday we will have a better understanding of this disease, and explore new ways to overcome it.

Julie's Endeavors

A few months after Julie graduated, she got a job working for a small solar energy company, World Water and Power. She has always believed in preserving our environment, protecting the trees, recycling bottles, cans, newspapers, and going green wherever possible. It was a natural choice for her to work for this solar energy company, and help put together the proposals for prospective clients.

And, because of Julie's understanding of mental health issues she has become an advocate for the mentally ill. She has taken several courses to learn how to help support family members who have someone in their home with mental health problems. She has even written letters to state representatives about providing parity for those who suffer from mental disorders.

I'm proud of her accomplishments and her desire to help those with mental health disabilities.

Midget

In late August of 1990, a dear elderly gentleman named Ed came to our front door. When I invited him in he said he had a present for our son Jason. He had his hand inside his shirt and when he pulled it out, there lying in the palm of his hand, was a small black and white dog. She was so tiny at only 6 weeks old. Ed told me she had been born on July 15th. I fell in love with her immediately!

Karl, on the other hand, was a little unsure about having a dog. I think it was partly due to the fact that no dog could measure up to Bonnie, his beloved childhood Collie. We'd tried several other dogs without success, so with great trepidation I finally accepted Ed's kind gift.

Just a few weeks earlier, Julie had gotten a beautiful longhaired calico kitten from the Dayton Fair that she named Cocoa. We needed to train them both, so we put them together in the same box in the kitchen at night.

We named our new dog "Midget." She was a toy fox-rat terrier mix and full-grown would weigh between 6-7 pounds.

Jason and the girls were in school all day, so I became the main person to train Midget. She soon became my "baby." She was the family dog, but Midget and I had a deep connection with each other.

As time went by, we went everywhere together. Midget was so empathic that when I got upset, she would sense it and try to make me feel better by licking my face or drying my tears. When Jason became agitated after he became ill, Midget would shake and get upset, too.

Midget was a loyal friend who was there for me when I needed her most. I also nursed her through several major illnesses. The most serious was a bout with Lyme's Disease in November 2002, when we were within hours of losing her. I, myself, had contracted the disease in May of 2002, and during my long recovery Midget stood by me. Through the proper medical treatment, my continued nursing skill and Midget's will to live, she survived her bout as well. She did sustain some kidney damage, but survived for another three years.

About a month before she died, Midget must have known she wasn't going to be with us much longer. I slept in the guest room so I could take her out at night without disturbing Karl. One night, I started to cry because I knew I'd miss her. She started to lick my eyes dry as she usually did, only this time she licked my face for more than an hour, as if to say "I won't be with you much longer in this world, so this is for all those times in the future when you need me, I'll be there." I was touched and moved at her devotion.

On March 4th, Midget was in such obvious pain we knew we couldn't let her suffer any more. We took her to the veterinarian where she went to "sleep" in my arms.

I was so distraught at her passing; I went to bed that night and prayed. In that semi-conscious meditative state Midget came to me, and I bent down to pet her. She was alive and well, young, healthy and best of all, happy! I touched her and she felt warm and soft.

I was so grateful for this experience because, even though I knew Midget was all right, seeing her that way was reassuring and helped me get through the worst part of her passing away.

Fibromyalgia

I received six weeks of antibiotics to treat the Lyme disease. What I couldn't understand was why I was not feeling any better after all that treatment. I had a series of tests for Lyme disease that all came back negative. Eventually, my doctor refused to give me any more antibiotics and suggested there might be something else going on, so he referred me to a rheumatologist. After my examination, he diagnosed me with Fibromyalgia. He also prescribed four more weeks of antibiotics to be sure the infection was under control.

Fibromyalgia syndrome can occur when there is an insult to the body such as that caused by Lyme disease, or an injury and it can create a condition where chronic pain occurs in the muscles and soft tissue which surrounds the joints. General fatigue and tenderness at 18 specific sites may occur. These points are used to help diagnose this condition. In my case, all 18 points were tender. I had difficulty sleeping, and a great deal of fatigue, as well as the constant pain that never seemed to abate.

The treatment for this condition is to address each symptom, such as pain with medication, a sleeping aid for sleeplessness, and yet another medication for depression, if needed. I found I had to be patient in learning to deal with this condition. It's difficult to wake up each morning and feel like you have been run over by a Mack Truck. It hurts to move when your body is wracked in pain. It's hard to do your duties as a Pastor's wife, handle the responsibilities of choir director and organist of the church, and report to work as a substitute school nurse while in so much pain. Sometimes, you can barely think straight! I had to rely on my faith in God to get me through the rough patches.

Over the years, I have gone through periods of remission and then relapse. Periodically, I would go to other doctors for a re-evaluation to make sure the Lyme disease had not returned or if I had been re-infected. I am still dealing with Fibromyalgia.

During one of these times of relapse, I participated in a study for a medication they were testing to alleviate the symptoms of Fibromyalgia. It was a double blind study, so participants didn't really know if they were getting the medication or a placebo, but I felt I was being given the drug as I did notice some improvement. The medication was later approved by the FDA to treat this condition, but unfortunately, I did not stay on it for long because it caused some side effects that I did not like.

Karl and I also had Companion Prayer, which was extremely beneficial in suggesting another path to follow, one with a more holistic approach. I have since embraced this holistic approach to living with Fibromyalgia. I go for massages every two to three weeks along with chiropractic adjustments, I've had acupuncture treatments which works well, I try to moderate my lifestyle to rest when I get tired, and I try to eat well including a lot of protein in my diet. I also exercise in moderation. But my greatest comfort comes from my faith in God and the support of loving family and friends. Karl is my right hand man, literally. When I have difficulty standing up, Karl is there to offer his arm for support. I have done much better following this program.

I have learned that you can live with a chronic condition, if you approach your problems with patience and don't give up. But you also must adapt your lifestyle to what you are dealing with, in order to live a productive and fruitful life. I believe God wants us to keep trying. We've seen others who, over and over again, deal with life's problems through faith. Somehow they plod on and their faith sustains them. But, we have also seen others who simply give up and are lost.

God has been there to direct me. Through Companion Prayer I follow a more helpful path, and with His help, I will continue to do the best I can to serve Him with a positive attitude, regardless of my limitations. God walks with all of us as we deal with the problems in our lives. We just have to listen for Him.

Camp Brainerd

As a member of the Lehigh Presbytery, I served on the Camp Brainerd Committee. It's a Presbyterian Youth Camp sponsored by the Presbytery. They had several worn out "boys' cabins" that were very old and falling apart. The committee was arguing about what to do with them, and admitted they had been rehashing this problem of the "boys' cabins" for years.

I spoke up and said, "Why don't you just build new ones?"

They looked at me closely since I was new on the committee and said, "Okay Karl, that's a good idea. Why don't you do it?"

I told them that we could build two large boys' cabins for under $20,000, and they were aghast. "You submit the plans, and we will submit them to the Presbytery for approval," they said.

I realized that I was taking on another major project, but I assured them that, if I started, I would see the project through to completion. I had construction experience, and with that, I figured out how it could be done, assuming we could count on the support of a local architect, several local contractors, help from building supply companies, and lots of volunteer help from the church and community!

The plan was approved by Presbytery, and with some key contractors helping me along, we were able to reach our goal just in time for the next camping season. It was a monumental task, but we finished the project on time and under budget, thanks to the many people who volunteered their time, labor, and resources.

The Camp Brainerd Youth Camp became one of the mission projects of the Shawnee Presbyterian Church, similar to a Habitat for Humanity project. It just proves that anything is possible when people work together. "How good and pleasant it is when people live together in unity!" (Psalm 133:1)

Painting the Interior of the Church

We then turned our attention to work that needed to be done to fix up the church. Painting the interior of the church is one task that some church volunteers can do successfully, and it makes people feel better about their church. A group of property committee members and other volunteers helped with the project.

The high walls were a challenge due to the difficulty in getting metal scaffolding in the church with the angled pews. So, we built our own scaffolding for one side of the church using 2 x 4's, and then we flipped them upside down for use on the opposite side of the Church. It worked just fine!

We were grateful to those who donated the paint, and to all the volunteers who helped. It was wonderful when people of the church volunteered to help out, and a good way for us to bond with our congregation.

Cornerstone Time Capsule

One unique thing we did to celebrate the 250th Anniversary of the Shawnee Presbyterian Church was to open the cornerstone of the church building, which was a time capsule, to review the items.

We had no idea what to expect, except that there were some old timers that remembered putting it in place 50 years before. The cornerstone had been removed once before and they had added a new time capsule, so there were now actually two time capsules in the cornerstone, one dated 1853 and the other 1952. We decided after reviewing the items, we would also add a new time capsule with the others dated 2002.

Following a special worship service with many special guests present, including the local newspaper, we removed the cornerstone. It was a beautiful summer day, and the sun was shining brightly. Our mason, Jim, had prepared the cornerstone the day before without actually moving it. However, it still took several strong people to remove the heavy stone. We sang songs while the mason worked at the stone, and when it was finally removed, we discovered two sealed metal containers inside the cornerstone.

We opened the boxes and placed the items on a table for inspection, asking people not to touch them. They contained money, newspaper articles, memoirs from those who contributed to the reconstruction of the church, and notes on the history of the church itself.

We took pictures of everything, and later placed the items back in three new containers, while adding new items to the 2002 time capsule. We included a newsletter article about the 9/11 tragedies, an important historical event.

Handicap Ramp

Another goal of the session was to build a handicap ramp for the church. It was an ambitious project but it did need to be done. The Shawnee Presbyterian Church had celebrated its 250th anniversary, and we wanted to complete something special for the church.

We started the ramp in 2002 and completed the project in 2004. We divided the work into several stages, and since we were doing the work ourselves with volunteer labor, it would take a little longer to accomplish.

In order to raise money for the project, we asked for donations from people who wanted the name of a loved one, or themselves engraved into "memorial bricks" that we would embed into the handicap ramp. We were able to raise over $12,000 for the construction.

The fellowship among the people who helped build the ramp was amazing. A bond was forming among the people who worked, and while we had obstacles to overcome, it was all built to code, with a concrete ramp and aluminum railings. We built it to last a lifetime! The church may eventually fall down, but that handicap ramp will last forever, and we dedicated the ramp with a ribbon cutting ceremony.

People Died After I Prayed

I was amazed that within a short period of time three people died after I prayed for them. After this happened, some of my pastoral friends said in jest that they did not want me to pray for their people. But, before jumping to conclusions, I need you to understand the circumstances behind what happened.

Sometimes, I get a nudge to act immediately upon hearing the news that someone is ill. I received one such call from a family member who informed me that their mother was very ill. It was quite a long trip, and I don't think the family expected me to go see her, but I wanted to support the family and be there in their hour of need.

So, I immediately left my office to make the two-hour drive. When I finally arrived, her family was all there, and they asked if I wanted a drink.

"No, thank you," I said. "I want to see your mother right away."

I went into the room where she lay, and their mother looked up at me. I had never seen her before. She had been bed-ridden for sometime, and was under care of a nurse. The family introduced me to her as the minister of one of her family members, and when she looked at me, a great big smile broke out on her face. She was very pleased to see me. It was then the family told me that she had requested to see a minister. She could barely speak, but managed to thank me for coming. She went in and out of consciousness and her breathing was labored. My heart went out to her, so I leaned over her and spoke into her ear, and said, "Your family is here with you, we all love you, and it is okay for you to let go."

I gathered the family around her bed and asked everyone to hold hands. I then placed my hand upon her forehead and proceeded to say a prayer. It was a long prayer, in which we gave thanks to God for the life that was given and we thanked Him for the love shared between family members. As I finished my prayer, she took one large breath.

We were all still holding hands, and when we all looked down at her we saw that she had stopped breathing. Nobody wanted to break the bond of holding hands, and tears began to form in everyone's eyes as we all realized that she had breathed her last breath. "I think she's gone," someone said. We quietly let go of each other's hands, and as we wiped our eyes someone else uttered, "I've never seen anything like it before in my whole life. It was the most beautiful way to pass away, surrounded by your family together in prayer."

My sense of urgency in seeing her was confirmed. I had been tempted to stop several times on the way, but somehow I knew I couldn't, and I went straight to their house.

The family was shocked, because they had been told that she could linger for several weeks, but they knew the time was close for their aged mother to die.

I later led the funeral service for her. She was truly a spiritual and beautiful woman who loved her family deeply, and I believe that because she was at peace with God and with her family, she was able to let go in prayer.

There was another family I ministered to in which the husband was suffering from Alzheimer's. They were very loyal to him, and they brought him home to be cared for by a hospice nurse because there wasn't anything more the medical profession could do for him.

Each day, his family would rally around him. It is always difficult to stand helplessly by as your loved one deteriorates before your very eyes.

Sometimes we all question why we must live when our quality of life is no longer there. However, I counsel that we are best served when we trust in God who is the author and finisher of life, no matter what the circumstances.

One could see that his condition was rapidly getting worse and his breathing was slowing. The family was called and those who could be there were present. He was "unconscious" and breathing deeply, and I came and stayed with the family. As we sat, I noticed that it was getting more difficult for him to breathe and wanted to pray before he passed over.

I gathered everyone together, knowing that there is great power in group prayer. We prayed a prayer of thanksgiving and praise to God. I told the man that it was okay to let go and be with God. A few minutes later, he passed over. It was a blessing that he did not have to suffer any longer.

Some days later, I presided over his funeral. What a devoted family! I was impressed that they supported one another throughout the whole grieving process.

We need one another, especially at funerals, to confirm and support one another during these times. The Bible says, "No one liveth or dieth unto themselves." (Romans 14:7) That is to say, we are dependent upon each other, and we need one another throughout life and death.

Not long after, another woman was in critical condition in the Intensive Care Unit. This person was in and out of the hospital several times. It appeared that on some days she was improving and speaking with me very clearly and coherently, but on other days, she was in a semi-comatose state.

The hospital called the family and told them that she could die at any time. I was informed about this and I left immediately for the hospital. When I arrived, the family was there, depressed about her condition. There was some discussion about whether she should be put on life support, but the family decided against it, knowing she would not want to live that way.

It was only a matter of time before her life's vital signs would stop, and once again I found myself praying for someone for whom the prognosis was not good, and who would probably die within a matter of hours. The best I could do was to console the family and reassure them of eternal life through our faith in Jesus Christ. I gathered the family around her bed and prayed for God to have mercy upon her. Within a matter of minutes, she passed away.

Shortly after, I performed her funeral and consoled the family.

Within a year, three persons had died almost immediately after my gathering the family to pray. Gathering the family around the bedside allowed the person to relax. When I told them it was okay to go, this was just what they needed. They could breathe their last breath.

Dying is like stepping from one room into another. When our bodies are in a weakened state, it is not difficult to "check out" as it were, from this earthly life to the Kingdom of Heaven. Even the apostle Paul admitted that he could be with God, but for our sake, he would stay. (Philippians 1:22-24)

Jesus said, "In my Father's house are many rooms, if it were not so, I would have told you. I go to prepare a place for you, and where I go, you may also go." (John 14:2-3) When I was younger, I recall praying to God to allow a person dear to me to die. I had visited our family doctor when he was very ill. In my mind's eye, I had remembered him as a smiling, vital, healthy healer. But when I saw him at the hospital, his face was wrinkled, he had aged remarkably, his eyes were closed, and he was confined to a bed. I was horrified by his deterioration. He was suffering terribly from a terminal autoimmune disease that attacked his body. He had gone blind, but he could still recognize my voice when I visited him. He said he wished that he did not have to suffer anymore, and wanted to die. I told him that I would pray for him.

I felt so sorry for him because he had been my family doctor for many years and had healed me from several illnesses I had as a child. He was the doctor who fixed up my finger after I drilled a hole through it, and pointed out the white spots on the x-ray of my hands. He was the doctor who helped me get better when I got chicken pox, measles, and tonsillitis.

After my visit, I went home and cried. I prayed to God to be merciful to him so he would not have to suffer anymore. I petitioned God that, here was a person that had helped so many other people get well, would God now be merciful to him? I prayed and prayed for mercy, mercy, mercy.

The very next day, he passed away. I was grateful that God had answered my prayer. Thank you, God.

Am I dead?

There was a wonderful woman who was active in the church and was kind to everyone. One day she suffered from an aneurism and was rushed to the hospital. She survived the first major burst of a blood vessel and was recovering. Unfortunately, she had a relapse and because she had high blood pressure, suffered another blood vessel break. While in the hospital she said, "I see people I know who are dead walking around. Am I dead?" she asked.

"No," replied the doctors.

"I just saw my dog that died. Am I dead?" She asked the doctors.

"No," they answered.

She was young, generous, loving, and kind, and before dying, she became aware of the next world around her. She called all her friends and family on the phone just hours before she passed away. She told them how much she loved them. I was sorry to see her leave us, she was such a beautiful person.

The Church Steeple

It never ceases to amaze me how mysteriously and wondrously God works. We needed to repair a hole in the steeple that was possibly caused by a woodpecker. Bats were entering the belfry through the hole and getting into the church. Besides that, the wood steeple was beginning to rot and several contractors in the congregation advised that the hole be fixed as soon as possible.

The property committee and session discussed the matter on numerous occasions, and arrived at several different opinions. But alas, nothing was done because each recommendation involved a great deal of money that the church didn't have.

A year and a half had gone by and still no one had any affordable solutions. I had been praying to God to help me serve the church, and if God wanted me to minister and help this particular church, would he not send me people to help build it up?

Then, after church one Sunday, as the summer was coming to a close, a man came up to me and asked for permission to paint the steeple of the church. I was dumbfounded, but eventually gained my composure.

"Well, yes, George!" I said. "I'm sure that would be fine with the session since they have wanted to fix and paint the steeple," I told him.

I was amazed, because George was 81 years old! He explained that to me he was a professional painter and had painted about 80 church steeples in his lifetime, and now that he would be 81 in two weeks he felt the need to paint another. When I spoke with the session they were also amazed, and agreed to let him paint the steeple.

George was a "snowbird" that came up to the Poconos during the summer months, and returned to Florida during the winter. I was amazed at his faith and his desire to fix the hole and paint the whole steeple. I would have been happy if he just fixed the hole, but he said, "No, the whole steeple needs to be painted."

Here was someone who came to us out of the blue and simply volunteered to paint the church steeple, after we had failed to figure out how to get up that high (about 60 feet) without expensive equipment.

I met with George soon after, and he told me what he needed to do the job. He apologized that all his ladders and brushes were in Florida, so I diligently wrote down everything he needed: ladders, paint, brushes, a power washer, wood planks, rope, etc.

"George, you are going to need some help doing this, right?" I asked him.

"Yes," he said. "I just need a little help with the ladders."

I knew then that God had sent him! George had complete faith in me that he would have everything he needed.

Wow, it was an amazing job! I was able to get everything he needed, and assisted him on the roof of the church by holding the ladder, and tying a few ropes. People gasped! I was grateful for his strong faith and ability. Here he was 81 years of age standing on the top step of the ladder I was holding, 60 feet up, and I couldn't get people half his age. In fact, several men in the church said to me, "I can't help you because my wife will not allow me to climb roofs."

I later found out that almost everyone felt the same way except for George's wife Bonnie, and my wife, Dale. I talked to Bonnie, and asked her, "Do you mind if George paints the steeple?"

"Oh, I wouldn't be able to stop him any way," she said. "George likes to be up high. He thinks the higher up he is, the closer he gets to God."

Whenever there has been a need in the church, I pray about it to God. He always manages to send me people to do the job, and to help the church in its ministry. This is the amazing grace of God that I have seen over and over again in my ministry. Somehow things get done. Maybe not always the way I think they should be done, but they do get done.

Even financially in the church, when things seem to get tight and gloomy, and I begin to wonder if I can complete the ministry I believe

God has called me to do, the Lord provides someone or something to help fulfill the task at hand.

Near Death Experience #3 - Unable to Breathe

The third threat on my life came not at the top of a church steeple, but in a bucket of shrimp. It was July 4, 2003, and Dale's brother Paul came up to visit us and brought with him a huge bucket of large fantail shrimp! We all ate the shrimp except for Dale because she is allergic to them. I commented to Paul, "I have never had this kind of shrimp." It was true that Dale had never served us huge fantail shrimp because she couldn't eat it. Occasionally we would have a few small shrimp mixed in a meal, but never the large ones.

Later that night, I woke up at 1:00 a.m. and was having trouble breathing. Dale told me to take Tylenol and go back to sleep.

"No," I told her. "I am really having trouble breathing!"

She turned on the light, took one look at me and said, "We're going to the hospital."

She immediately gave me two Benadryl tablets, and drove me to the emergency room at the Pocono Medical Center. She could see that my face and neck were puffy and I was showing signs of anaphylactic shock. When we got there, we told them I was having trouble breathing, and they took me in immediately. The Doctor asked me if I was allergic to anything. "IVP dye," I told him. Then he asked me what I had to eat recently. "Huge fantail shrimp," I told him.

The doctor laughed and said, "Don't you know that they make the IVP dye from shrimp?" Then he said, "Didn't anyone tell you not to eat shrimp?"

"No!" I told him.

Meanwhile the nurses were administering to me a large amount of Benadryl through an IV bag. Immediately, I began to breathe easier. As the doctor was talking to me, I became dizzy, and felt like I was floating on air. I also noticed a group of people standing at the foot of the bed staring at me! Who were these people and why were they standing at the foot of my bed in the emergency room? One woman was standing there, just looking at me with great concern on her face. She had regular "street" clothes on, as did the other people.

Then, I heard the voice of my mother, Frances, "Now don't be in such a hurry to see me," she said.

Wow! I had not heard my mother's voice in many years. It was amazing to me, but also affirming, that they were not quite ready for me to be on the other side.

Later, I asked Dale whether she saw any other people standing in the room with us at the hospital. "No one was in the room but the doctor and me," she replied.

It seemed that once again I had a near death experience where I was between this world and the next. My mother, with a touch of humor, sent me back among the living.

Radio Ministry

In my ministry, I am always asking God, "What would you have me do, Lord?" It is something I believe every servant of the Lord should do.

I knew we had several people in the congregation who were "shut-ins" at nursing homes or even in their own homes. I was meditating and praying to God about how best to reach out and touch them in a meaningful way, when it occurred to me that radio programming could be the way to go. With it we could bring our services right to their bedsides. After all, I had developed the TV ministry for shut-ins in a previous church, so why wouldn't it work here in Shawnee on Delaware? I didn't feel TV was the answer, at least not until the technology caught up, but what about radio? This is a very mountainous area, what if we could use the mountains to help us reach out to others?

I visited Paul, a shut-in and faithful member of the Church. "What do you think about me developing a radio ministry?" I asked him.

"It would be wonderful if I could hear you on the radio. I'd listen to it all the time," he said.

So, I made some inquires and then made a proposal before the session. Some of the members of session remember the day that I first made the pitch, and they frankly thought I was nuts! For me it was a leap of faith. I laid out how I would first get approval from the FCC, and then the church could raise the money through institutional and private sources. What did the Shawnee Church have to lose?

With the support of the session, we prayed about it and placed it in God's hands. It took 3 years to get approval from the FCC, but it finally came. We were granted a license for a low power 100-Watt station that would transmit on 104.9 FM. It took another nine months to raise the money and purchase the equipment necessary to go on the air. Fortunately, we had members of the church with electrical, computer, and amateur radio experience.

We designed a station that was 100% digital and could operate automatically. We built the computer component by component with parts we picked up at various computer shows. We would have to master the computer programs that operated the radio station, and encourage volunteers to learn the system. Fortunately, the technology was available to do what we wanted. I had some of the greatest volunteers to operate the station. We began to air 24 hours a day, seven days a week playing Christian, and other great music.

One of the inspirations for bringing radio to Shawnee was the fact that Fred Waring and the Pennsylvanians used to broadcast radio programs from Shawnee many years ago. He was a famous music director who was popular across the country. He was also the recipient of the "Congressional Gold Medal" in 1983 for Music Achievement, and is buried in our church cemetery. We play his music on our radio station every day, in his honor!

It is my hope to reach out to the masses using the radio to broadcast Christian music, hourly scripture readings, stories of hope and encouragement, and the preaching of the Word. We put together a variety of music programs that are aired throughout the day and try to reach out to all generations by being inspirational. For me, it has been a test of faith. Everyday, I try to touch someone's life in a positive way. It has been a real effort on the part of the church to be a light to the community we serve.

Struggling To Get Out of Debt

Just as we work together as a team, so we take on debt together. It seems like we have always struggled to pay our bills and we have created a considerable debt. Yet, God has blessed us in many ways. As we have given help to others, God has returned the blessing to us.

Helping our children get through college and pay the myriad medical bills was difficult. It was also very expensive trying to help Jason in various ways by going to the best doctors we could find, and following different treatments. Many times, we were forced to charge the medical treatments on credit cards.

However, as I became deeper in debt it became a form of slavery! If you have ever been in debt, you know exactly what I am talking about. The credit card companies often charge outrageous interest rates that I believe is a form of Biblical usury! Then it is almost impossible to get out of debt.

Thus, I have worked very hard to pay off the debt that we have accrued over the years, and fortunately, I've still been able to provide for my family, to tithe, and to give something to those in need as well. Even with these hardships, God still helped us to meet our needs.

I considered declaring bankruptcy at one time, but I decided against it because I believe that if I owe an obligation to those from whom I borrowed, I must pay it back. This is the Christian work ethic I believe in, although somehow there were times that the harder I worked the deeper I got in debt. It's been a hard financial journey for our family, but we realize that there are people who have it far worse than we do. When I compare our situation with others throughout the world, we are truly fortunate.

Working for the Lord does not mean you will receive much money for the long hours worked. That's why one of my favorite aphorisms is: "Work for the Lord. The pay isn't much, but the retirement plan is out of this world."

The Floods at Shawnee on Delaware

Trying to meet the spiritual and physical needs of others is always a challenge. Preparing to meet those needs before a disaster occurs is even more difficult. I remember Dale and me talking about how important it was for us to prepare for a disaster. This was in September of 2004. I didn't know exactly in what form these disasters were going to manifest themselves but I knew something was going to happen.

There had already been times when people needed an emergency place to stay because of the loss of power during severe ice storms, and because we lived up North, it was likely to happen again. So, I talked to the session about equipping our church Christian Education building as an emergency facility, and they agreed to make preparations. With the help of an electrician, we installed a transfer switch and purchased an electric generator. We had a well for water, and propane gas to fuel the stove. We had mats for people to sleep on, and a collection of blankets, towels, and sheets. We also kept a well-stocked food pantry.

Dale and I also documented everything we owned realizing we could lose everything. So, we took pictures of our belongings with a digital camera, and I went to my insurance agent and drew up a policy that would cover everything. We talked about flood insurance, but because we live in the mountains, we didn't feel we needed it.

I told Dale that I felt that we had done everything we could to prepare for whatever might happen. One month later, after we had completed our preparations, Hurricane Katrina was heading for the Gulf coast. "Everyone should evacuate right away!" I said. As I watched the terrible storm hit, there was an incredible devastation that wiped out much of New Orleans and the surrounding areas. I couldn't believe that the storm hadn't affected us. I wanted to help people, but there wasn't much I could do. I felt that I was picking up on the imminence of a disaster of huge proportions, but I didn't know exactly where and what form it would take.

There were three floods that did hit the Shawnee area, and on one occasion, the Delaware River was rising so fast that the community went into action. We called on people that lived close to the water and helped them move everything of value out of their basements. We even made human chains to pass items from person to person to try to save the belongings people had in their homes. The flooding was so widespread, and came on so fast, that only those who acted quickly had a chance of saving a few items. After several hours, it was too late and all we could do was to make way for the water that was rising fast.

After the flood of 2004, there was a clean-up in the town of Shawnee. There were many homes and businesses that had been devastated by the flooding, so we all chipped in as a community and helped one another.

The tragedy is that many families lost a great deal of property in the flooding. However, we are thankful to God that no one in our community lost their lives.

I felt that I had somehow misunderstood my intuitive feelings about preparing for a disaster. Our church was high and dry and we had only a little water, nothing that we couldn't mop up. We had prepared for an emergency, but the devastation had occurred somewhere else.

However, there was another flood to hit in April of 2005. One woman in our town that had been hit hard by the earlier flood had just settled back into her renovated apartment. Then again officials were saying that another flood was on its way. "What should I do?" the woman asked me. I said a quick prayer and told her, "Unfortunately, you should get everything you value out of the apartment." I told her that we would help her, and we loaded up our van with everything she wanted to save. The next day her apartment was totally under water. She was glad she got out what she could in time.

However, a third flood hit the Shawnee Village again in June of 2006 that caused more damage. By this time, many of the people knew exactly what to do to prepare for the flooding. One person said, "You know it's scary, but I think we're getting better at coping with the flooding." We are still grateful again, that God gave us strength to get through the difficult times.

Christiana's Teeth

There were times when we had a problem, and we tried everything to solve the situation, but nothing seemed to work. These are the times when we turned to God and asked for His help in prayer.

Christiana asked us to help her and we agreed we would do our best. Christiana has always had problems with her teeth. They were soft and she had had many cavities. She also had a problem with a tooth that had ankylosed on the upper right side of her mouth. This meant the tooth would not come down out of her gums and was wrapped around the bone in her jaw. She always took diligent care of her teeth, but she needed to have some work done which required a root canal. Unfortunately, the dentist had over-filled the tooth and Christiana was in constant, excruciating pain. She tried different medications and different dentists to no avail.

She was desperate for help, so she came to her father and me and asked for Companion Prayer. We had prayer with Christiana present, and we were advised that she needed to have a surgical procedure to correct the problem. No amount of medication, heat or ice treatments would relieve her pain.

During our prayer session we asked for a recommendation for a dental surgeon who could perform the surgery, and were given several names of different doctors in New York City, none of which we knew existed. Christiana checked them out and found one surgeon that was covered by her insurance. She made an appointment, had her surgery and the problem was corrected.

We were eternally grateful for the advice we received in the Companion Prayer session. Each time we go through this process, we take a leap of faith in which we have to completely trust in God to guide us.

The Mixed-Up Rings

Marriage is a covenant between two people and God, and it is a commitment that a couple makes between one another. As a sign of their love and commitment, a bride and groom will usually exchange rings; however, sometimes the ring ceremony gets mixed up. I remember two wedding ceremonies where the bride and groom just couldn't get it right. One bride was furious, but the other bride was very cool.

In one instance, when the time came for the ring ceremony, I asked the groom, "What sign do you give of your love?"

"A ring," the groom answered, and he got the ring from the best man and handed it to me. When the bride saw it she said under her breath in a harsh way, "That's the wrong ring! That's the wrong ring!" As I looked at it I realized she was right. It was definitely the wrong ring.

"Where's the right ring?" I asked. The Maid of honor quickly produced the correct ring. So, I took the correct ring and proceeded with the ceremony.

At another wedding, I asked the groom, "What sign do you give of your love?" And the groom turned and received the ring from the best man and then placed it in my hand. I then raised the ring up and said a prayer, "Bless this ring that he who gives it and she who wears it may abide in thy peace, for ever and ever, Amen."

I handed the ring to the groom who then placed it on the bride's finger. The bride looked at me with a look of surprise and whispered under her breath, "Shall we continue with the service like this?" and pointed to the ring which was on her finger – her new husband's ring! She shrugged her shoulder indicating it did not matter to her whether we used the wrong rings or not, but she wanted a cue from me to make the call.

Should we continue the wedding with the wrong rings? I was a bit surprised because no one, including me, had noticed that it was the wrong ring!

I wanted to do things right, and asked, "Where's the other ring?"

At that, everybody looked at the Maid of Honor, and she was stunned to realize she had the ring we needed, and handed it to me.

"It's nice for a couple to start out sharing, but we are going to do this one right," I said.

I took the right ring and started over again. I blessed the ring and gave it to the groom, and asked the groom to repeat after me, "This ring I give thee, in token and pledge of our constant faith and abiding love."

Then, when I asked the bride, "What sign do you give of your love?"

She could hardly contain her laughter, and said, "This ring."

I blessed the ring and gave it to her and when I asked her to repeat after me, she could barely speak for her laughter. After a few more moments of giggles, we continued with the ceremony.

Wedding Mishaps

There are times when no matter how hard a couple plans a wedding, something can go wrong.

There was one wedding that was to begin at 3:00 p.m. Unfortunately, the ushers did not show up until 3:00 p.m. so when the guests arrived earlier, there was no one there to show them to their seats or hand out a bulletin. When asked where they had been they responded, "We thought the wedding was at 3:00 p.m."

During another ceremony, the ushers forgot to hand out the wedding programs, and they handed them out as people left the church!

There was a wedding that was proceeding just as planned, when all of a sudden, the maid of honor whispered excitedly something to the bride, and I saw the bride turn pale. I knew that was not a good sign.

I stopped what I was saying and asked gently, "What's the problem?"

"I forgot the ring!" the maid of honor said.

"Where is it?" I asked.

"It's in the car," she said.

"Go get it!" I told her.

I briefly explained to the congregation that we would learn one of the first lessons in marriage - patience. Sometimes we need to wait patiently until everything comes together.

Within a minute, she hurried back with the ring, and although she'd only been gone a minute she was certainly teased about her forgetfulness during the reception. Sometimes we just forget things.

At some weddings, the ushers have forgotten to pull the runner down the aisle before the bride enters the church.

On one such occasion, when the ushers pulled the runner down the middle of the aisle it came up considerably short. They needed a 100-foot runner, but they were 75 feet short! To top it all off, the wedding was outside and the wind kept blowing the 25 foot runner to one side. Frankly, it would have been better if there were no runner at all!

In fact, I have seen so many problems with runners, I don't recommend them. Sometimes they are too wide to fit down the aisle. Sometimes women get their heels caught on the runners which can be very dangerous. Most of the runners are made out of a very thin plastic. I've seen garbage bags made of better material than the runners they make today.

I traveled to Los Angeles, CA to perform the wedding for my niece, Colleen, at the beautiful "Inn of the Seventh Ray." It was a wonderful outside wedding; however, when Julie went to light the candles at the beginning of the service, the candles kept blowing out no matter how hard she tried.

There are a variety of things that happen when people get married, but it finally boils down to the wedding vows: "I do promise before God and these witnesses to be thy loving and faithful wife or husband, in plenty and in want, in joy and in sorrow, in sickness and in health, as long as we both shall live."

There were many funny and strange things that have happened during some of the weddings I performed. Some were embarrassing, while others were absolutely hilarious.

The Ring Bearers – Delight or Disaster

Ring bearers can be a total delight or a demonic disaster, and we've seen both types in our weddings.

Some children, while very cute, make it half-way down the aisle and suddenly they discover that everyone is looking at them! They think, "Oh, no! Not me! I'm getting out of here," and they run for the hills.

Other children are well behaved and do fine, because they seem to know that something important is going on.

You can usually tell which kids are used to going to church because they have been taught how to behave during a formal worship service. Others will run wild throughout the service.

I have seen some children who are traumatized when asked to walk down the church aisle alone. But then there are others that take everything in stride and walk down the aisle with no problems at all.

Getting the children to stand up in front of the church and remain still the whole time is the next challenge. Even after a carefully planned wedding rehearsal, I advise the couple getting married not to be surprised if the children don't make it through the whole ceremony.

At one wedding, the couple had a child actually carry the rings on a pillow. At this wedding, the child's behavior was not the problem, but someone had tied so many knots, possibly 10 or more, that held the rings to the pillow, that the couple had trouble getting the rings free. The groom was a wreck, and his hands started shaking, so the bride got into the act and started undoing the knots so they could get to the rings. The groom mentioned that he should have brought a knife with him, to cut the rings off the pillow. The bride was also getting angrier by the minute because someone must have deliberately sabotaged their wedding by tying the knots tightly.

I then got into the act and started undoing the knots, and meanwhile, the congregation was waiting for the ring ceremony, so I explained that we needed to get the rings off the pillow, and it would take just a minute. Trusting in my own ability to undo the knots, I assured the couple that I would get the knots undone, as both the bride and groom were visibly shaken at this point.

In most cases, artificial rings are tied on the ring pillow for the children to bring forward and the best man and the maid of honor are charged with holding the real rings. But this couple wanted to do it by the book and have the real rings on the pillow.

I finally got the last knot undone and we proceeded with the ceremony. "It may have taken some time to get the rings off the pillow, but that does not compare to the eternal symbolism this ring represents," I explained. "It is a circle that has no end, and as long as you live together in the eternal love of God in Christ Jesus, your relationship will have no end."

I always tried to take every situation that could have turned into a disaster, and create a delightful situation that would have lasting value. As children of God, our heavenly Father loves us even though in our human frailty we make mistakes.

The Wedding on the Ski Slope

This was one of the most exciting weddings that I have ever performed. The couple were avid skiers and snowboarders; even the grandmother was a cross-country skier.

So they asked me if it was okay with me to perform the wedding on a ski slope. They talked with the Shawnee Mountain Ski Resort officials, and they agreed to allow their "first" wedding there at the bottom of one of the ski runs which was in a fairly flat area.

After a long talk with this wonderful couple, we set the time for the rehearsal. It was going to be only the three of us, because they wanted the wedding plans to be a secret to the family. The couple was going to ski down the mountain just before the wedding. However, I would be the first to ski down to the designated spot.

I insisted on a trial run, and during the rehearsal run, the bride fell, and I spun around just before the bottom of the hill.

"It's a good thing we are practicing," I commented. "We had better take it slowly the day of the wedding." It was agreed that we would ski down "Pennsylvania," one of the easier trails.

Then came the day of the wedding and it was a beautiful day! The temperature was about 32 degrees. Perfect! Instead of wearing my robe, and risk being called "Superman Pastor" with my robe flapping in the wind, I decided to wear my collar as I skied down. As I was the first to ski down, I could see the people gathered at the bottom of the hill, and there was an announcer on the loudspeaker telling people what was going on. I skied to the back of the crowd and there I put on my robe.

Then I walked to the arbor, still in my ski boots, because the ground was covered with snow. Next, the groom came down the hill on his snowboard, fully dressed in his tuxedo.

It was exciting as the announcer said, "Here comes the groom." He came down perfectly and stopped to my left, kicking off his snowboard. Then the bride in her full wedding dress and white coat came gracefully down the hill.

The announcer over the PA system said, "Here comes the bride."

All the skiers on the slope came to a complete stop. A great cheer arose from all parts of the ski slope. Family, friends, and bystanders on and off skies were in awe of the bride coming down the slope in her wedding gown.

I felt as if I were at a football game! Never before had I seen a bride receive such an ovation! They cheered and clapped! Without a falter, she snowboarded to the base of the hill to the back of the crowd where she was greeted by her father.

The aisle was marked with ski poles sticking up from the snow every two feet leading up to the metal arbor where I was standing with the groom. Then, up walked the bride with her father. The faces of the people were of smiles, grins, and astonishment as there were many people who, being curious automatically became part of the ceremony. After all, we were in the middle of a public ski resort at the height of the ski season.

As the bride came forward, I opened the ceremony with a prayer. Then it began to snow lightly. It was a perfect day for a ski slope wedding. When I asked for the rings, I was handed a snowball where each ring was placed. The couple also had instructed me to tell the guests, to throw snowballs at them as they left.

At the reception, the wedding cake was a white sparkly ski slope with a trail gradually running down the cake; and, at the bottom of the cake, there were the bride and groom upside down with skies crossed. It was the most unusual, delightful wedding I had every performed. Everyone enjoyed celebrating with the bride and groom.

Angelic Appearance

Dale and I were on vacation and trying to relax, rejuvenating ourselves. We decided after our daughter's wedding in January to take a three-week vacation to Florida and get some sun.

During this time, we took a day trip to Disney World. This would be our first visit without our children and we could enjoy the park at our leisure without the wild rides. We took our time and enjoyed the sights.

While we were at the Animal Kingdom, walking from one exhibit to another, a beautiful woman came up to me on my right side, tapped me on my shoulder, and said, "I want to wish you a happy birthday!" I was stunned and speechless. Not only was my birthday in a few days, but she was a total stranger. She smiled at me, as she walked away. I turned to Dale who was on my left and said, "Did you see that woman, she just wished me a happy birthday?"

"What woman?" Dale said. I turned around to look at the angelic woman and she was gone.

"She was right here," I said to Dale.

"Who was?" Dale said.

"A beautiful woman was just here and wished me a happy birthday," I said.

Who could she be? She didn't look like the other people in our midst. She wasn't in a rush and she was serene and pleasant, and for some reason had taken time to single me out for my special day.

"Could this have been an angel?" I asked Dale.

"Yes," Dale said. "She was probably giving you encouragement."

Then the strangest feeling overcame me. This was déjà vu! And it all came flooding back to me. I recalled that when I was in Disney World, at Epcot 28 years earlier, the very same thing had happened to me. A very good-looking woman had come up to me, wished me a happy birthday, and disappeared. No one saw her but me. What a nice treat, but why? It seemed to me that God was showing me that He cared for me, and was encouraging me to keep doing whatever I was doing! Now, it had happened to me again! Several nights later, I was sleeping and the same woman who had wished me happy birthday appeared in my dream. I said in the dream, "You are the woman who wished me a happy birthday!" She just smiled at me.

The next day, I told Dale how the beautiful woman with the angelic presence had appeared in a dream and just smiled at me. "That confirms that she was from the other side and probably one of God's angels," Dale said. I was in a state of amazement.

Several days later, toward the end of our vacation, Dale and I visited our niece, Crystal, in Atlanta, Georgia. We went to an art museum, where we saw a special exhibit from the Louvre in Paris. When I saw the picture that Rembrandt had painted of Matthew and the angel, I got chills. There in the picture was my angel whispering in Matthew's ear giving him the inspiration to write the Gospel of Matthew. She looked just like the angel that had wished me happy birthday. Rembrandt had painted the angel on the right side of Matthew just as she appeared to me. I was stunned. Perhaps she was whispering in my ear giving me inspiration for this book.

The scriptures tell us that we should, "Not neglect to show hospitality to strangers, for some have entertained angels unawares." (Hebrews 13:2) I think we all encounter many angels. It is just one more way God sends His guidance, His encouragement, His help, and His comfort.

THE END

Epilogue

As we have experienced what God has called us to accomplish, may you, the reader come to a greater awakening of God's presence. God is here. We pray that the sharing of our story has blessed you in some way: made you laugh, opened your imagination for you to use your intuition, and has inspired you to develop a deeper relationship with God.

www.ingramcontent.com/pod-product-compliance
Lightning Source LLC
Chambersburg PA
CBHW030413100426